Poor People's Lawyers in Transition

A Volume in the
Crime, Law, and Deviance
Series

Jack Katz

Poor People's Lawyers in Transition

Rutgers University Press
New Brunswick, New Jersey

Library of Congress Cataloging in Publication Data

Katz, Jack, 1944–
Poor people's lawyers in transition.

(Crime, law, and deviance)
Bibliography: p.
Includes index.
1. Legal assistance to the poor—Illinois—Chicago.
2. Legal aid—Illinois—Chicago. 3. Lawyers—Illinois—
Chicago. I. Title. II. Series.
KF337.C45K38 344.773'1103258 81–15399
ISBN 0–8135–0943–2 347.730411103258 AACR2

Manufactured in the United States of America

To my father, Charles R. Katz

Contents

Acknowledgments ix

Introduction:
The Social Construction of Equal Justice 1

1 Poor People's Conflicts and Lawyers' Work Problems 17

2 The Decline of Reform and the Emergence of Legal Aid 34

3 Becoming a Legal Aid Lawyer 51

4 Legal Services Programs and the Sixties: Complementarity and Dependence 65

5 Legal Services Programs and the Sixties: Tension and Independence 90

6 Becoming a Poverty Lawyer 105

7 Personal Careers and the Persistence of Group Character 123

8 Legal Services Programs Eclipse Legal Aid 136

9 Legal Services in the Seventies: Instability and Reform within a Declining Social Movement 160

10 Legalizing Poverty 179

Appendix:
A Theory of Qualitative Methodology:
The Social System of Analytic Fieldwork 197

Notes 219

References 247

Index 263

Acknowledgments

Acknowledgments are unquestionably the single most important part of academic books: they are usually the first thing read; for many readers, they are often the only thing that is read; and ironically in sociology they often afford readers their last glimpse of human reality. Out of respect for the importance of the tradition, I have sorted my thanks carefully into five categories: those who took the risk of permitting inquiry into their lives; those who pointed me or kept me pointed in new directions with comments usually prefaced by "that reminds me of . . ."; a the-problem-with-that-is crowd of critics who, in reacting to prior drafts, overcame what had been, and probably really is, my best judgment; a rich set of institutional supporters; and invaluable research assistants.

Those who took a risk. I began this study at a time when I learned that the legal assistance organizations in Chicago were about to merge. As a graduate of the University of Chicago Law School and a graduate student at Northwestern, I knew several of the staff lawyers, had old school ties to some others, and calculated I could win the acquiescence of organization leaders by implicitly threatening to make an end run and contact the staff directly. This proved largely unnecessary. Kenneth Howell, then the leader of one of the merging organizations, Community Legal Counsel, was instantly encouraging, surprisingly open, and—drawing on his background in corporate law practice—repeatedly helpful with comparative sociological thinking. At the other merging organization, the Legal Aid Bureau of United Charities, staff leaders and board officials never did quite authorize my entry. Ellis Ballard, Gordon Scott, A. Gerald Erickson, and the late Arthur Young were always gracious and accommodating, but none deserves the blame for letting me in. I apparently approached the United Charities at a point in the merger when the lines of authority were so confused that none felt he had a complete right to deny me entry. After being told four times, "I don't think it'll work, but I can't tell you no," I began asking secretaries for organizational documents, requesting that staff lawyers permit me to sit in on client interviews, and assuming the position of a "fly on the wall" (as one lawyer put it) at group meetings, all with a presumptive air of legitimacy and the apprehension, which lasted the 18 months of fieldwork, that the next minute I would be thrown out.

Some 70 staff lawyers cooperated in a variety of ways: allowing me to accompany them through a morning in court; managing my presence in client interviews; and participating in personal interviews, often for several hours. It seems inappropriate to thank each here; one or more might consider the reference a breach of promised anonymity. I trust there is no risk in offering public thanks to Sheldon Roodman, Elnor Greenfield, and James Weill for supplying organizational documents and background information on Chicago's Legal Assistance Foundation.

I learned of the merger before it was general public knowledge, over dinner with my wife, Marilyn Katz, who was then just beginning to practice law as a Vista lawyer at Community Legal Counsel. Subsequently, as a poverty lawyer in Connecticut and California, Marilyn continued to be an invaluable source of leads to people and information in Legal Services. With amazing insight, Marilyn has always offered unqualified praise and encouragement.

The that-reminds-me-of set. Howard S. Becker, the late John Henry Schlegel, Arthur Leff, and Robert Cover provoked me to new lines of thought, usually with extremely casual comments. Because, for the most part, they believed they were talking about their own work, they have no identifiable responsibility for what I have done here.

The the-problem-with-that-is set. More numerous but equally innocent are those who read late or early drafts and offered thoughtful criticism. They are: Richard Abel, Howard Becker, Egon Bittner, Thomas Ehrlich, Howard Erlanger, Oscar Grusky, Geoffrey Hazard, John Kitsuse, Gary Marx, Carrie Menkel-Meadow, Philippe Nonet, Allan Schnaiberg, James Weill, Stanton Wheeler, and Mayer Zald. For reactions to earlier drafts of the Appendix, I would like to thank Howard Becker, John Kitsuse, Peter Manning, Mel Pollner, Allan Schnaiberg, Michael Schudson, Ralph Turner, and Stanton Wheeler.

For financial and organizational support, I owe generous thanks to NIMH and Northwestern University, the Russell Sage Foundation and Yale Law School, and the Academic Senate of the University of California at Los Angeles. I must also thank Jane Bitar, who managed heavy typing burdens with an attitude that always invited more work.

Research assistance. Four graduate students at UCLA provided indispensable help. Sheila Balkan traveled to the Chicago Historical Society and discovered crucial materials for chapter 2. Nancy Fix and Judith Saxon combed the manuscript several times with keen eyes. Man Tsun Chang organized the bibliography. Nancy Fix and a law student, Doug Canfield, coded the data presented in chapter 10. Saxon also composed the Index.

A few passages in chapters 1 and 6 appeared previously in an article, "Lawyers for the Poor in Transition," in *Law and Society Review* 12(1978): 275–300. I thank the editors for permission to reprint.

Poor People's Lawyers in Transition

Introduction

The Social Construction of Equal Justice

A statement of law that warned "But these rights apply only to those who can obtain the legal skills necessary to invoke them" would be absurd. An affirmation of unequal access to the law would nullify the moral claim of any constitutional provision, statute, administrative regulation, or judicial decision. As an empirical matter, not just as a contention of philosophy, the value of equal access is an essential element of the commonsense understanding of a legal system, just as are the virtues of a general, public, intelligible, and consistent reasoning.[1] Phenomenologically, proclamations of law imply commitments to equal justice. Reflecting this universal common sense, pronouncements of the moral value of law have, "from the dawn of Anglo-Saxon legal history," embodied symbols of equal justice.[2]

Despite the timelessness of the aspiration, and quite apart from political realities and other bothersome practical constraints, it is impossible even to conceive of a legal system that could demonstrate it has achieved equal justice. Like other grand moral quests, equal justice is inevitably elusive.[3] The most idealistic lawyer may sense the impossibility of realizing equal justice through the everyday contradiction he perceives between self-regard and regard for the rule of law. Consider the dilemma of one who supplies rare legal skills to people unusually disadvantaged in protecting their rights. Employing an exceptional ability, the altruist wins an apparently hopeless case for an unpopular indigent. Heroically vindicating the rule of law against heavy odds, his triumph at once earns a celebration of self and justifies dismay for the legality of a system that implements rights on such unpredictable, extraordinary contingencies.[4]

At the most general level, the aspiration for equal justice appears irrationally blind to the processual, emergent nature of law. Suppose there were a firm popular vote to realize fully, at any cost, equal access to the law. How might government proceed? It might survey the rightful claims and grievances of all citizens and then allocate lawyers' services either to meet the whole need or according to some proportional formula that would disregard differences in wealth, respectability, and subjective perception of need.[5] The primary difficulty with such a final solution to the problem of equal justice is that the law would not stand still for it. Depending on their sophistication, surveyors could discover or invent an infinite variety of previously unperceived, rightful claims and grievances. Put as an administrative problem, how would government determine how much legal skill and research to allocate to each person and group in order to measure the extent of his, her, or its unmet legal need? And the dilemma would reappear immediately following the initial allocation, however it were brought off. Once the lawyers were dispatched, their work would not only meet needs previously defined but alter official and lay understandings of the distribution of rights. New suits would be brought, and unprecedented decisions would be rendered, inevitably provoking renewed discontents over inequity in the distribution of legal resources.

The simplistic survey solution is ill conceived because law is not a static distribution of rights but a process of arguing what the law is. A system of equal access to law is, at best, an ongoing argument about whether equal access exists. Law must aspire to equal justice in order to merit the moral quality we attribute to it; yet, the social agencies of implementation will inevitably contradict the aspiration.

Put another way, the goal of achieving a state of equal justice is mythical, but that this is so does not justify cynical disgust, for such a goal can neither be realized empirically nor proven hopeless. Indeed, one could always make the radically complacent argument that all those who lack access to lawyers, courts, the halls of legislatures, and the other agencies for legal redress actually have no significant legitimate claims not now being met. Of course, this conservative argument could not be proved without being abandoned—for the only way to be sure would be to assign lawyers and wait for all their cases to lose—but it could be believed. The aspiration to equal justice gives an equal logical status to beliefs that the current condition of access to the law is and is not equal.

In the philosophy and the politics of both the criminal and the civil law, the meaning of equal justice has remained elusive. The intellectual and practical difficulties have been especially great as they pertain to plaintiffs. Although the meaning of "equal quality" for defense service is, of course, always debatable, the initiation of civil and criminal suits against the poor at least creates a moral framework in which something must be done by publicly sponsored lawyers if the value of equal justice is to be honored. Furthermore, the incidence of such prosecutions provides a minimal definition of how many, how often, when, and where publicly sponsored lawyers must do something. There are no similar benchmarks for establishing the requirements of equal justice for plaintiffs.

Jurisprudence has offered no theory defining how the concept of equal justice could govern the access of the poor to the right to bring civil suit. Nor have legal philosophers given substantive meaning to the value of prosecutive equality on the criminal side. (Although the phrase is common, no one knows what it would mean to have "even-handed" enforcement against white-collar and common, or "street," crime.) The processual nature of law creates a fundamental dilemma of legitimacy that is shared by civil and criminal public lawyers: before they succeed in prosecuting the wrongs of the rich or achieving recognition of the rights of the poor, public lawyers are unable to establish that their initiatives are required by equal justice. Yet, soon after they have taken novel initiatives, poverty lawyers and white-collar crime prosecutors have quite consistently won judicial sanction for expanding civil protections for the poor and criminal prohibitions against the privileged. Public lawyers in the United States must, and often quite effectively do, use bootstrap efforts to achieve legitimacy for their plaintiffs.

I do not mean to suggest that the inherently elusive quality of equal justice is philosophic news but, rather, to set up a line of sociological research into personal and collective commitments toward equal justice. It is not immediately clear how anyone involved in the legal system could ever be proud of the state of equal justice; yet this inherently problematic outlook has long been routine. How can both prosecutors and lawyers engaged in providing legal assistance to the poor convince themselves that the current allocation of resources in the legal system is morally tolerable? Conversely, how do lawyers and law offices take on and sustain the morally indignant perspective that equal justice is grossly lacking? Before they win judicial victories validating their assertions of unprosecuted wrongs or unprotected rights, how can they become animated by the concern that white-collar criminals are getting away with their crimes or by the claim that poor people have rights that are being violated? Under what conditions do lawyers and organizations of lawyers mobilize against reprehensible inadequacies in equal justice; what determines how long they will persist in their animus?

In this book I address a small part of these large questions by reporting a historical case study of the professional staffs and organizations that have specialized in providing civil legal service to the poor. There are many,

many topics relevant to the larger inquiry which I do not take up.[6] I say nothing here, for instance, about the social organization of perspectives on equal criminal justice for the poor. The U.S. histories of attempts to organize remedies for unequal access to the civil and to the criminal law are in some respects strikingly similar and in others notably different. Over the last 100 years, organizations exclusively serving the poor have grown into seemingly permanent resources for the defense of the poor in criminal and civil cases. At first, private contributors supplied the money. (Charitable resources came to civil legal assistance organizations somewhat faster than to criminal defender agencies—Brownell 1951.) In the 1960s, broadly stated federal legislation sent public funds first to the criminal defense of the poor—a congressional act set up a defender system in U.S. district courts after the Supreme Court produced the *Gideon* decision—and then, through the Office of Economic Opportunity (OEO), to civil legal service for the poor.

On the plaintiff side, the value of equal justice has advanced in sharply different forms in the organization of U.S. civil and criminal law. Criminal prosecution, which had been a privately governed function in the English common law tradition, had, in the United States, become virtually the exclusive prerogative of public officials by the nineteenth century. The establishment of the public prosecutor's office apparently did not proceed from concerns about equality in the institution of criminal cases, but it did mark a turn toward what has become a firm public commitment, at least on the formal or ideological level, to overcome the differential influence of complainants' private resources.[7] Apparently no institution for the overall public control of the right to institute *civil* suits has ever been even seriously debated in the United States.[8] As a result, equal civil justice for the poor has been pursued primarily through a separate service facility segregated by social class, a legal assistance organization serving exclusively an indigent clientele. In criminal courts, the poor are now segregated to a separate staff of lawyers only for defense services, whereas in civil law matters, they are segregated to a separate agency both for instituting and for resisting legal advocacy.

Of course, personal injury suits sometimes promise sufficient rewards for lawyers in private practice to become somewhat indifferent to the economic status of their clients. Particularly in cases of race discrimination and through the U.S. Justice Department, the government also has provided plaintiff services to the poor in certain specialized matters. But there are not many exceptions to the statement that poor people have recourse only to a legal assistance agency—a law office serving only poor people—both to press and to resist civil claims. As a result, the study of the social organization of complacence and indignation in the civil representation of the poor is largely a study of the history of the perspectives on equal justice that have been enacted by civil legal assistance organizations and their lawyers.

In sociology, the study of evolutionary changes in organizational mission is often termed *institutional analysis*. The history of legal assistance to the poor cannot be explained fully by an institutional analysis. U.S. organizational commitments toward equal justice have advanced sporadically and in response to broad movements for social reform. Legal assistance agencies were born with an aggressive reform mandate in the Progressive Era and turned toward passivity as that era faded into the 1920s. Complacence governed the institution until the formation, within the civil-rights, welfare-activist, and war-protest milieu of the sixties, of the Legal Services Program as an arm of the War on Poverty. As of this writing, in 1981, the movement toward equal civil justice is gravely threatened by the tide of conservative victories in the elections of 1980. An institutional analysis looks at an institution's world through the experience of its members—essentially from the inside out. It cannot explain changes in the institution's political and economic context. Such macrochanges may seem of controlling significance in the study of changing commitments to equal justice.

But the influence of economic and political events has been neither so direct nor so decisive as to render spurious an institutional analysis of civil legal assistance. For one thing, legal assistance offices have been complacent during times, such as the thirties, when some lawyers outside were allied with radical movements for general social change. For another, it is not obvious how a politically dominant mood of complacency about the rights of the poor could be translated into a taken-for-granted, everyday working attitude of lawyers representing the poor. It is not true that just any organizational social structure can arrange complacence in the legal staff. Nor is it obvious how individual legal assistance lawyers could, while confronting the problems of the poor, manage to shape a work life free of righteous indignation. Similarly, in periods of vigorous social movements and dominant political sympathies for the poor, it has been quite problematic whether lawyers employed in legal assistance organizations could acquire and sustain an aggressive posture against unequal justice. In the sixties, most who tried soon felt "burned out." Conversely, after the decline of the sixties, in the relatively quiescent seventies, the thrust toward reform among legal assistance lawyers did not die out. In fact, I will argue, it increased.

In short, despite the influence on legal assistance to the poor of national political changes and externally determined social movements, there is a great deal of unexplained variance in organizational structure and in personal response. This is work for an institutional analysis. Moreover, a close look does not reveal a simple and certain correlation between fluctuations in legal institutional commitments and changes in the national political mood. The heightened concentration of law enforcement agencies on white-collar crime found ways to persist through the seventies, well after the end of the Watergate scandal (Katz 1980). In 1974, after the dissolution of the broad movements of the sixties and in the middle of the dismemberment of OEO, the national Legal Services Corporation was created. U.S. movements toward equal justice have required a push from external crises to start them off, but they have shown a capacity for self-sustained momentum once in progress.

The recent period of progressive movement may now be ending. Soon after taking office, President Reagan requested that Congress eliminate the Legal Services Corporation (and his attorney general announced that he would downgrade concern about white-collar crime). Yet there is now an elaborate body of case law in which the judiciary has committed itself on the side of the poor in civil matters. There has also appeared among news media leaders and in the elites of the legal profession a powerful constituency on behalf of federal funding for legal assistance. There was no such case law, judicial experience, or organized constituency in favor of federally funded legal assistance lawyers before the creation of the Legal Services Program in the 1960s. Whatever its immediate consequence for the Legal Services Corporation, the current political environment makes especially relevant the ability of an institutional analysis to examine closely the ways in which a reform thrust in legal assistance agencies has been dependent on and independent from the force and fate of surrounding social and political movements.

In this book I examine the history of legal assistance lawyers and agencies in order to address two sets of issues. I try to determine the contingencies in organizational structure and personal experience for the maintenance by legal assistance lawyers of complacent or indignant perspectives on the state of equal justice for the poor. I try too to specify the ways in which the philosophies characterizing legal assistance work have been independent of and dependent on social and political movements. The site of my study is Chicago.

The Chicago Experience

This study traces through four stages the social foundations of the aspiration to equal justice as it has been enacted by Chicago's legal assistance organizations. The pioneering civil legal assistance organizations, especially those in Chicago, were agents against social injustice in battles led by progressives in the late nineteenth century. The institution's founders were not primarily lawyers, and they were not primarily concerned with the procedural ideal of equal access to the courts. Prominent among the initial emotional and practical concerns were classic problems of class oppression, such as refusals by employers to pay workers their earned wages.

By 1920, legal assistance organizations had replaced their original plaintiff's role with a defensive posture. Funded through city-wide civic charity drives and controlled by elite members of the bar, Legal Aid societies were dedicated to the procedural goal of providing "a day in court" for poor people who had been sued. In Chicago, civil legal assistance to the poor was provided through the United Charities of Chicago, an agency dominated by professional social workers and dedicated to "family service" as its first priority.

The institution turned back to substantive goals of social justice in the 1960s with the development of the national Legal Services Program, which quickly funded about 300 local programs in the War on Poverty. In Chicago, about 50 new staff jobs for civil legal assistance were added to the 14 operating on charitable contributions: a handful in the Appellate and Test Case Division, plus some 30 positioned to serve large volumes of walk-in clients in eight poor neighborhoods, all within the United Charities' Legal Aid Bureau; and 12 or so in Community Legal Counsel, an independent Legal Services program initiated to work with groups of the poor.

After struggling for independence from city Democratic machines and a host of other political opponents, Legal Services programs faced frozen budgets and a national leadership poised to dismantle their reform capability as the second Nixon administration took hold. Watergate intervened to break that hold, and under the Ford administration the Legal Services Program was placed in a corporation format: it was funded by the federal government and headed by a board kept at a distance from sudden changes in partisan politics through a system of staggered presidential appointments. Subsequently, with a friendlier national administration in office (Walter Mondale had been one of the strongest Senate supporters of the Legal Services Program), the appropriation for Legal Services jumped from 70 to 300 million dollars, and the number of Legal Services lawyers increased from 2000 to 5000 (Legal Services Corporation 1979, pp. 4, 8). In Chicago, the Legal Services staffs consolidated, broke completely from the United Charities and its Legal Aid Bureau, tripled in funds, and doubled in personnel.

In the late seventies, the political controversies that surrounded the new reform thrusts of legal assistance lawyers in the sixties greatly diminished, suggesting that the aggressiveness of the plaintiff role had been toned down. Actually, types of reform actions that often brought highly publicized political attacks in the late sixties became far more widespread and continuous in Legal Services throughout the seventies. By becoming increasingly professional in the seventies, Legal Services and the impetus toward reform survived the decline of the activist movements of the sixties; indeed, in places like Chicago, reform lawyering became far more powerful than ever before.

But the professionalization of reform may have meant a change in the character of reform. There is no better site to study this change than Chicago, which in 1980 had the largest, most experienced litigating staff anywhere in Legal Services. Although Legal Services lawyers originally were styled "antipoverty" warriors, their reform activities increasingly appeared to have less success in eliminating poverty than in legalizing the state's definition, organization, and maintenance of the poor as a segregated economic class.[9]

Overview

After an analysis in the first chapter of the problems lawyers face in representing the poor, chapter topics roughly follow the history of legal assistance. Why not a straight historical sequence? Although chapter 1 is based largely on observations made in the early 1970s, it argues that certain pressures to limit the scope of legal representation follow from the social reality of poverty; my contention is that, in working out roles as representatives of the poor, legal assistance lawyers have always had to struggle with these pressures. Until the common problems faced by legal assistance lawyers and organizations are understood, one cannot appreciate the strategic significance of the different responses that have been fashioned in organizational structure and personal careers. The material in chapter 1 becomes the basis for understanding the meaning of many themes taken up in later chapters, such as the Legal Aid lawyer's posture of reasonableness; the Legal Services lawyer's culture of significance; the social distance that developed between Legal Aid's staff and the lawyers on its board; and the mistaken assumptions behind the format of neighborhood offices for Legal Services programs.

Some readers may want to avoid the shock of jumping from the contemporary scenes portrayed in chapter 1 to the events in the 1880s which begin chapter 2. Those already familiar with the dilemmas of legal assistance work on the front lines of client intake might begin with chapter 2. Those interested primarily in examining personal strategies for coping with the dilemmas of human service work might skip the historical chapters and read in sequence chapters 1, 3, and 6.

Chapter 1 examines the interpretation of equal justice that legal assistance lawyers are expected to assume by their proximate environment of indigent clients and adversaries. The contention is that poverty, as presented in the form of individual requests for assistance, typically implies that very little need be done to achieve equal access to the law; legal assistance lawyers are routinely called to a quite limited professional role. Although the limits have been transcended in varying degrees at various times, legal assistance lawyers have, throughout the history of the institution, been pressed to limit the significance of their work, as well as the development of their occupational careers, essentially to the local social environment.

Poor people bring expectations that are routine in a sense that is almost universally recognized in the institution yet not articulated in its literature. Chapter 1 attempts to locate precisely the meaning and source of the experience of "routine." The experience of routine stems not from any inherent similarity among the people or among the problems brought to poverty law offices (for the personal and technical variations are inexhaustibly rich) but from structural boundaries that make it especially difficult for the lawyers to extend their efforts. For almost 100 years now, young attorneys have become dismayed at the prospects for developing careers in legal assistance work after a year or two of struggling to shape their work with the poor into crescive patterns. Their frustrations come from a concentric series of problems: in linking time spent in the social world of the poor to futures in the larger society; in linking work on one povery law case to work on the next; and in linking efforts over the various stages of relationships with given clients.

Chapter 2 begins in the 1880s with a brief account of the reform-spirited agencies that first represented the institution in Chicago. The focus is on two themes missing from the existing literature on legal assistance: the initial convergence of drives for legal and social-class justice; and the association between the impetus toward substantive reform and ties to surrounding social movements in the Progressive Era. I then review the transition between 1890 and 1920 from the pioneering agencies to the quiescent Legal Aid Bureau of the United Charities. Here, the focus is on the connections among the emergent patterns in staff demographics, organizational design, and institutional purpose.

Legal Aid societies were a quiet but extraordinary sociological achievement. They not only banished the earlier spirit of indignation over social-class injustice; they managed to eradicate the memory of a more aggressive advocacy and to socialize a staff that would regard its primarily passive representative role as fulfilling the profession's highest aspirations to equal justice. Based on organizational records and interviews with senior members, chapter 3 depicts the Chicago Legal Aid Bureau as it existed from 1950 to the early 1960s, just before the advent of the Legal Services Program. I attempt to show how the lawyers' personal careers were shaped into vehicles for Legal Aid's collective day-in-court philosophy. My analysis is based on descriptions of staff demographics and staff culture, including the culture of "reasonableness," a culture which functioned as a working ethic and a collective ethos to make severely limited advocacy a subject fit for moral celebration.

The next two chapters describe the structure of Legal Services programs and examine their early days in Chicago. Taken together, these chapters specify the relationship between the initial "antipoverty" thrust toward substantive social reform and the surrounding, protean social movement. Chapter 4 emphasizes the origins of the reform impetus of Legal Services in the social movements of the sixties. Chapter 5 quickly counters the reading that the surrounding social-movement context may have sustained, as well as originated, the reform impetus in Legal Services. It examines the many ways in which ties between Legal Services programs and aspects of "the Movement" of the sixties impeded aggressive Legal Services action for social change. There was no simple, positive, direct relationship between the strength of sixties movements for social change and the aggressiveness with which lawyers for the poor interpreted the requirements of equal justice. By challenging the simplistic correlation, I begin to show how the impetus toward reform survived through the generally conservative political environment of the late seventies. The rest of the book is addressed to the question of the persistence of reform.

Chapter 6 turns from the influence of external social forces to examine internal dynamics, presenting a theory of the poverty lawyer's "involvement." Originally, I began searching for biographical and contextual background features differentiating lawyers who did and did not remain in Legal Services staff jobs for more than two years. This proved an artificial focus and an unsatisfactory strategy for isolating the contingencies that determine the persistence of aggressive personal careers in poverty law. After a series of revisions in the definition of the problem (see the Appendix), I settled on an explanation of the experience of "involvement" on the institution's front lines. Chapter 6 explains the maintenance of involvement as a matter of three individually necessary and jointly sufficient conditions: (1) participation in reform litigation, (2) with personal responsibility for its fate, (3) within a collectively generated culture of "significance." Here is another reason that reform was able to survive into the eighties: none of these conditions of involvement requires the context of a social movement.

In the early 1960s, 400 lawyers were employed nationally by Legal Aid organizations on a combined budget of less than $4 million. By the early 1970s, over 2000 lawyers were employed on a Legal Services budget of $70 million. The superior resources enjoyed by Legal Services lawyers suggest that they would inevitably displace Legal Aid's officials as leaders of the shared institution. This generally occurred, although in Chicago, an extreme case, the transfer of power required almost a decade. But the triumph of Legal Services lawyers was much more clearly one of personal advantage than one of philosophic dominance. Considered as personal career perspectives and as collective conceptions of mission, Legal Aid and Legal Services still define a central tension in the institution. Throughout the country for the last 15 years, there has been a shifting balance from year to year and from program to program between, on the one hand, the use of a working ethic of "reasonableness" to implement a day-in-court philosophy; and on the other, the demand for personal involvement in substantive social reform.

Chapter 7 begins by laying out a framework for an extended examination of the persistence of the perspectives historically associated with Legal Aid and Legal Services. The bulk of chapter 7 compares the implications of the two types of personal careers for what I term *organizational persistence*, the problematic continuity of collective efforts among lawyers who work in a legal assistance organization either from different positions or at different times. In competition with lawyers bent on reform, the Legal Aid perspective has survived largely because of its superior organizational strength. Chapter 7 ends by starting a comparison of the *institutional strengths* of the two career perspectives, their differential capacities for acquiring new resources and for expanding the acceptance of their roles in external domains. Chapter 8 demonstrates in detail the superiority on this dimension of lawyers who manifest a perspective on involvement. It traces the strategic resources employed by a small group of about 10 Legal Services lawyers, those in Community Legal Counsel, who entered a merger with the 45 lawyers of the United Charities' Legal Aid Bureau expecting to be swallowed up and soon took over the entire legal assistance operation in the city.

Chapter 9 examines patterns of organizational and institutional development in the 1970s. I touch on the United Charities Legal Aid Bureau, which returned to its pre-1965 autonomy and size, and I then review the many changes that occurred in the independent, consolidated Legal Services program, the Legal Assistance Foundation of Chicago. Internal authority systems in Legal Services programs became less stable in the late seventies; instability frequently became full-blown crisis. I attribute new patterns of organizational instability to a loosening of ties to the external constituencies that originally anchored internal hierarchies of power. The second half of chapter 9 documents the dramatic expansion of poverty reform litigation in Chicago after 1974.

Chapter 10 examines the evolution of Legal Services' initial commitments to institutionalize an expanded conception of equal justice and to reduce poverty. Originally fused, the two purposes became separated; arguably even opposed. I propose a coherent theme underlying the apparent diversity of reform litigation objectives: the thrust of the most aggressive, innovative, professionally sophisticated work performed by Legal Services lawyers has been to transfer the social organization of poverty from relations in the private economy to relations between citizens and government. In 1980, Legal Services lawyers were using reform litigation primarily for two complementary goals: blocking and dismantling the private market's distinctive methods for organizing economic relations with the poor, such as summary evictions and actions to repossess consumer goods bought on credit; and constructing procedurally smooth operations by public agencies that institutionally segregate the poor as a common means of subsidizing their cash income, health, housing, and food supplies. From their origins in an "anti-poverty" movement, poverty lawyers appeared increasingly to provide professional expertise to rationalize the state's organization of the poor as a homogeneous, segregated social class. Throughout the seventies, poverty lawyers did not change their litigation objectives, but the structural implications of their reform role changed as the tenor of the times became progressively more conservative. To understand this ironic process, I locate the modern role of poverty reform lawyer within the century-long transformation of poverty from an occasionally prosecuted crime to an officially sanctioned, routinely administered legal status.

Over the course of the book, a number of topics in the sociologies of work, organization, and social movements become relevant: the nature of a career as a personal experience; the phenomenology of involvement as a method of persisting in a line of action; the role of caste systems of stratification in mediating relations between elites and disreputable lower classes; the relation between the fate of social movements and the organizations they spawn; the relation between the careers of members in organizations and the collective careers of their organizations; the stages and contingencies of merger as a process of transforming two autonomous formal organizations into one. To signal the possible relevancies of this case study for various fields of sociology without distracting the reader from the narrative focus, my discussion of the sociological literature is conducted largely in the notes.

There is little direct description of methods in the text. What I did and how I did it are usually implied by the context. The methodology I followed, a variant of analytic induction, is described in the Appendix.

Terminology

As may already be apparent, the terminology for describing legal assistance organizations and lawyers can be confusing. There are good sociological reasons for the difficulties. In some places, New York City for example, the Legal Aid Society is familiar as an agency for the criminal defense of the poor. In Chicago, "Legal Aid" means civil legal service. In some cities, the traditional Legal Aid agency became the exclusive vehicle for receiving federal Legal Services funds. In Chicago, the Legal Aid Bureau of United Charities initially held the city's major Legal Services grant but lost it after seven years. Thus, for several years, many "Legal Services" lawyers in Chicago worked in "Legal Aid." To many of them, the Legal "Aid" name was a disgraced reminder of the traditional view that legal assistance for the poor was a charitable gift, not a legal obligation of the state and a personal right of the poor. Even while on the Legal Aid Bureau's staff, they preferred to think of themselves as "Legal Services" or "poverty" lawyers.

It is likely that the federal OEO–poverty law program was initially given the name "Legal Services" to distinguish it from "Legal Aid" societies. But to outsiders, "Legal Services" often seems an uninformative and oddly redundant preface for lawyers. To make matters worse, when the federally funded lawyers on the Chicago Legal Aid Bureau's staff broke away to form a new organization, they named it the Legal Assistance Foundation of Chicago. In some of the discussions which led to the choice of the new name, there was mention of the possibility that a title close to "Legal Aid" might give traditional supporters of the Legal Aid Bureau pause to reflect on whether their contributions were going to the right place.

I use the following conventions more or less consistently. All organizations and lawyers in the business of providing legal services to poor people who do not pay them are in the institution of "legal assistance." "Legal Aid," a bureau of the United Charities in Chicago and an independent "society" elsewhere, is an old, charitably funded agency traditionally committed to individual service, not reform. "Legal Services" programs are sets of law jobs that are federally funded, whether the jobs are located within the Legal Aid Bureau or within organizations such as the Legal Assistance Foundation which do not receive any substantial private funding. Most "Legal Services" jobs are located in neighborhood offices, but many are located in downtown specialized litigation units. "Legal Services lawyers" are distinguished by their location in a federally funded neighborhood office or their concern with reform litigation. Many, including a few young lawyers who are described as working in the Legal Aid Bureau, like to call themselves "poverty lawyers." "Legal Aid" lawyers express a passive perspective on the problems of the poor. Most "Legal Aid" lawyers described in this book worked in the Legal Aid Bureau, but some were in Legal Services neighborhood offices.

In rough summary, everyone described below is in "legal assistance" work; "Legal Aid" lawyers and organizations are distinctively committed to individual service; "Legal Services" lawyers and offices are distinguished by a neighborhood practice or a concern with reform.

In chapter 8, the metamorphoses of organizational identity produce almost hopeless terminological confusion. The chronology which soon follows may help.

Typographical Conventions

Excerpts from documents follow the standard conventions: they are not italicized and they are verbatim. Field notes appear in two different forms. Italicized indented material represents my observations. Nonitalicized indented material represents my paraphrase of a study member's statement. Within each type of material, quotation marks contain verbatim, often tape-recorded, members' statements, and brackets contain my interpolations. In the paraphrases, my questions are set off by italics. Lawyers are often identified with the abbreviation "L"; clients, with "Cl."

Chronology of Chicago Legal Assistance Organizations

1886	Protective Agency for Women and Children: sponsored by Chicago Woman's Club; funded by personal solicitation
1888	Bureau of Justice: sponsored by Ethical Cultural Society; funded by personal solicitation
1905	Legal Aid Society: formed in the merger of the Protective Agency and the Bureau of Justice; funded through sale of "memberships"
1919	Legal Aid Bureau of the United Charities of Chicago: created from the takeover of the Legal Aid Society by United Charities; funded through professionally organized charity appeals
1930	Chicago Community Fund created; its city-wide, United Way–style campaigns soon supplying the major part of the Legal Aid Bureau's funds
1965–1967	Legal Aid Bureau of United Charities develops the Neighborhood Legal Services Program and the Appellate and Test Case Division; funds come from the Chicago Committee for Urban Opportunity (CCUO), which receives its funds from the OEO Office of Legal Services
1967	Community Legal Counsel (CLC): created by a lawyer paid by the National Legal Aid and Defender Association to stimulate applications for OEO Legal Services grants; funded directly by OEO Legal Services; branches in Chicago and Detroit
1970	United Charities displaces CCUO as the direct grantee of the OEO Office of Legal Services
1972	Legal Aid Society: resurrection of the long-dormant corporate shell of the Legal Aid Society; the vehicle for a merger of CLC and the United Charities Legal Aid Bureau; the pre-1965 Legal Aid Bureau work unit retains a special rela-

	tionship with United Charities and a special independence from the board of the Legal Aid Society
1973	Legal Assistance Foundation of Chicago: the Legal Aid Society disintegrates into the United Charities–funded Legal Aid Bureau and the new Legal Assistance Foundation, which receives all the OEO Legal Services funds for Chicago
1974	The Legal Services program is transferred out of OEO into a national Legal Services Corporation created by congressional legislation; the Legal Services Corporation funds the Legal Assistance Foundation in Chicago
March 1981	President Reagan proposes zero-funding for the Legal Services Corporation.

Chapter 1

Poor People's Conflicts and Lawyers' Work Problems

Legal assistance lawyers have often complained that their work is personally confining, of limited significance, or "routine." A conventional explanation cites heavy case loads. Virtually all legal assistance offices have strikingly large case loads. According to organizational statistics, 48 lawyers in Chicago's Legal Aid and Legal Services programs handled 43,803 "active cases" in 1972; only about 10 percent were "in litigation" (United Charities of Chicago, Legal Aid Bureau 1973).[1] But such figures can mislead; heavy case load is a spurious explanation. Legal assistance offices increasingly have employed paraprofessionals, law student interviewers, appointment systems, and priority rules to screen clients and create small case loads for their lawyers. Yet the phenomenon of routine treatment persists (Bellow 1977, p. 52).[2]

Another spurious explanation of the complaint of routine is that, despite their talk of altruism and self-sacrifice, legal assistance lawyers ultimately are governed by "straight" models of professionalism and traditional aspirations for high income and prestige.[3] There is substantial evidence that frustration with routine cannot be explained by reference to "professional" identity, at least not with any *substantive* reading of the concept. Not uncommonly, Legal Services lawyers who protest loudly against "a lack of growth" were uncertain while in school that they wanted to be lawyers. Many leave legal assistance organizations bemoaning "the routine," only to switch not to more prestigious or challenging law jobs but to managing businesses; practicing journalism; cultivating farms, fisheries, or children; or other unlawyerlike occupations.

If "professionalism" does not seem sufficient to explain complaints about routine work, it also does not seem necessary. Discontent with routine is by no means confined to professionals. Given mechanical roles, factory workers often struggle ingeniously to create diversions and brief escapes (Garson

1975). If reference to traditional professional models is not a necessary explanation of the complaint against "routine," neither is the work of the legal assistance lawyer so similar to that of the factory worker as to justify an explanation by a common human drive for variation in experience. After all, legal assistance lawyers are engaged not on an assembly line but in "people work";[4] poor people may be treated without differentiation, but they never present themselves identically. The lawyers' complaints reflect personal career expectations that are not democratically distributed in their society.

What are the career aspirations that the context of legal assistance work tends to frustrate? Many young lawyers, like other novice professionals, anticipate a career of a sort typically unavailable to factory workers. They expect work to transform their abilities and sensitivities into higher states which they cannot as yet visualize. In pursuit of a *process* of developing presumably latent competences, they look not simply for cases that are different but for cases that will *make* a difference for their futures.[5]

Experience may take on a crescive aspect, a sometimes euphoric, motivating sense of clarifying, in quite practical ways, a future that before had been only dimly seen. In the course of acting to meet immediate demands, a person may acquire resources, make investments, or otherwise promote possibilities for acting in subsequent situations. As clients, poor people typically set up social relations that undermine crescive patterns in lawyers' work. When encountering clients—and the social environment of adverse parties, opposing counsel, and local courts that often surrounds their clients—civil lawyers for the poor repeatedly experience discontinuity within cases; discontinuity between cases; and continuity in pressures to limit the significance of cases to the people immediately involved.

Examining the role of everyday problems in giving cumulative significance to work resolves the paradox that many young legal assistance lawyers, even while expressing indifference about their long-range careers, still experience severe career limitations. Of greater importance for the overall argument of the book, viewing lawyers' work as defined by an indigent clientele reveals a fundamental, historically constant feature of the institution. Routine treatment is not inevitable in legal assistance, but pressure to treat legal problems without making much of their differences *is* systematically implied by the social meaning of poverty. However important as a political or moral issue, poverty is presented to legal assistance offices in a stream of individual problems, each of which already has been defined as insignificant in its social ramifications. So long as he or she is poor, a person's civil conduct will rarely affect the interests of more than a small circle of others. Changes in personal status, as in divorce, will not involve the disposition of holdings that aggregate the interests of many others. A poor person's liability to pay a debt, continuance of a tenancy, or gain of a governmental benefit will not make many others either losers or winners in the transaction; and those who will win or lose will not win or lose much in cold, material terms. When poor people today seek civil legal assistance, they bring the same invitation they have brought for almost 100 years, an invitation to enter small social worlds that have little patience for remedial attentions.[6] This chapter portrays the background of legal assistance work, a background against which subsequent chapters highlight the historically changing roles shaped by several generations of legal assistance lawyers and organizations.

Confinement to the Proximate Social Environment

The setting for civil legal work for the poor contrasts dramatically with the setting in which lawyers work for wealthy corporate and individual clients. There is much variation at either pole, and some phenomena are common wherever legal advocacy is practiced; but there are also distinctive problems faced by lawyers for the poor. Whatever their own inclinations and abilities, lawyers for wealthy clients are expected, assisted, and at times formally directed to treat their work as significant. This expectational environment has its fundamental source not in client preferences but in the social networks that attend wealth and other sources of power. Conversely, lawyers for the poor, regardless of their competence and values, confront an everyday environment that treats their work as routine by assuming, suggesting, and at times demanding that it ought to be regarded as insignificant.

Lawyers for large corporations, unions, and government agencies represent representatives. Often they represent representatives of representatives. When arguing in court, a labor lawyer may be representing the interests expressed by a union official, who represents the trustees of a pension fund, who represent the interests of the rank-and-file. When drawing up a contract for private negotiations, a lawyer in a corporate law firm may be embodying the desires of a company president, who is the agent of the board of directors, which answers to advisers employed by institutional investors, who invest money on behalf of others, including some corporate entities. . . . A staff lawyer in a regulatory agency who is drafting a set of rules for public comment can anticipate that his product will go up an internal hierarchy, over to a few key legislators, then under the scrutiny of lobbyists, whose reports will be reviewed by numerous interest groups. Before the lawyer begins the oral argument, starts to write the contract, or outlines the regulatory scheme, a series of interrelated audiences stand more or less attentive to whatever emerges.

The work of a lawyer situated in such a network may be deemed unpleasant for any number of reasons, including boredom, but it is significant in a strict empirical sense. The lawyer's actions will signify broadly; they will ramify in implications throughout the social relations that create his or her client's social status. More important, so will the lawyer's inaction. He or she will often be told of a significant problem and even instructed in a detailed solution by an outside interest. A definition of his work as broadly significant may literally be served up to a corporation lawyer in the form of papers beginning a federal class-action lawsuit by an attorney for stockholders or by a public interest law firm. Elaborate problems and solutions are often handed to young lawyers at regulatory agencies in the form of regulations drafted by counsel for major industries. Part of the strategic work of the Washington lawyer is to make it simple and easy for government lawyers to act as though they administer a complex and demanding supervisory apparatus.[7]

In some of the most remunerative civil legal practices, it is unusually easy to treat work as unusually difficult. Lawyers for clients with significant interests often create a collegial environment in which each encourages the other to see complexity in the situation at hand. Two business lawyers may combine efforts to anticipate the ramifications of a planned course of action for each other's clients as well as for parties who do not have representatives present. In negotiations, each lawyer may find reasons to look beyond the client he actually meets—the executor, trustee, union official, or corporation executive—because the latter represents removed parties—heirs, beneficiaries, rank-and-file members, stockholders—who may subsequently object that they have not been properly represented. Each lawyer will often, for his own client's advantage, use his knowledge about the institutions the other parties operate in order to advise those parties how they might better represent themselves. The selfish motive for mutual assistance in anticipating the responses of socially distant audiences is the hope of increasing the probability that the other party will be able to live up to his part of the bargain. Consider the tenor of collegial relations in the following description of a New York City real estate practice.

> What ordinarily happens in major (real estate) sales transactions is that a prospective buyer and seller are brought together, often by a broker, and

> they bargain on the essential terms without consulting their lawyers. These bargained-for terms . . . are generally monetary, invariably including purchase price, and frequently include amount of the down payment, and the date of closing. . . . The matter is then referred to their attorneys for negotiation of details and drafting of necessary documents. . . . The lawyers are expected to iron out minor differences and put the whole deal in legally acceptable form. At times, a basic conceptual underpinning must be found for the entire transaction, as the principals have agreed on terms that do not readily fit traditional legal concepts ordinarily applicable to real estate agreements. When this kind of problem exists, the lawyers are not so concerned with trying to get the best of one another as jointly trying to dream up a legal theory that will hold the deal together. . . . they . . . start suggesting to one another problems that may arise and clauses that should be included to cover contingencies. (Johnstone and Hopson 1967, pp. 84–85)

There is typically no elaborate social network attending problems when they are presented to legal assistance lawyers. The poor seek out lawyers for assistance with personal troubles which are often in or near a crisis state: having been denied public aid, having received an eviction notice, having had utilities shut off, having had a violent domestic argument. Often the situation is within or at the edge of litigation, the client with court papers or "final" dunning letters in hand. This context of personal conflict initially gives the work of the legal assistance lawyer a very local setting. The client's emotions typically are focused on recent events and on particularistic features of current adversaries. In such a practice, it is unusually difficult to treat problems as of far-reaching significance.

Poor clients may insist their problems are of unsurpassed importance, and their lawyers may agree; but the latter will not be urged to that opinion by adverse parties and opposing counsel. Typical adversaries for legal assistance lawyers include other poor people, as for example, in domestic relations conflicts; small real estate owners, as in disputes between tenants and resident landlords; and the lower echelons of workers in public-aid bureaucracies, retail stores, and debt-collection agencies. An adversary-spouse of a legal assistance client usually will not pay a lawyer much to gather evidence for domestic relations court. In battles over evictions, the poverty lawyer's tenant-client may be fighting an unrepresented landlord who knows nothing of eviction law.[8] Among adversaries who are represented, the modal opposing counsel is the collection lawyer who bases the economics of his practice on high volume and low unit costs.[9] A poor person usually will have a great deal to lose from litigation but not enough to make it worthwhile for an adversary to expend substantial legal resources to take it from him.

Jurisdictional rules embody economic judgments that the legal problems of the poor should be handled as local matters. A legal assistance lawyer cannot reasonably expect ever to be handed papers inviting him to defend a poor person in the generally more sophisticated federal court system. Poor people are unlikely targets for attempts to collect the $10,000 that is a minimum condition (among other equally inapplicable conditions) for federal jurisdiction.

Economic forces also discourage legal assistance lawyers from investing in the avoidance of conflict. Because the costs a poor person can impose in conflict are relatively low, the transaction costs to others for avoiding conflict with the poor are relatively high. Suppose a legal assistance lawyer were to articulate idiosyncratic sources of conflict and imaginatively draft a consumer contract or lease tailored to the particular tensions at hand. Who would care? Retailers and landlords would find no compelling reason not to continue to treat the poor cheaply, on routine forms. A legal assistance lawyer cannot expect adversaries to care to anticipate and avoid conflicts.[10]

Radical differences in clients' social worlds follow systematically from extreme differences in their economic status. A person's status as "poor" stimulates expectations in a series of social relations that his or her legal problems will be treated routinely. I have suggested that adversaries are not likely to treat conflicts with the poor as worth much investment. Courts often follow suit. When Legal Services lawyers began bringing unprecedented questions of law to state courts, they found judges dominated by local perspectives and geared to summary treatments. Dramatic conflicts sometimes followed. As indicated in the following report by a Chicago Legal Services lawyer of his experience in 1968, the reason for judicial hostility may not be antipathy to the poor so much as an insistence on everyday predictability.

> I went into [judge] Hermes' court with a motion, not a long one but the longest one he had on his desk, and he rolled it up into a ball and threw it at me. *Literally?* Yes. A hundred lawyers in the courtroom were laughing. They would decide things without ever reading them. He just wasn't going to do that kind of work in his court. Later, when I came back down from the Supreme Court with an order, he enforced it without hesitation. That was the normal order of work he was used to. But on that motion he said, "If you want this decided, take it to the Supreme Court." (Cf. Stumpf and Janowitz 1969.)

Because poverty is taken as a reason for routine treatment by adversaries, opposing counsel, and even courts, it is reasonable for the poor themselves, who live constantly in this environment, not to expect more than summary service from legal assistance lawyers. The statement by clients "I only came here because I couldn't afford a real lawyer" has become a stock and somewhat bitter joke among legal assistance lawyers. Examining recurrent patterns in lawyer–client interaction confirms that the poor typically do not expect much from legal assistance lawyers.

Accurate descriptions of lawyer–client relations rarely show a client presenting a demand for a given amount of legal services and a lawyer responding in kind. The relation typically is an interactive process in which definitions of client demands are produced through negotiations. In a cyclical process, a legal assistance client will begin with some explanation for having come to the office; the lawyer will offer an interpretation of the client's concerns; the client will treat that interpretation as a proposal subject to revision; the lawyer will respond by offering a modified definition of the situation; and so on, until a tacit agreement is reached. To see whether poor people call for far-reaching legal solutions to their problems, it is necessary to look at what they accept as proper endings for a lawyer's involvement in their lives. Put as a matter for field observation, the question is, On what definitions of the lawyer's role do clients leave the office peacefully?

First, they often accept "eligibility rules" as precluding further service. Prospective clients may be induced to leave by the citation of rules limiting eligibility by income or organizational priorities. As examples of the latter, the Chicago programs in the early 1970s officially refused to perform bankruptcies for the unemployed and to prosecute uncontested divorces where there were no minor children in the family.

Poor people also often accept "hard realities" as a reason they should not expect to receive elaborate legal assistance. They may be told, "You need more evidence," "You haven't been damaged enough," or simply, "It's not fair, but there's no legal remedy."

A client claims "pain and suffering" from a slip on a banana peel in front of a grocery store. She is told she must get medical evidence of the harm before a lawyer can do anything to obtain a recovery.

A secretary who has recently been fired complains that her ex-employer has "false things" on file. She rejects the suggestion that sex or race discrimination might have played a part in her discharge, and she does not want her job back. She leaves after being told that she must incur further damage, such as a substantial period of unemployment and sub-

sequent job denials, before a lawyer could sue to remove the "false things."

A client whose new car was stolen during a servicing, when an auto dealer locked and parked it on the street overnight, does not protest the advice that there is no remedy.

A taxi driver who retired after 30 years on the job complains about a pension denial. His union and employer agreed that his suspension for 1 year, 24 years ago, constitutes a "break-in-service," depriving him of the necessary 25 years continuous service. He leaves quietly after the legal assistance lawyer commiserates and concludes that there is nothing he can do.

A client, insisting that he was the innocent party in an auto accident, has been told by the state that he must now get liability insurance to keep his license. A widow complains about her meager social security benefits and about the official explanation that she did not contribute enough during her working years to qualify for more. A 20-year-old identifies himself as a truck driver and complains of a vicious circle: he will soon be evicted because he can't pay rent, but he can't afford the transportation costs to get to job sites. He has been sent welfare checks but refuses to accept them. After a few minutes of explanation that nothing can be done, each of these people leaves.

If the legal assistance lawyer accepts the client's objective as within the organization's competence and advises that something can be done about it, the client will often be content with the advice that not much need be done. The following are examples of summary assists I observed that ended initial client interviews amicably.

A widow claims that her husband died owing her $8000 in support payments. She balks at the statement that the potential recovery is too large for eligibility at Legal Aid. The lawyer discovers that she has been unsuccessful in obtaining a death certificate from Wisconsin and offers to help by writing a letter. She then leaves gratefully.

A client asks for advice on what to do with a deed that was left in her possession when the property owner died. The deed names two other people as joint tenants. To whom should she send it? She is told that copies should be made and sent to both by registered mail.

A welfare recipient complains that his check was reduced. A call is made to his caseworker, who explains that his social security check was increased. The client then thanks the lawyer and leaves.

A woman reports that her son damaged the family car when using it against her orders. She says she wants him "to take his medicine" and is reassured by the advice that she is not personally liable.

Two friends explain that they have been unable to make contact with a door-to-door salesman after they made "down payments" on TV sets. When the lawyer phones the salesman and relates his promise of imminent delivery, they are reassured.

A husband and wife complain that, although they were until recently entitled to Medicaid, the wife's year-old Indiana hospital bill has been refused payment by Illinois public aid. They leave after receiving a form to start an administrative appeal within the Illinois public-aid bureaucracy.

A woman announces she wants a divorce and leaves satisfied after a three-minute interview. In this time, the lawyer asked about a dozen questions and placed the answers on a form. He anticipates using the form to elicit testimony from the client in a summary court proceeding.

Unless clients become "obstinate," repeating demands for service that already have been rejected, the lawyer will not end the interview with a request that the client leave.[11] Contacts between legal assistance lawyers and clients typically are not ended unilaterally nor even by making it clear that they have ended. Just the opposite: poor people are often content to leave legal assistance offices without receiving commitments for far-reaching or long-lasting service, provided they obtain an indication that the end of the current contact does not end the relationship. Legal assistance lawyers quickly learn that an effective way to overcome a client's reluctance to leave is to announce open-ended conditions for another contact:

Don't worry about their threat to evict you, but if you're sued come back.

If a private lawyer won't take your case, give me a call.

If the judge doesn't dismiss the case against you after you tell him (A, B, C), contact me immediately.

After you get more evidence, you could come back.

If they don't deliver the TV, let me know.

We don't do bankruptcies for people without jobs, but after you start working . . .

Discontinuities between Cases

Through clients and the adversaries and court settings they bring, legal assistance offices are presented with a social environment predisposed to treat the legal problems of the poor as if narrowly circumscribed. Poverty lawyers are thus encouraged to develop the implications of conflicts little further than their immediate face-to-face environment. This wall of expectations defines the outermost boundary confining a legal assistance lawyer's work. A second boundary separates the lawyer's conduct in handling a given case from his or her conduct in other cases.

In any contact with a client, a lawyer may have to negotiate an understanding of what the client wants, determine what the relevant facts are, and convey comprehensible advice. For lawyers who have long-term relations with clients, the accomplishment of these tasks on any given occasion is also an investment in subsequent work. The requests for help typical at legal assistance offices center on crises; the urgency implies that the lawyer–client relation will be short term or one-shot. Moving from one short-term client to the next, legal assistance lawyers experience problems in making work on one problem useful for the next.

Large organizations and wealthy people often place their lawyers "in house" or on retainer. In such relations, the lawyer may provide service without the client even perceiving a need for it; for extended periods of work, the lawyer may avoid the need to negotiate a definition of service with the client. For example, the lawyer may discover a problem (new regulations or new statutes) in the course of routinely keeping up with changes in the relevant legal framework and business climate. He may provide service—for example, by incorporating a new tax-avoidance strategy into a standard contract—in his ordinary management of the client's interests.

In contrast, the stream of personal crises brought to legal assistance offices makes the task of learning what the client wants an everyday experience. The following excerpt is taken from an intake interview conducted by a lawyer who at the time had two years of experience in legal assistance. It indicates how idiosyncrasies in perception and style of expression limit the ability to use the experience of one client interview in the next.

Cl. enters L.'s office with the standard intake card. It has been filled out by a secretary, and it indicates that his problem is "social security," his income is a bit over scale, there's one in his family, and he's 66. L. at first assumes Cl. has a social security problem. Cl., realizing that

L. is basing his questions on a reading of the card, says: "No, I don't care what she puts down there."

L. finds Cl. difficult to understand, as do I. He mumbles and seems to be talking on irrelevant tacks about his family, his first and second wives and their relatives. Social security seems somehow relevant; he keeps referring to what "the man at Social Security" told him. L. keeps asking, "What's the problem?" *Cl. keeps saying,* "I don't have a problem. I'm here because you white folks have common sense, and I don't."

Cl. mentions something about being taken for less than 65 at Social Security. He is 65, he insists, although his birth certificate shows him to be younger. L. pursues this, trying to pin down his age and what was determined about his age at Social Security. But Cl. frustrates this line of questioning. He indicates that he's got a job for the next few months, and then he'll be 65 even according to his birth certificate.

Cl. also mentions that he got married without divorcing his first wife. His second wife died. The Social Security guy told him he was a bigamist. He doesn't want to break the law, and he realizes that bigamy is illegal. He never has broken the law, and "I don't want you white folks to throw me in jail." *At first L. brushes this aside as irrelevant but then tries the idea that divorce is the reason he came in. But no, he doesn't want a divorce.*

Now L. is enjoying this fellow and the struggle to figure out why he came in. He asks a series of questions on family history and status. At least that's a line of questions he can pursue in an orderly fashion, and it seems somehow relevant. At various points, L., concerned that he's misinterpreting Cl., reads back his interpretation of Cl.'s statements: "OK, now look, you're married now, you've got two kids, you never were divorced from the first marriage. . . . Right?"

Finally L. figures that when Cl. went to Social Security, someone jokingly told him he was a bigamist. Cl., afraid of being a "criminal," came in to see if he needed a divorce to avoid jail. L. reads this back. Cl. nods "yes." L. tells him there's nothing to fear, that he should return if he wants to remarry but otherwise "there's no problem." As Cl. is leaving, L., thinking of claims that the first wife might make against him, asks if he has any property. Cl.: "Just the clothes on my back. Thank you, white folks."

Irrespective of interviewing styles, the need to negotiate mutual understandings poses a common problem. Once they realize that interpretive difficulties are to be expected, legal assistance lawyers must decide how "hard" or "soft" they will be with clients. The "soft" posture would be to listen patiently as a new client unfolds his story by describing 14 years of affection for his dog; how his concern grew as the dog began to show signs of disease; the state of fright in which he drove the dog to a public hospital for emergency surgery; how this trauma explains why he got drunk after leaving the dog at the hospital; how this explains why he had an accident and got arrested for drunken driving. . . . The "hard" response quickly cuts in with, "In one sentence, what's your problem?" (In this case, the client wanted to know if he had to pay a $500 fee requested by a lawyer who had represented him when the other party to the accident threatened suit.) The "hard" response may cut down the length of the interview, but it will not make it a resource for comprehending the next.

Closely related to the task of learning what the client wants is the task of establishing the relevant facts. For lawyers who work in long-term relations with clients, knowledge gained about a client's affairs forms a useful basis for dealing with a succession of problems. A common thread also can be woven through a lawyer's career if clients change but the adversary stays the same, as in the case of lawyers who specialize in matters under the jurisdiction of federal regulatory agencies. They become lay historians and sociologists, developing a feeling for an institution's sense of its mission which they can use to predict its responses to a client's plans (Horsky 1952, pp. 71–73).

As I demonstrate in describing reform activities in chapter 6, legal assistance lawyers may also develop long-term relations with clients and adversaries. But my point here is that the form in which work is presented to legal assistance offices implies short-term relations. A given national corporation or a given public bureaucracy may be the common and therefore long-term adversary behind the complaints of numerous clients. But clients typically come in after unsuccessful attempts to influence the discretion of particular collection agents and caseworkers. The development of long-term relations with adversaries depends on transcending an initial focus on the idiosyncrasies of local personalities.

For example, despite their desire to develop a cumulative expertise, legal assistance lawyers specializing in housing receive a series of complaints each framed initially as disputes over particular tenancy relations. A client will come in with a bundle of receipts, and the lawyer will be invited to reconstruct the rental relation by interpreting barely legible scribbles and imputing dates to receipts. One need not resort to culture-of-poverty explanations or the "personal disorganization" of the poor to understand why legal assistance lawyers must struggle repeatedly to elicit the facts. Where lawyers have short-term relations with clients, they have relatively little opportunity to influence clients' record-keeping practices, much less to follow the example of many lawyers for resourceful clients and keep the records themselves.[12]

Discontinuities within Cases

Pressed by expectations to remain within a local social environment, hemmed in by difficulties in making efforts on one case relevant to the next, legal assistance lawyers run into still tighter restrictions on their work: extraordinary risks that investments made in the initial or preparatory stages of cases will never be realized. Because of structural characteristics of their relations with clients, legal assistance lawyers are unusually powerless to prevent the destruction of the apparent value of early stages of representation.

Legal assistance lawyers must become reconciled to their restricted ability to determine the meaning of their work to clients. Short-term relations preclude supervision of how clients use advice beyond the office doors. I interviewed L. after he completed his first month in a neighborhood office.

> I feel a tremendous pressure to do something that'll be of value for people who come in. I feel I'm not doing my job if I just tell them that there's nothing to do. Maybe they've been waiting for weeks for an appointment, or an hour in the waiting room; they've spent some money to get here, or they're taking the time off work and losing money that way. So I do a lot of social work. . . . But then if I don't make a case out of it, when they leave the office I don't know how their lives are going to be affected. I don't even know if they understood me. You know, sometimes I'll be going on, telling them where to go and what to do to handle something on their own, and then when they're smiling, about to leave, I'll ask them something and it's clear they never knew what I was talking about. And—I thought of this for a while—I guess it's not my place to call them up and find out what happened. That's too paternalistic.

Legal assistance lawyers believe that their clientele contains a sizeable percentage of "crazies." Whether or not they are crazy before coming to legal assistance offices, poor people often *appear* crazy when they leave before the lawyer is able to grasp their perspective;[13] and given the pattern of short-term relations with unscreened clients, this is a frequent event. For the lawyer, the upshot is a sense—sometimes bitter, sometimes absurd—of wasted effort. The lawyer may render his experience of incomprehensibility and absurdity comprehensible and rational by imputing craziness to clients. Here are two examples of clients who were labeled "crazy" when the lawyer failed to grasp the client's perspective on the lawyer's role.

> *After getting off the phone, L. laughs and reports as follows:* All the caller said was, "Forget that. I wasn't supposed to be involved with it." We really get some crazies. She came in with a news article on the Penn Central Railroad, and she asked me to explain it to her. She wouldn't tell me what she wanted, except she kept asking me to explain the article to her. I did, the best I could. She really came in for money; I referred her to Public Aid, and she's got some social security problems. When I asked her, "Why do you want me to explain it? Do you have some stock in it?" she said: "I did but it was stolen. Just explain it please." OK. Now she calls and says that.
>
> *After establishing Cl.'s income and family status, L. tells her:* "Unfortunately, we have a policy against taking divorces where there are no children. Unfortunately, all I can advise you is to save your money and get a private attorney."
>
> Cl.: "I have a private attorney, and I don't want a divorce. He remarried. Can any man just go and do that?"
>
> L.: "You were never divorced?"
>
> Cl.: "No. I don't want a divorce. You mean to tell me that any man can just go off and do that?"
>
> L.: "He can't remarry, but that's his problem."
>
> Cl.: "You mean, I can't do anything?"
>
> L.: "*I* can't do anything. . . . *You* can get him prosecuted for bigamy. It's against the law in this state to marry again when you're already married."
>
> Cl.: [getting angry] "Now you're contradicting yourself. You said you couldn't do anything."
>
> L.: "*I* can't do anything, but *you* can ask the state's attorney to prosecute him for bigamy. Or you can get support; you can go to the court of domestic relations."
>
> Cl. and L. repeat two more rounds of this, and Cl. then storms out. I ask: "What was it that she wanted?"
>
> L.: "I don't know *what* she wanted. She seemed slightly .24. Do you

know what that is? [It is the office's code number for the category, "Incompetents' Estates."] That desk really gets a mess of things, everything the others don't know what to do with."

He doesn't seem to want to talk about this further, appearing annoyed by the scene. I let my question go unasked: because this is a public institution, might she have thought he was the "state's attorney"?

As the effort to identify client objectives may be rendered futile by "crazy" clients, so the effort to establish facts may be undercut by "clients who lie." Several lies are said to be typical: a husband's insistence that he cannot pay support because he is unemployed; the claim by a defendant in an auto accident damage suit that his car was stolen on the fateful day and later returned, all mysteriously; a tenant's claim that he did not receive the notice required by statute to initiate an eviction.

Whether or not poor people do lie to lawyers with unusual frequency, the legal assistance lawyer is in a relatively impotent position for protecting himself against client deceit. In contrast to "clean" law practices, which arrange the use of organizational property or power on the basis of documentary evidence, legal assistance lawyers primarily handle "dirty" work. They can be suddenly and visibly stained by an unexpected appearance of client immorality. Like private practitioners of divorce, personal-injury, and criminal law, legal assistance lawyers are expected to take disputes over personal incidents toward trial, where they must often take a posture based on a client's credibility. A legal assistance practice is systematically biased away from the opportunity to investigate a client's story before acting on it. For self-protection, lawyers for the poor develop strategies—but never foolproof remedies—to avoid "getting burned."

> The first month I was here . . . I believed everything my clients said. I would get several cases a week where the client said she didn't get a five-day notice. . . . So I'd go in for a hearing on a five-day notice. I remember one case in particular in which I was so sure of winning I had already written "won case" in the file. I had asked her several times, and she kept saying she hadn't gotten the notice. The day of the hearing, I had her near me, and I was saying to her, "Now remember, you just say that you didn't get the five-day notice and it'll be all right." [Then judge] Sampson takes a copy of a five-day notice and puts it in front of the client and says, "Did you get one of these?" And she folds. . . . And after she's been lying to me all along, when [the judge] looks down, she tells the truth. This kept happening to me,

> again and again. Now I don't trust a fucking one. I assume they got it; if they didn't, I'll find out. *How?* I'll ask the other attorney for a copy. *But what if she still insists?* If she insists, I'll go to a hearing.

Some legal assistance lawyers believe that they face special problems from clients who stand them up because their services are free. For this recurrent dilemma as well, they devise tactics:

> Clients are notorious about changing their minds about divorces, adoptions, name changes. Even though he's broken her ribs, he's kicked her ass so bad you can see it, still she'll say, "Oh, he promised not to do it again." We try and protect ourselves against having our work wasted by having the client come in with the court costs before we'll do the forms and type up the pleadings. This money gives clients a stake in the suit. They may not even realize that they can sometimes get their money back and may think they're committed to continuing with the suit. But there are no sure-fire protections against clients wasting your work by changing their minds, or just not coming back and moving so you can't find them.

Again, this boundary on the ability to build up the meaning of work can be attributed more confidently to the structure of lawyer–client relations than to the psychology of the poor. It is not at all clear that clients receiving free legal assistance change their minds more often than clients who pay for service. But the absence of a fee allows the event to become an unequivocal "stand up"; work on the initial stages is completely "wasted."

Conclusion

The statement "The legal problems of the poor are routine" is universally controversial in legal assistance circles. There are two things wrong with it. "Routine" misses the human diversity of the clientele and the intricacies of intervening in their lives. Insofar as "routine" suggests redundancy, a repetition of the past in the present, it does not accurately describe the flow of problems into legal assistance offices. Each client and case contains innumerable unique features; each may be taken to require a somewhat unprecedented response. For decades, legal assistance lawyers have avoided boredom by taking interest in the work of interpreting clients' styles of personal expression and the meaning of uniform legal remedies as they fit into idiosyncratic biographies.

The question addressed in this chapter is not whether the civil problems of the poor are "redundant" but whether they turn up at legal assistance offices in a form that restricts the development of cumulative patterns in work. Legal assistance lawyers must often act differently in the present case than they have in the past, but not necessarily in a way that will make a difference for their future. The ambience into which the legal assistance lawyer walks every day is one that implies that the problems of the poor are insignificant, can be handled satisfactorily without reaching far beyond a poor person's small social world; that summary advice and assistance will often be satisfactory; that conflicts should be negotiated without making "a big deal" of them; and that if a dispute goes to litigation, he should not make a federal case of it.

The second problem with the assertion "The problems of the poor are routine" is its passive voice. The analysis in this chapter is directed not at what legal assistance work "is" but at the boundaries defined for it by the institution's social environment. Legal assistance offices may be organized in ways such that the experiences of the lawyers are shaped "on the front line," where these boundaries are experienced directly. They may also be organized with eligibility screens and paraprofessionals which insulate the lawyers from confining pressures. And they may be organized to promote reform strategies that overcome prevailing limitations. The personal and collective response is not determined by the environment. In the following chapters, I use this analysis of the institutional environment at legal assistance offices as a background against which to pose the different responses that have been made over the history of legal assistance to the poor.

Chapter 2

The Decline of Reform and the Emergence of Legal Aid

In 1919, Reginald Heber Smith published the first of a series of surveys and policy documents describing a growing, national Legal Aid community. The history he outlined conveyed the legitimating aura of tradition by claiming an essential continuity with organizations in the late nineteenth century. But "Legal Aid" societies, the universally agreed upon vehicles for delivering civil legal service to the poor from 1920 to 1965, constituted a second and significantly new stage in the institution's history.

Two fundamental, related institutional patterns were transformed from 1885 to 1920: an emphasis on social-class reform declined with the waning of a surrounding social movement; and the staff became socially distant from its formal leaders and sources of funds. An examination of this first transformation in purpose and structure should throw into relief the social foundations of Legal Aid. In later chapters, when I examine the transition in the 1960s from the format of the Legal Aid society to that of the Legal Services program, these patterns reverse. The following account thus provides an initial, rough sketch of social factors which, for almost 100 years, have been important influences on organized interpretations of equal justice for the poor.

Reform Origins

Two nineteenth-century organizations are usually cited as predecessors of Legal Aid in Chicago. Both prominently displayed features that were lost in the development of Legal Aid. Mixing outrage with idealism about oppression of the poor, the founders made law reform an initial objective; and they struck a close relationship between public exhortation and legislative lobbying on the one hand and daily service to walk-in clients on the other.

Members of the Chicago Woman's Club established the Protective Agency for Women and Children in 1886. They staffed the agency with social workers from among their own number, hired a lawyer, and personally solicited funds. The first calls to action spoke of "the great number of seductions and debaucheries of young girls under guise of offered and needed employment." Initially, then, the concern was narrow and only marginally about social-class injustice; the agency would attempt to limit class exploitation only at the boundaries of traditional sexual morality. The intake process was not, however, limited to this special "protective" concern; and as it brought in a broader representation of the urban poor, the agency widened its vision and addressed more general forms of economic exploitation. Particular attention soon was paid to wage claims and to "chattel mortgage extortions threatening families with losing their little all" (Conover 1898, p. 287).

During the agency's life, female board members routinely reviewed individual cases and served in staff capacities. Board and staff roles were also combined in special projects. In one, board committees assigned members to oversee proceedings at boys' courts, which led in turn to requests that lawyer-directors provide voluntary defense representation. In another special project, board members were stationed at "criminal assault" trials to provide "the shrinking victim" with "moral support" (Conover 1898, p. 288). This service was related to the board's program of lobbying for legislation to strengthen the punishment of rape and child molestation.[1]

The other nineteenth-century predecessor of Legal Aid in Chicago was the Bureau of Justice. It was founded in 1888, not by lawyers, as its name might suggest, but by reform-minded members of the Ethical Cultural Society of Chicago, primarily businessmen. They responded to a call to action in a speech on "gross abuses" of which "the friendless and the poor were the victims . . ." (Ethical Culture Society 1926, p. 236).

> The atmosphere of that year was charged with a great current of public interest concerning justice to the poor and unfortunate, and conferences of well-to-do and thinking men were frequent to devise ways and means of clearing a situation made world known because of the so-called Anarchist riots, trials, and executions which followed in rapid succession. Out of this environment the Bureau of Justice was ushered as one of the factors which sought to provide a remedy.[2]

The bureau did not develop a formal affiliation with the Ethical Society, although dual memberships were common. It was obvious that the Ethical Society would be a precarious supporting base. Only recently, the Ethical Society had begun a struggle for its own existence when its leader joined the highly visible Henry Demarest Lloyd in a public campaign to petition gubernatorial clemency for the Haymarket bombers. For this principled stance on what was for years the leading *cause célèbre* in Illinois, the Ethical Society was labeled "anarchist" and drew the hostility of much of Chicago's business community (Radest 1969, pp. 63–64, 154). The bureau depended financially on personal solicitations by leaders of the local social, business, and civic elites. So did the Legal Aid Society, which was created in a 1905 merger of the bureau and the Protective Agency. The Legal Aid Society received its funds from the same sources and in the same way as had the bureau—through purchases of individual memberships—and with the same financial concern to avoid controversy.

While the Bureau of Justice avoided an image as radical, it maintained a program for reform. Between 1896 and 1917, two long-term presidents led the bureau and then the Legal Aid Society, and they both had activist backgrounds. The first, Frank Tobey, was a New England abolitionist who became a wealthy furniture dealer in Chicago (*Book of Chicagoans* 1905, p. 571). The second, Rudolph Matz, was a lawyer from a philanthropically prominent Chicago family who had developed a reputation for litigating public-interest issues. Matz had received publicity in the 1890s by suing factory owners on behalf of the Society for the Prevention of Smoke (Chicago Legal Aid Society 1910, p. 11).

As in the Protective Agency, the bureau and the Legal Aid Society operated with relatively little social distance between the voluntary governing levels and the paid staff. Attorneys employed by the organization were appointed to board positions. Both ex-staff lawyers and board members had prominent local legal careers.[3]

Reform activities included publicizing outrageous conditions, drafting legislation, coordinating political support, and mounting lobbying campaigns. Law reform was stated in two of the bureau's three formally announced purposes; and throughout the bureau's history and the life of the Legal Aid Society, the year's progress in legislative reform was a leading feature in annual reports. Conspiratorial arrangements between constables, justices of the peace, and creditors were among the earliest targets. Decrying as "nefarious" the routine corruption of the courts in collection practices, the bureau moved to reform the state constitution and the city charter so as to abolish the use of a fee system to compensate the officials.

Wage assignments were attacked by drafting a succession of bills to bar their enforcement, to increase their notice and disclosure obligations, and to inhibit their creation (for example, by requiring signature of the spouse).

Related campaigns sought prohibitions against charging interest on salary loans. By promoting such restrictive economic legislation, the organization placed itself at the heart of what was perhaps the most significant contemporary politicolegal issue: the constitutionality of statutes regulating business practices. After the Illinois Supreme Court reversed some of the organization's legislative victories as unconstitutional, alternatives to statutory remedies were tried. The *Tribune* was induced to refuse advertisement from designated loan companies. In cooperation with the Chicago Association of Commerce, then a strong force for civic reform (Wiebe 1962, p. 19), a wage loan society was formed to operate at rates that would undercut loan sharks.

By 1920, law reform activities were placed in low profile and divorced from staff responsibility. In the late 1930s, they were largely abandoned. From the outset, procedural justice and substantive reform had competed as goals. The procedural ideology finally took over in the form of a distinctively passive interpretation of "equal justice" as access to a day in court.

The change of emphasis was made in the face of opposition from some who had become members of the Legal Aid community by following tangents of their earlier, primary commitments to Progressive movements. Matz represented the conservative position. President of Chicago's Legal Aid Society from 1908, he had persistently backed legislative reform activities; but he gradually turned against prohibitive and toward permissive statutes that encouraged free-market answers to usury and other credit abuses. At the national Legal Aid convention in 1916, the more radical view was represented by Professor Graham Taylor of the Chicago Commons. Taylor, an important figure in the settlement houses and among social workers at the University of Chicago, had been a prominent participant in the reform campaigns of the Legal Aid Society. He now urged Legal Aid societies generally to return to law reform by mobilizing public concern about oppressive applications of the law to the poor and by promoting remedial legislation directly (Taylor 1916, pp. 128–129). Matz, supporting the position taken at the convention by Reginald Heber Smith, a young Harvard-trained lawyer associated with Boston's Legal Aid Society, rejected Taylor's views. In the Chicago Legal Aid Society's (1917) annual report for 1916, he recorded his reasons and revealed a discomfort with radical movements and associations:

> To my mind it is a mistake for the Legal Aid Society to attempt preventative legislation except in an incidental way. The primary object of the Society is not to try to bring about the reform of certain laws. The minute

> we begin to do that, the minute that becomes the primary object of the Society in the eyes of the public, we are going to be known as reformers who "have a mission," or we are going to be considered "visionary."

From Working Class Advocate to Counselor for the Pathological Poor

In 1919, the Chicago Legal Aid Society became the Legal Aid Bureau of the United Charities of Chicago. The United Charities had developed out of nineteenth-century relief-and-aid societies into a charity-organization society—a "scientific" liaison between charities and the poor—and then it became a professional social work agency featuring family counseling and psychologically oriented casework.[4] Legal Aid was now subordinated in an organization which saw its role as intervening with the detachment of expertise between charitably inclined but naïvely sympathetic citizens and the morally untrustworthy poor. Public alerts to conditions especially oppressive of the poor and accounts of campaigns for remedial legislation dropped out of Legal Aid's reports.

In 1922, a recently expanded United Charities was consolidating its power among local private philanthropies. Legal Aid, no longer part of an effort to exhort the public toward outraged concern, was now part of a program organized to discount the public's experiences with the apparently compelling needs of the poor. A major theme projected by United Charities was the risk to the moral character of the poor posed by the foolish indulgence of laymen.

> Occasionally reports are received of women and children begging at the door. One hundred and five such cases were received last year, which it was [*sic*] impossible to locate. The person begging had evidently given an incorrect address. Here is a case in point:
>
> A child appealed for aid to a minister. The minister telephoned the nearest United Charities district office and was asked to detain the child a few minutes. Shortly he was told that the residents at the address the little boy gave knew no such family, nor was the family known in the neighborhood. As a result of the minister's interest, the child's real home was discovered and the little fellow checked in his "Artful Dodger" enterprises.
>
> FAMILY BEGGING IS UNNECESSARY
>
> *It may be authoritatively stated that no family need beg in Chicago because of destitution. The United Charities is able to give ample*

relief in these cases. Behind every instance of child begging are dissolute and depraved parents profiting therefrom. (United Charities of Chicago 1922, p. 22)

In later years, United Charities emphasized an image as a family-service agency. By official design, the Chicago Legal Aid Bureau served social work goals, attending to client problems as reflections of personal pathology rather than structural injustice:

> Legal Aid looks at the whole problem of the client. Its lawyers are aware that in many instances, such as family matters and deep involvement in debt, the legal problem is symptomatic of deeper emotional disturbances. To aid them in these situations, a group of competent caseworkers with special training have been assigned to the Legal Aid Bureau as a cooperative function of the Legal Aid Bureau and the Family Service Bureau of United Charities. (United Charities of Chicago 1957, p. 15)

In an ironic way, Legal Aid's increasingly conservative posture was self-consciously promoted as the fulfillment of its initial progressive impulses. In economic disputes, Legal Aid's nineteenth-century predecessors had intervened in social-class relations predominantly as debt collectors for the poor, frequently enforcing workers' wage and injury claims against employers. When governmental agencies were created to moderate these class tensions, Legal Aid let them have the business.

Even before the proliferation of federal ameliorative agencies in the 1930s, Legal Aid began referring plaintiff actions to external remedial agencies such as unions and state labor and industrial-accident commissions as these alternatives became available.[5] But Legal Aid did not passively acquire what became its characteristically passive, defensive posture toward the rights of the poor. In her 1918 superintendent's annual report for the Legal Aid Society of Chicago,[6] Maud Parcells Boyes noted that loan shark, chattel mortgage cases had been declining in the society's work load as a direct result of remedial legislation which Legal Aid had itself proposed and pushed. In a sporadic but consistent line of development that culminated in the late 1930s, Legal Aid lost portions of its plaintiff case load to remedial alternatives which its board members helped draft and enact. In a speech in 1938, the chairman of the Legal Aid Committee of the United Charities noted how laws they had promoted, such as a wage payment act which gave the state's Department of Labor criminal penalties to enforce wage claims, were relieving Legal Aid of a heavy collection-agency role (Chicago Historical Society 1938, p. 19).

Over the first third of this century, legal assistance lawyers essentially abandoned what originally had been their primary role of aggressively attacking exploitation of the working class in the private economy and took up a defensive role of counseling assistance to the pathological poor. In 1910, the Chicago Legal Aid Society received 5102 "applicants," of which 1804 had wage claims and 445 had other claims for collection, including a large percentage of workman's compensation (Chicago Legal Aid Society 1910). Thus, in almost 50 percent of its case load, Legal Aid had represented the working poor as *plaintiffs and creditors*; and in this work, it stood primarily against their social-class superiors. As late as 1918, the Legal Aid Society collected almost $40,000 for its clients, a figure almost twice the size of the society's whole budget [Chicago Historical Society n.d. (1919?), p. 4]. By the 1950s, Legal Aid had become largely a *defender of debtors* against retail creditors and a party to conflicts *among the poor*, largely in domestic-relations matters. In the early 1960s, wage claims and other collections comprised a small part of 1 of the 12 "desks" at the United Charities of Chicago's Legal Aid Bureau. The symbolic placement of the plaintiff economic case load, as well as its size, is notable: six desks were in the Family and Probate Division, with part of one desk in this division devoted to claims before administrative agencies (public aid, veterans, social security); six were in the Economic Division, with all but the "miscellaneous" desk, which covered wage claims, consisting of defense work.

Legal Aid's Passivity and Its Professional Honor

Although the inclusion of Chicago's Legal Aid within a charity administered by a professional social worker was unique among modern Legal Aids, the character of its work was not.[7] As in other Legal Aids, the Chicago staff pursued the dispassionate goal of a day in court rather than the substantive interests of the poor as a social group or class. As in Chicago, Legal Aids nationally shaped their commitment to this procedural ideal in quiescent deference both to the economic interests represented by the organized bar and to the conservative moral and social values of those who supplied their funds.[8]

Throughout Legal Aid's modern period, it avoided the controversial poor, whether in criminal, labor-relations, or civil rights cases. To avoid even minor controversy, Legal Aid showed a special deference to the local bar. Income eligibility scales and restrictive policies on accepting fee-generating cases were periodically submitted for bar approval. Even where bar associations had failed to designate lawyers who would represent, for fees, clients deemed ineligible at Legal Aid, some Legal Aids, fearing charges of favoritism, still refused to refer clients to a lawyer (Smith and Bradway 1936, p. 124).

When the Chicago Legal Aid Society became a bureau of United Charities, the superintendent (executive director) of United Charities, Joel D. Hunter, moved quickly to formalize symbolic support from the elite of the bar. In 1923, reviewing his first three years of experience with Legal Aid, Hunter listed new ties with the profession as two of his four major accomplishments:

> The handling of domestic cases by the experienced social workers of the United Charities; the relationship which has been established with the Northwestern University School of Law, resulting in the Legal Aid Bureau having a member of the faculty as advisory counsel; the appointment of a standing committee of . . . the Chicago Bar Association [with] . . . an equal voice with the standing committee of . . . the United Charities in determining the policies of the Legal Aid Bureau; and economy in the saving of some overhead expenses. [Chicago Historical Society n.d. (1923?), pp. 11–12]

The Chicago Bar Association had, thus, become a full partner in the governance of Legal Aid. The relationship established with Northwestern's law school reflected even more intimate ties of sentiment between Legal Aid and the top echelons of the legal profession. In 1919, an agreement was struck whereby all Northwestern law students would be required to work at the Legal Aid Bureau at some point in their student careers (Chicago Historical Society 1919). Soon there were an average of 25 law students a day working under Legal Aid's five staff lawyers. Dean John Wigmore, who negotiated the arrangement for Northwestern, was then perhaps the most prominent law academic in the country and was related by marriage to the leadership of the United Charities.

In a national pattern, Legal Aid judiciously qualified its adversarial posture. Percentages of cases litigated were pointedly reported as low; the implication was that relevant outsiders might otherwise criticize the agency as too aggressive. In the same defensive vein, Legal Aid was characterized as a court of last resort for the poor. The lawyer's relation with clients was styled as judicial and mediating rather than partial and militant. In this, as in most ideological matters, Smith formalized the rhetoric that became standard in the Legal Aid community.

Writing in 1919, Smith faced a difficult ideological problem. He wanted to deflect suspicion that Legal Aid's "free" services would enable the poor to litigate frivolously either for unfair bargaining advantage in economic relations or for spite in personal relations. But he also wanted to portray Legal Aid as governed by professional standards rather than the moral criteria of charity. Because service at Legal Aid would lack the usual economic restraint, some other restraint was necessary to avoid the first pitfall; but restraint based on moral, social, religious, or political values would not avoid the second.

Smith's solution was to stress the lawyer's status as officer of the court; professional ethics would thus be the moderating influence. Legal Aid lawyers would reject clients or cases only on "professional" standards, thus acting as court in determining whether the client had a "meritorious" case—meritorious in contrast, that is, to litigation that was ethically improper because it exploited technicalities for "delay" or "frivolous" claims although courts would entertain it as proper. In other words, Legal Aid would avoid the excesses potential in its unique financial relations with clients by being more meticulous in ethical restraint than the state's courts would require. To avoid restrictions based on invidious standards, Legal Aid would have as its first commitment a purely legal ideal: the provision to clients of a day in court. Fashioning restraint with a lawyer's unique moral symbols, Legal Aid was immune to criticism from professional circles.

Smith's achievement is represented in the following passage, in which he moves from guarding one vulnerability to the other, apparently unaware of his contradiction:

> *The office of a legal aid organization is like any ordinary private law office*. The only objective signs of difference that impress the observer are the modesty of the appointments and the steady procession of persons coming and going. *In general the organizations, through their attorneys, conduct their cases just as any attorney conducts his practice*. . . . As the legal aid organizations stand in a quasi-public position . . . they are confronted with certain peculiar problems which have led to the adoption of several interesting principles concerning the conduct of the work. Realizing that their work was in the field of the law and that they were taking a part in the administration of justice, the organizations have wisely refrained from erecting any moral standard which applicants must satisfy before being entitled to assistance. The only test is the intrinsic merit of the claim plus a due regard for those restrictions which good ethics im-

> pose on all members of the bar. Suits for reasons of spite, vexatious proceedings taken for delay, technical defenses to just claims, will not be undertaken. . . . The societies institute or defend cases in court only when they are reasonably convinced that truth is on their side. Their appearance in court depends on the merits of the case as they understand it and not on the payment of fees. They have established a standard of conduct which is likely to exert a powerful influence in the future. *The standard accords with the best ethics, but it unquestionably is far in advance of the average attitude of the bar. They deal with the old and vexing question of duty by frankly placing their duty to the court before their duty to the client* (emphasis supplied). (Smith 1919, pp. 161–162, 164–165)[9]

In the Legal Aid philosophy, equal justice was to be the distinctive mission of a specialized organization that would operate as an island of idealism in a profession governed by the ability to pay. But as long as privately compensated lawyers served their clients' substantive goals and did not limit their services to a procedural, day-in-court standard, Legal Aid's dedication to equal access to the legal system could only be an exaggerated professionalism. By segregating the poor to separate facilities at which the dispensation of legal service would be governed by a unique commitment to equal justice, Legal Aid's services necessarily would be unequal to those available for a fee.

The inherent contradiction in this separate-but-equal ideology grew as the private profession grew. In the 1920s and 1930s, the movement of ideas in Legal Aid ran opposite to philosophic currents at the top of the profession. Legal Aid professed an idealistic jurisprudence that assumed a radical division between the process and substance of law. Poor people, the theory went, were properly served by advocates who would first consult "the law," assess substantive rights, and then judiciously invoke legal procedures. Meanwhile, in the major law schools, where the professional elite of the next generation was being trained, "legal realism" (Twining 1973) was blasting away at the formalistic jurisprudence of the nineteenth century. Law students who would graduate to Wall Street and to New Deal positions shaping the welfare state were being socialized in a highly pragmatic atmosphere full of ridicule for distinctions between what the law is and what it turns out in practice to be (Auerbach and Bardach 1973). They would learn that to exploit every opportunity for delay and to seize on every technicality that would give strategic advantage to a client could constitute an ethical obligation and a measure of professional acumen.

The contradictory character of Legal Aid's unequal commitment to equal justice—its masking of substantive values by a procedural ideal—was less subtly represented in the formal rules of Legal Aid societies. "Spiteful" claims and "vexatious proceedings" permit broad interpretation. Representation of plaintiffs in divorces was severely restricted on the view that requests for such services indicated personal pathology. So was representation in bankruptcy, which was often seen as a "technical defense to just claims." In the 1950s, Chicago's Legal Aid lawyers were required to win the assent of social workers for these cases, and financial supporters were assured that assent was not given liberally. Under the title "it is a matter of PRIDE that . . .," the Chicago agency reported in 1957 (for 1956): "As usual, the largest single type of cases involved family matters. Out of the 8,398 family cases only 31 were plaintiff's divorce cases. These were filed after investigation and recommendation by a recognized social agency" (United Charities of Chicago, Legal Aid Bureau 1957, p. 3). The next annual report explained:

> In 1957 21 bankruptcy petitions and 52 divorce complaints were filed. Policy on these kinds of cases is established in cooperation with the Family Service Bureau of the United Charities, and no affirmative action is taken unless the client is given an opportunity for casework assistance through Legal Aid Bureau–Social Service Department. It may seem strange that divorce and debt problems should be treated in the same fashion, yet studies indicate that habitual indebtedness or overexpenditure of family income are frequently the result of emotional disturbance and social maladjustment in either one or both spouses. (United Charities of Chicago, Legal Aid Bureau 1958, p. 4)

Much of Legal Aid's domestic-relations work served the "community's" interests more clearly than the client's. An important example was the enforcement of support obligations against husbands on behalf of poor women who, if enforcement were successful, would find their public-aid benefits decreased correspondingly. If clients did not gain, taxpayers did. The policy had powerful supporters, such as the *Chicago Tribune,* which showed its appreciation in an obituary:

> In her twenty-seven years as a lawyer with Legal Aid she . . . saved taxpayers about $500,000 by collecting support money from husbands who desert their families. If the money had not been collected, public relief funds would have been used to clothe, feed and shelter the mothers and their children. She also reinstated many marriages by winning vacat-

> ing orders on divorces fraudulently obtained. . . . She often fought divorce actions filed by husbands in other states. She thwarted one man three times in as many states in his efforts to get a divorce without adequate grounds. ("Legal Advisor" 1962, p. 10)

Legal Aid's Social Structure

Legal Aid's day-in-court philosophy was institutionalized in its social structure. The staff that represented the poor was separated sharply from the organization's governing officials and its supporting financial base. The division of labor between Legal Aid's board and staff reflected the caste stratification that characterized the U.S. legal profession through the first half of the twentieth century. Staff and board were assigned separate tasks, and personnel for the two groups were drawn, respectively, from the lower and the upper strata in the profession.

The board members of the nineteenth-century legal assistance agencies had personally approached external audiences on behalf of the agencies' substantive organizational goals. Social distance between staff and board functions grew as external organizations intervened between them to specialize in policy leadership and fund raising. In 1930, in a process led by Hunter and the United Charities, Chicago's Community Fund was formed. Like United Way and Community Chest organizations elsewhere, the Community Fund acted as an externally located agent for raising the major portion of Legal Aid's income. This change brought Legal Aid unprecedented financial security and a lowered public profile. In a national pattern,[10] the case for Legal Aid became muffled in amorphous, omnibus solicitations of the public.[11]

As Legal Aid abandoned the role of exhorting the public on behalf of the poor, it opened another channel of symbolic expression, one with ritual significance. Now, eminent judges and public executives would routinely portray Legal Aid's virtues, generally to the profession and in particular to Legal Aid's own governing bodies. An institutional voice speaking toward the public on systematic oppressions of the poor had been replaced by ceremonial speech largely by and to the elite of the bar.[12] Bar leaders viewed the bar's connection with Legal Aid as helping to raise the occupation of lawyer to the honored status of a profession. The following inspirational note is from the 1940 president of the American Bar Association.

> Looking back across the forty years of my membership in the American Bar Association, four episodes stand out vividly. The first is that of a

> slender young man by the name of Reginald Heber Smith leading a symposium on the subject of legal aid in the old Shubert Theatre in St. Louis at the 1920 meeting. It was the first time that the idea of a clear social opportunity as a national objective, big enough and practical enough to challenge the organized Bar of America, had ever been presented in my hearing. (Charles A. Beardsley, quoted in Brownell 1961, pp. 19–20)

As already noted, the Legal Aid Committee of the Chicago Bar Association worked with the Legal Aid Committee of United Charities to supervise the "professional activities" of the Legal Aid staff (Gariepy 1926). Both committees were composed of volunteers (mainly senior partners) from large law firms, and they usually met together bimonthly. Minutes of meetings from 1955 to 1962 show their routine concerns: the annual fund-raising program in "leading firms"; plans (which were unsuccessful) to attract young associates from firms to Legal Aid committee work; personnel policies (salary scales, cost of living increases); budgetary matters; adjustments of the income scales determining client eligibility and arrangements for referring clients out; and administrative policies governing such matters as client registration fees and agency payment of court costs. No issues of the professional quality or reform significance of staff work were mentioned. The sole subject of recurrent controversy was the "social needs" restriction on divorces, a policy that was continuously and painstakingly modified.

The staff carried out the everyday tasks of representing poor people, and committee members periodically exercised administrative oversight. The relations between the two groups were ethnically as well as formally stratified. Legal Aid came to exhibit a common pattern in handling relations between members of an elite (in this case, the corporate board lawyers) and members of lower economic classes (here, the indigent clientele) that differ by ethnicity, nationality, race, or caste. Personal service to such lower strata is considered dirty work and relegated to members of pariah groups kept permanently outside the elite (Shibutani and Kwan 1971, pp. 190–193).

The change in staffing patterns came quickly at the time of the First World War. In contrast to the relatively slow succession of staff lawyers who were closely related to board members in origin, who joined with board members in the conduct of organizational work, and who shared occupational futures with their formal superiors, the staff—but not the board—became non-Protestant and female and began to turn over completely almost every year. Female, Jewish, and non–Anglo-Saxon names began appearing on staff rosters in 1915. Whereas the first staff lawyers were employed for about 10 years, and in the early 1900s staff lawyers typically left after 3–5 years, the modal tenure declined to less than 2 years. Patterns of staffing toward the end of the decade were summarized by Boyes, the long-term social worker "superintendent" of the Legal Aid Society:

> During the year our staff of attorneys has changed and we have no one today who was with us a year ago. Miss Markley left us in May to be married and since that time Miss Brody has had her place, and I wish to say in regard to Miss Brody that no one ever worked on the legal staff who has accomplished what she has. . . . She has left us this month to open an office of her own. Our staff of attorneys now consists of [three]. . . . It is always a source of gratification to the Superintendent that there are few changes made in the office staff, except among the attorneys; we expect that they will not stay with us long, but while they are here they bring all the enthusiasm of the beginner. (Chicago Legal Aid Society 1917, pp. 24–25)

In later years, about half the staff became "permanent," and a demographic differentiation of board and staff lawyers became traditional. Legal Aid's social structure became a harmonious unity of opposites, just as did its symbolic mission, which honored the profession's elite by reinforcing the moral disrepute of its most marginal clients. The social composition of the internal Legal Aid hierarchy exaggerated the stratification of the bar as a whole. Studies of lawyers from the late 1940s to the early 1960s consistently found demographic characteristics distributed among occupational positions in a hierarchical pattern,[13] a pattern especially pronounced in Legal Aid.

Legal Aid was governed formally by senior members of large law firms, a group of male, white, native-born, Protestant lawyers. Senior Legal Aid staff lawyers described the typical United Charities Legal Aid Committee member as a white, male, Protestant, Republican, graduate of an exclusive private college and a prestigious national law school who was a partner in a large corporate law firm or who was general counsel and perhaps also executive officer of a large corporation, "with a background that reads like *Who's Who*."[14] Their work world rarely if ever brought them in contact with the kinds of clients, forums, opposing counsel, and even legal problems (domestic relations and consumer debt) which formed the daily environment for Legal Aid's staff.

Legal Aid staff lawyers were mostly young and almost all from minority groups. Occasionally one was a first-generation Eastern European immigrant. Personnel files on the 14 staff lawyers employed in 1955 showed that each fit one or more of the following categories: female, black, Jewish, Catholic. Seven were graduates of proprietary or Catholic law schools; all but one was locally educated and, in contrast to the educational backgrounds of 13 of the 18 Legal Aid Committee members, none had received a degree from an Ivy League school.

Occupational careers in the two groups rarely began in the same schools and virtually never developed over the same positions. There was no occupational mobility between the two groups: committee members from large law firms had not worked in Legal Aid; Legal Aid lawyers did not move into large law firms. No member of the United Charities Legal Aid Committee for 1955 (or ever, in the recollection of senior staff) had been a Legal Aid staff member. Of the 18, 14 had av ratings in the 1955 Martindale-Hubbell, and 10 were partners in major law firms (as indicated by the listing of the firm in the volume's biographical section). Of the 55 lawyers on the Legal Aid staff from 1955 to 1964, none received av ratings; none had been, nor did any become, associates of major law firms (according to my checking of the Martindale-Hubbells for 1960, 1965, and 1973). Most ex–Legal Aid staff lawyers went on instead to solo practices or office-sharing arrangements in Loop or neighborhood locations.[15]

Within the staff, a flexible integration contrasted with the staff's rigid hierarchical segregation from the board. From 1920 to 1960, Legal Aid mixed lawyers by race, sex, religion, and ethnicity into one staff to an extent that perhaps surpassed all other lawyers' work organizations. In 1955, 8 of the 14 Legal Aid lawyers were women; for many years, women composed about 50 percent of the staff (U.S. Dept. of Commerce 1950).[16] This made the staff as demographically bizarre in the legal profession as its moral mission was extraordinary. In 1950, women made up only about 3.3 percent (n = 331) of the 10,006 lawyers employed in Chicago. There were at least three black women lawyers employed by the Chicago Legal Aid Bureau in the early fifties. Legal Aid had a staff that was about 14 percent black, and 14 percent female black, when blacks were about 2.5 percent of the city's lawyer population and when female blacks were .1 percent of the city's lawyers. To belabor the point, in the early fifties, Legal Aid employed about 33 percent of the black female lawyers in the city and about .07 percent of the city's white male lawyers.[17]

On sex, race, and ethnicity, staff and board lawyers were closer to their respective proximate social environments (clients, opposing counsel, judges) than to each other. This suggests the immediate background which board lawyers brought to their relations with the staff. The Legal Aid staff, largely

Jewish and Catholic, locally educated, and occupied with the task of managing cases in lower city courts, was similar in origin and function to the docket clerks in large law firms. About Wall Street lawyers in the early 1960s, Smigel (1964) wrote:

> The large law firms also need men who act as managing clerks. These men are expected to know the courts and their routine. If they are lawyers they usually come from the local schools—often from local night schools such as Brooklyn, Fordham, and St. John's. Many of them come from Jewish and Irish families. Partners feel these men can get along best with the clerks in the New York courts, who generally stem from the same background. In effect, they serve as liaison between the lower level bureaucrats of the courts and the Ivy League lawyers in the firm. (p. 42)[18]

Conclusion

Students of U.S. institutions may well wonder whether Legal Aid's transformation of purpose was correlated with a change in the racial identity of clients. Indeed, blacks formed a relatively insignificant minority of legal assistance clients in the early decades and became the single dominant group during Legal Aid's flourishing in the 1950s. But the coincidence was not close, and the racial change does not seem causal. In 1918, just before the symbolic submergence of Legal Aid under the social work leadership of the United Charities, "American Negro" characterized only 10 percent of the year's new applications, or 923 of 9361. (Another 4000 were characterized as "American white," and 3700 more were spread over 20 ethnic categories, such as Bohemian, German, Magyar, Italian, Polish, Russian (i.e. Jewish), and Scandinavian.)[19] Legal assistance clients did not become black in large numbers until well after the change in the institution's direction had been substantially accomplished.[20]

In a longer view, the racial identity of legal assistance clients seems even less valuable as a key to understanding changes in the institution's direction. There was certainly no racial change in the clientele sufficiently dramatic to account for the shift back to an aggressive, social-reform mission in the mid 1960s nor for another reversal—the decline of the antipoverty thrust in the 1970s. More illuminating explanatory factors can be located in the changing relations between legal assistance organizations and surrounding social movements.

Originally a product of moral energies which typified the Progressive Era, legal assistance organizations turned in a conservative direction as the Progressive Era came to an end around the First World War. The process, however, was not simply one of abandoning reform objectives when the external, societal mood for reform deteriorated. On the contrary, persistent support for reform led to the change. Remedial laws and agencies were called for by a line of legal assistance leaders running from the 1880s to the 1930s. As governmental alternatives were established, first in the Progressive Era and then in a culminating burst of legislation in the 1930s, state agencies took over the business of constraining tensions growing out of private employment relations; charitably funded Legal Aid societies turned instead toward a passive advocacy and the profession of social work to help what was often seen as a psychologically weak clientele. Although it is easy to make too much of the parallel, a similarly ironic pattern may be perceived in the recent relation between the decline of the antipoverty mission of Legal Services programs and the decline of the social movements of the 1960s (see chapters 9, 10): a gradual, unannounced change in thematic direction toward professionalizing the maintenance of poverty, which is specifically achieved by increasing, not reducing, the mobilization of law reform.

Chapter 3

Becoming a Legal Aid Lawyer

Staff lawyers took on Legal Aid's interpretation of its organizational mission in a three-stage process. The day-in-court philosophy required that legal assistance lawyers work within the narrow boundaries defined by the local social environment. The first feature of a staff that would carry this philosophy was that it must be drawn from the low-opportunity margins of the profession.

A felt need for the job would not in itself equip staff lawyers with a way of interpreting the problems of representing the poor, however. The most important resource for smoothing out the everyday experience of legal assistance work was an ethic of "reasonableness." Given Legal Aid's view of its normative dilemma, "reasonableness" played a special role in the collective drama. The dilemma, as I have said, arose with the removal of economic restraints on the provision of legal services: poor people, given free legal services in the name of equal justice, might exploit their now paradoxically unequal access to counsel to harass their fee-paying adversaries. Because neither law nor institutional ideology could define when representation became harassment, "commonsense" moral restraint was essential.

These two conditions were necessary but not sufficient for shaping members who would give life to the collective philosophy. For Legal Aid was not a factory nor an impersonal bureaucracy in which management's interest in its labor force was limited to worker satisfaction: Legal Aid was a project of professional honor. If the staff were to represent the moral concerns of the legal profession, staff lawyers had to learn not just to live comfortably with their professional environment but to embrace it. In the third stage of their careers, Legal Aid lawyers came to identify with the expectations of opposing counsel and judges. The regard of the local professional environment became the basis of the Legal Aid lawyer's self-esteem.

The primary purpose of this chapter is to explain how lawyers in Legal Aid societies developed careers which embodied a complacent perspective on the requirements of equal justice for the poor. A secondary purpose is to show how Legal Aid homogenized its staff. Chapter 4 shows how, in contrast, Legal Services has promoted among its lawyers a heterogeneity in philosophic perspectives on the institution.[1]

To obtain my data, I examined the personnel files of all 55 lawyers employed in the Legal Aid Bureau (LAB) from 1950 through 1973. The quotations that follow are taken from interviews with 20 lawyers. Of these 20, 14 were on the LAB staff during the field study; the other 6 interviewees were on the Legal Services payroll. This may seem an odd data base for an analysis of the personal career which served as a vehicle for the institutional philosophy distinctive to *Legal Aid,* but institutions are not bounded by organizational payrolls. Careers characteristic of Legal Aid can be found in the biographies of some who formally have been members of Legal Services organizations. Conversely, subsequent chapters on the careers of "Legal Services" lawyers draw on the experiences of several young lawyers who were hired by the LAB after 1965.

Entry: A Step Up

Separated by widely divergent personal backgrounds, lawyers came to Legal Aid out of a common perception of marginal market position. For a Jewish graduate of Northwestern Law School during the Depression, for a middle-aged black woman who graduated from De Paul in the 1950s, and for a 1970s graduate of a night program at a local proprietary law school, Legal Aid was a good job. Apart from an occasional daughter of the professional or upper classes,[2] lawyers joining the staff did not initially understand Legal Aid work in the rhetoric of altruism.

Even though my interviews were conducted at a time when many Legal Services lawyers were outspoken about their moral motives, Legal Aid lawyers did not recall their original motives as morally compelling. Arthur Young, director of the Legal Aid Bureau from the mid 1950s to the early 1970s, recalled:

> "I graduated from Northwestern in the days of the Depression. I came from a family with no particular means to get into the practice of law, and having done my clinical work here, I thought I'd come here while I was looking around for a job." *How did you get here, did you. . . ?*
> "I offered my services as a volunteer, which of course—in those days, I think we had 14 lawyers, and the case load, as I say that was the big Depression, 12 or 14 lawyers—everybody had four or five volunteers. Because jobs, getting jobs in the law was impossible. I know my

> brother, who preceded me out of Northwestern by a year, was working for the magnanimous sum of $5 a week for a law firm."

Those who did speak of acquiring moral motives indicated that they had acquired altruism after entering.

> I graduated law school in '53. I had no plans where to go. In school, I just wanted to be a lawyer. A schoolmate of mine at De Paul Law, R., had attempted to get me into a legal society, when they wouldn't take blacks. I didn't get in, but I went to all the sorority affairs. They didn't accept blacks and Jews then. But I knew all the sorority officers. R. came here as a volunteer, and I came to Legal Aid as a volunteer, following her. This was before I passed the bar. After I passed, I stayed as a volunteer. By then, I was committed to doing this kind of work, and I liked it. By the time I passed the bar I was hooked on Legal Aid.

If recruits previously had not shown any distinctive concern with equal justice, still, officials at Legal Aid did want the staff to represent moral concerns. Sometimes officials prompted retrospective discoveries of altruistic purpose within the recruitment process.

> I was going at night to law school, and then working . . . a half day at a . . . big prestigious firm. . . . I was a docket clerk; that's mainly what I was. . . . It was obvious that, when it came to permanent hiring, they would hire either people from Harvard or the people first in their class from local law schools. So when [a friend on the Legal Aid staff] said, "There's an opening down here," I said, "I'll take it." *Was there an interview?* Yes, with the assistant Legal Aid staff director. *What did you talk about?* He wanted to find out if I was interested in the poor. He asked if I was in Vista, or did anything like that. I didn't have anything like that, but we talked about what I had done, and I had participated in a juvenile workshop, and that was an interest in the poor. Then . . . I remembered that when I was young I'd get a shirt back from the laundry with a hole in it, and I'd ask my father what could be done about it. He'd tell me that nothing could be done, because it would cost too much to sue; it wouldn't be worth paying a lawyer. [The Legal Aid official] liked that. He said that showed an interest in the problems of the poor.

In Legal Services, as chapter 4 shows, moral and philosophic commitments in staff backgrounds have supplied conflicting perspectives and idioms for interpreting the everyday world of legal assistance. At Legal Aid, because moral perspectives typically emerged after entry, they emerged in a uniform, organizationally controlled context. When Legal Aid lawyers did mention previously established moral motives for entry, they reflected not on what they had intended to do for the poor but on what previous jobs had done to them. Legal Aid may have been dirty work in the profession's moral division of labor in that clients brought messy emotional problems to be handled in the courts of least competence against disreputable opposing counsel, but the ambience was a relief to some staff. Several had come in from still dirtier work.

> After I graduated, I worked for a law firm that bordered on the unscrupulous. . . . I didn't know shit about law then. It appeared to me to be a general law firm. . . . Well, it turned out they were a bit too aggressive. *(I have to pry out what he found objectionable.)* For the first six months there, I did collection work for them. Then I told them that if they didn't switch me off that, I'd quit. I wanted to change into corporate law. The unethical stuff was in their client relations. They sued their own clients a lot.

Legal Aid had a staff that was national in background but that had not attended national law schools. This indicates another homogenizing function. Most Legal Aid lawyers were educated at "local" law schools, but not necessarily in the Chicago area. Legal Aid offered a valuable entry to lawyers with no personal or institutional ties to the Chicago legal community.

> I came to Chicago because my husband was coming here. A friend of mine from home had a cousin who had contacts in the Daley machine. He said that you can't get a job there without connections, and I didn't have enough. But, he said, he heard that the Legal Aid Bureau was hiring people, and maybe I could try there.

> I came right from [Fordham]. I took the New York bar, and then came out. I came [to Legal Aid] . . . after two years in private practice. I was working for a wholesale collection agency and then this position came open. . . . *What were your ideas in going into private practice?* I wanted to be a fantastic rich trial lawyer, I guess. . . . But I didn't like private practice. I had to take the cases I didn't want, like little misdemeanors, little assault cases. I was a stranger in Chicago, and I needed to gain a following. To do that if you don't know people you

have to become politically affiliated, or become affiliated with organizations.

One of the most striking differences between the Legal Aid staff and the staff that Legal Services developed was the much greater age differentiation in Legal Aid.[3] Yet in a subjectively significant respect, the Legal Aid staff was, even on this dimension, more homogenized. First, those who entered Legal Aid past the age of 30 usually were new lawyers. Many old and young entrants alike had been concerned to obtain a "lawyer's" identity. For them, the job had a minimal occupational career meaning that cut across age grades.

I was with an insurance company since '55. I stayed there until May of '66, three months after I started this job. *How did you come to decide to go to law school?* I was 30 and getting married, so I thought I'd learn a trade. I'd been with the insurance company for years, and there was no future there. *What kind of work did you do there?* Clerical, you might call it. That's all it was. *If you had stayed on, what might your future have been?* Oh, I guess like in all bureaucracies, you move up to be a manager of other clerks, like a supervisor, then a supervisor of supervisors. I'd always had difficulty filling out the "occupations" slot on motel cards. Now the occupation name has become easier. I just put down "lawyer."

I graduated from Wisconsin Law School in 1970. Then I went to work for the Continental Bank here, in the trust department. *What were you doing there?* It wasn't legal work. What there'd be to do was to look at a trustee's proposed payment and see if it was OK in terms of the trust document. What you'd do would be to write a memo on it. . . . You see, as a bank they aren't allowed to practice law. So if it was a point that required legal work, they'd send it to their law firm and they'd do it. In two weeks I knew I wasn't going to stay and I started looking around for something else. The problem was that I was losing my identity as a lawyer. I remember that I asked them if I could go to court. Nothing I was doing was taking me to court. They said, OK, but don't tell anybody where you're from. And then, you see, they'd hire people to do the same work who had only B.A.s or M.A.s. The work didn't require legal training, but you thought that after three years of that you should be better able to do it than someone without that training.

Legal Aid hired a staff with highly diversified backgrounds and gave them jobs that made little use of their background differences. As I show later, relatively minor differences in the prior occupational experiences of Legal Services lawyers made major differences in the perspectives they adopted on legal assistance work. For new graduates as well as for those who had long been on other career tracks, Legal Aid marked a new beginning. Prior occupational experiences were rendered irrelevant, in most cases thankfully. Lawyers more often came to Legal Aid in search of career discontinuity than continuity. Typical among them was a lawyer who had been reviewing district-level administrative decisions on social security claims. He recalled his relief at escaping an invisible job:

> It was just paper work, all done from the files. I had no personal contact with people. It was an impersonal bureaucracy. The director of the office might not even know who you were.

When occupational background *was* made relevant to a staff lawyer's assignment, it was likely to be over his objection.

> I graduated from law school in 1956, from Creighton University, in Omaha, Nebraska. Then I took the bar there, and then became a claims adjuster for two insurance companies, both in Nebraska. I did that until I came to Chicago in 1960, when I began working as a revenue officer for the IRS . . . and then I worked as a claims adjuster for [seven years]. I was put on here, on this desk, because of my insurance background and because of the medical reports you have to deal with on this desk. I knew about them from claims adjusting. Since I've been on this desk, I've been trying to get out because it's like claims adjusting, and that's why I left that.

Becoming Reasonable

An appreciation of a Legal Aid job as a step up in occupational mobility does not equip one to feel comfortable in it. By adopting "reasonableness" as a working ethic, Legal Aid lawyers translate the procedural, day-in-court jurisprudence into a means for personally accepting everyday professional and moral limitations. The following quotation from a domestic-relations lawyer shows how learning to accept unreasonable clients is part of becoming reasonable.

> *What about problem clients?* We have a special problem. We can't kick the client out. . . . If the clients want to be unreasonable, that's it.

> You have to let them. You know that they can't get more than $20 support; but they insist on asking for $40, so you ask for $40. I don't care because I see this job as a procedural thing. It's my job to get them into court, win or lose. . . . There's no law in these cases, and there's not much property so there's no contest there. That means there's no need for depositions, interrogatories, etc. Mainly, you just must make sure that the allegations on income get in. You don't have to worry about convincing the judge or influencing him. The judges see so many of these, they have a schedule. I don't try and win the judge over or anything like that. I get the client a hearing and let the judge decide. . . . I don't consider myself a divorce attorney on this job. What I do is run around with the volume. I wouldn't *be* a divorce attorney in private practice. If you work for a fee, you have to identify with the client or the client will go to another attorney. You needn't *do* that here.

This perspective both constructs and resolves the moral dilemma defined by Smith. The view is that the case turns not on a legal issue (there is "no law" involved) nor on a complex evidentiary presentation but on judicial discretion. If so, there is not much for a lawyer to do. There is however the danger of creating spurious litigation by too readily providing representation and the inverse danger of restricting representation on moral grounds. The ethic of reasonableness recognizes and avoids the dangers of falling into one or another of the two pitfalls. One accepts clients and takes positions one thinks wrong, but one does not push matters beyond what adversaries and local courts consider appropriate boundaries.

Most of the senior Legal Aid attorneys had been on domestic-relations desks for several years at some point in their careers. Each could give examples of the recurrent need for the ethic of reasonableness in custody and support battles. But, as I argued in chapter 1, any specialty in legal assistance will involve "no law" and no factual disputes of complexity if the lawyer accepts problems as they are presented to the organization. The specialist in personal injury and property damage and the lawyer with responsibility for public aid and union pension claims spelled out the same philosophy. Others spoke of representing clients "without a defense" by "pleading equities" in order to sway an adversary's discretion over the scheduling of debt payments, the number of days tenants would have to vacate, and the amount of proof a public-aid official would require before increasing benefits.

Legal Aid lawyers do not operate as lonely day-in-court philosophers in a thoroughly hostile environment. Reasonableness is a working ethic; not just a self-tranquilizing attitude, it has practical advantages for managing the case load. Conduct is "unreasonable" when it produces bothersome noise on the way to predictable outcomes. Threats of unreasonable conduct are regularly presented by unsocialized newcomers—transient clients, infrequently encountered adversaries, and new judges. Maintaining a posture of reasonableness, keeping a distance from unreasonable opposing counsel, helps keep clients in line:

> Lots of times the clients will have second thoughts about the case when it comes time to go to trial. . . . One important thing: don't fight with lawyers at the bench. If the lawyers can't keep their cool, how can the clients? I never retaliate if I'm being abused. I just look at the judge with soulful eyes, sort of to say, "I wonder when he will stop this nonsense." I just keep quiet.

Another lawyer reported that he would hum a tune to himself until an adversary's tirade subsided.

Judges with whom one has established a reputation for reasonableness may support the effort to make everyone reasonable. Clients may entertain unreasonable expectations, and judges can assist the socialization process.

> Judge L. often says, "you've got Mrs. L. as your attorney, and you should feel lucky, because she's one of the best lawyers in the city of Chicago." He's very nice to me. And that helps. If the judge knows that the client might be unhappy with the result of the case, he will say that so that the client won't feel that he had bad representation.

Reasonableness, a commitment to prevailing norms, lends predictability to negotiations. Accurately predicted outcomes are more readily accepted by clients than disappointing results.

> One of the things I always felt was an advantage. . . . When you got to working in a particular field [here, consumer defense], you got to know the particular lawyers, and it was easier working. You understood their styles; you knew what to expect from them. You could tell when a lawyer came on a case that you could settle it for $5 a month, and you could tell a client that.

"Reasonableness" is not an ethic peculiar to lawyer's work for the poor; but in the context of legal assistance work, it has a very special meaning. Smith noted that the following Lincoln saying, one famous among lawyers everywhere, was displayed on placards in each of the six offices of the New York Legal Aid Society in 1907: "Discourage litigation. Persuade your neighbors to compromise whenever you can. Point out to them how the nominal winner is often the real loser—in fees, expenses, and waste of time. As a peacemaker the lawyer has a superior opportunity of being a good man." Two lawyers of the Chicago Legal Aid Bureau had this saying on display in their offices in the early 1970s. Consider who the audience was. Unlike most lawyers in private practice, legal assistance lawyers virtually never meet with adversaries or opposing counsel in the home offices of either. The absence of office conferences reflects the lack of cooperative preparatory and drafting work. It also means that the Legal Aid lawyers and their clients were the exclusive readers of Lincoln's admonition to restraint.

Identification

An effort to be reasonable implies that others have complementary capacities. For legal assistance lawyers, the effort treats the local professional environment as a moral community. Reasonableness as a means of control works both ways; it indicates a readiness to use the expectations of adversaries and local courts as a basis for self-conception and self-respect. In Legal Aid, organizational character was incorporated deeply into the personal careers of its staff. Legal Aid lawyers transformed their initially cold calculations of occupational alternatives into emotional commitments to the day-in-court philosophy.

Senior Legal Aid lawyers revealed the depth of their identification with the local professional environment most dramatically when it appeared that the respect of familiar adversaries or judges was in doubt. There were many reports of "embarrassment." One Legal Aid lawyer's memories of embarrassment lasted over 25 years.

> *(We've been discussing everyday work problems, and I ask) "How about people who lie?"* "Yes, that's a big problem. At first I believed everything I heard. All my clients were in the right; they were all telling the truth. I remember one time, it was an eviction action, and during the OPA—when you could get extra time, there was a freeze—well, I told the story to the judge that the client had told me—I forget just what it was, the story I had believed. Well, this judge was a real actor. And the judge said to me: 'Even if you are with the Legal Aid Bureau, do you have to be that gullible?' "

The risk of embarrassment is an everyday feature of a Legal Aid practice. When a case involves "no law" and there has been no pretrial investigation, the lawyer must base his arguments on the facts as asserted by the client. In this circumstance, virtually any adverse decision by a judge can be an occasion for embarrassment; for it shows disbelief of the client and implies that the lawyer has been either disingenuous or taken in.

Embarrassment, rather than outrage, follows on the presumption that a judge's rejection of the client's account is right. As a practical matter, the judge's determination will indeed be the final truth. When a case that has been given this shape is lost, typically there will be nothing to appeal. As a proposition valid far beyond Legal Aid, no matter how a case is advocated, there will only be proof to a moral certainty, proof sufficient "for all practical purposes."[4] In Legal Aid, the ethic of reasonableness gives cases a form that severely limits the practical purpose of continuing the argument after the trial court's determination. In this way, reasonableness leads to identification with the local professional environment.

Consider the Legal Aid lawyer's resolution of "typical client lies." Poor people often claim as a defense to a debt-collection action that they never received service. This is not always a lie. Criminal convictions of process servers for "sewer service" were won in New York in the late 1960s.[5] But LAB lawyers would become embarrassed when it was "proven" that their clients were lying.

> *(I mention that it's necessary to find if the client is lying, because you can get embarrassed if a lie comes out in court.)* I'm embarrassed so much. I go in with a petition that there was no summons served. I'll get the deputy in—oh, you have to fight it out if that's what they say; you can't make the judgment that they're lying and not do it—you can cross [examine] the deputy, but he always served the client.

Of course, an unqualified identification with the local professional environment would often mean clients would not get any representation. Here again, the phenomenology of Legal Aid is a product of the dialectic outlined by Smith. The daily struggle is to go toward reasonableness without going over to the other side. When the case is to be decided on the credibility of the client, the conscientious Legal Aid lawyer must choose between running the risks of embarrassment and prejudice.

> This just happened and it's fresh on my mind. A middle-aged hippy came in, a Jewish man with a beard and hippy clothing and all. On this

> one, I was taken in. Usually I'd be more wary, but this time the general interviewer had written on the [form]: "I believe he is sincere." It was a custody matter. He was being denied visitation. She [the wife] said that he had subjected the kids to pot and that, when he came over, he would sleep there with his girl friend. He was really something. He was a big health-food nut, a real bug on health food. In court the wife brought in some of his health food, and the judge asked him if he didn't think he wasn't overdoing it a bit. . . . I argued very strongly, and I was so embarrassed when we were confronted with the fact that the child said that there was a woman there. Then, he admitted it! [Later] More and more I'm trying to use my own judgment. This is something that I'm learning. The court has such a great volume that they demand that you must be reasonable. I've made a few exceptions to this, and when I have, I've made a fool of myself. This hippy case again. What happened there was that I thought, Well I can't be against him just because he's a hippy; so I leaned over backwards to go along with him, just because he was so hippy-ish. The judge, who never says that to me, said, "L., I have a lot of respect for you, but how come you're so unreasonable for once?" I felt just terrible.

Policies and structures internal to the LAB also promoted identification with the local professional environment. Formal evaluations were an annual occasion for officially defining the desired perspective. I reviewed over 20 years of staff evaluations and found a constant deference to the local professional environment. Staff lawyers were commended with such phrases as: "well liked by court people"; "been complimented by judges"; "handles himself well in court and is cooperative and well-thought-of by opposing attorneys"; "favorable reports from judges and lawyers"; "The judges, court attaches and other attorneys always speak highly of Mr. L. and he has a good working relationship with them."

Elaborate evaluation procedures made this deference a collective ritual. For an evaluation to be complete, it had to be signed by the lawyer reviewed and by officials at several hierarchical levels. Supervisors felt hard pressed to say something new about those they had evaluated for over 10 or even 20 years. Content was highly redundant; year after year, staff lawyers would thus be reminded of the importance to the organization of their local professional reputations.

But these were formalities. Crucial encouragement was given by an organizational structure which exploited the identifications made by the local professional environment in order to promote long-range careers. In the mid 1950s, the staff was divided into two groups, "permanent" and "rotating" lawyers. As reflected in Legal Aid Committee minutes and as recalled by Young, the director of the LAB during this period, the division was made specifically for the purpose of influencing the development of staff careers. For years, the staff had been split informally between those who wanted to make careers in Legal Aid and those who wanted to use Legal Aid as a stepping-stone to private practice. In the old system, the more experienced lawyers had the "trial" positions, and the newer members worked as their assistants. In the revised system, new staff lawyers rotated between desks, each with a substantively specialized case load and each with "trial" (court-appearance) responsibilities. Most of the permanent staff assumed supervisory positions. By rule, new lawyers rotated from desk to desk each six months, out of the organization after two years.

For their part, the rotating lawyers had the opportunity to carry personally a variety of cases into a variety of local courts and to meet a large number of opposing counsel. They were expected to use the practical experience and personal contacts gained in a minimally prepared, high-volume court practice to start careers on the other side. This was literally a process of building a career by accepting the way the local professional environment defined the problems of the poor.

The permanent lawyers faced an environment in which their expertise would be recognized constantly. A six-month maximum on the time a rotating lawyer could occupy a given desk meant that supervisors were always in demand. The everyday experience of the permanent staff was a stream of requests for advice by deferential subordinates. With about two-thirds of the staff kept at low tenures, there was also more room in the budget to reward the one-third with greater experience.

The other side of the everyday experience of their expertise was constructed in relations to outside professionals. Legal Aid took the cases the private bar found insufficiently worthy for economic or public-service ends, and the disinterest of the private bar was the source of the Legal Aid lawyer's distinction. Long-term Legal Aid lawyers developed an exceptional expertise for practicing before lower state courts and administrative agencies on a uniquely high volume of certain types of cases. Given the reputation of the economically marginal lawyers who had practices analogous to Legal Aid's, organization officials could proudly claim without fear of contradiction that one staff member was "the best Social Security lawyer in Chicago," another the most expert lawyer in handling paupers' estates, another unparalleled in the defense of consumer credit contracts.

Among their external colleagues, Legal Aid lawyers also enjoyed pristine reputations for ethical, "professional" conduct. Judges singled out their reasonableness for praise, and court clerks understandingly overlooked their failure to provide the usual consideration at Christmas.

> It would be easier I guess if I paid off like the private attorneys do. But I am ethical! I keep a high standard of integrity. I never take up a bailiff's offer. *What kind of an offer?* Oh, they'll ask, "Would you like me to talk to the judge for you?" It may be baloney, that they have any influence, but I stop it right away. . . . I said to the clerks at Christmas, I felt awful, they were so good to me, showing me the ropes and all, that I couldn't give them anything. . . . They said to me, "We understand. We know you're not working for a for-profit business. All we want from you is your thanks."

Several phrases commonly used in the LAB capture the way institutional constraints were turned into personal resources in staff careers. Smith had instructed that Legal Aid should look like any private lawyer's practice. Legal Aid was fondly termed "the largest law office in town" in annual reports, board meetings, and staff vocabulary. The image paradoxically used the "large" number of clients, an indicator of the limited sophistication of service, to draw on the prestige of corporate law firms, which are in fact "larger" in number of staff and average client size.

In a phrase frequently used by the assistant LAB director to describe hiring criteria, the Legal Aid lawyer was "someone who liked to work with people." A commitment to reasonableness required restraint in representation, but not impersonality. When obliged to represent a vindictive parent in a custody battle, the Legal Aid lawyer would strain to bring into the negotiations a reasonable perspective on the interests of the child. With adversaries, a lawyer could draw on a reputation for disinterested reasonableness to make special arrangements for clients. For example, a collection lawyer might hold off suit if an LAB lawyer would keep a running account and collect the debt payments. Or the Legal Aid lawyer with responsibility to administer an incompetent's estate might encourage a social worker to care for a client's household needs.

The Legal Aid culture identified staff lawyers as people with highly differentiated concerns for the incapacities of clients. Throughout the working day, opportunities were available to "humanize" cold, unqualified rules. Rules governing eligibility for service were interpreted in daily consultations between Legal Aid staff and officials. Legal Aid's eligibility rules functioned less certainly to impose uniformity on staff behavior than as a politically defensible face to outsiders and as a precondition for the exercise of the power to make exceptions, which was a treasured daily ritual.

Long-term staff lawyers spoke of Legal Aid as a "home" and a "family" with a "heart." Smith had warned that the organization's mission would be undermined if legally viable representation were restricted on moral grounds or if litigation proceeded on spurious grounds. But neither the day-in-court philosophy nor the local environment's expectations would be threatened by extending oneself in the direction of the defenseless poor outside of contested litigation.

Chapter 4

Legal Services Programs and the Sixties: Complementarity and Dependence

In 1961, Legal Aid leaders reviewed with pride the growth and the increasingly national distribution of their institution. There were 92 cities with Legal Aid societies in 1950, 209 in 1960 (Brownell 1961, p. 10); 194 lawyers worked in Legal Aid societies in 1947, 292 in 1959 (Brownell 1961, p. 47). Quantitatively, the institution had been expanding very rapidly for decades. "In the three decades, 1920–1950, the rate of growth (measuring offices) had been roughly forty percent for each, but for the decade 1950–1960, it was over 250%" (Brownell 1961, p. 10). With the advent of federally funded OEO Legal Services, the expansion of legal assistance to the poor accelerated dramatically. By 1970, 300 Legal Services projects, employing about 2000 lawyers, had been established.[1] In Chicago, the LAB had 20 lawyers on staff in 1963 (United Charities of Chicago, Legal Aid Bureau 1964); in 1970, Legal Services funds in Chicago supported an additional 50 lawyers.[2]

Nationwide, Legal Services brought a tenfold increase in the number of lawyers and significant changes in organization and purpose. In several key respects—mission, relations with a broader social movement, social distance between staff and board—Legal Services represented a return to patterns characteristic of the late nineteenth century. Substantive reform was again a top priority. The Legal Services Program was one element in the War on Poverty, which itself was diffusely related to other antiestablishment movements of the sixties. Leadership for Legal Services programs (LSPs) often came from would-be staff lawyers who had developed alliances with representatives of the poor and created governing boards.[3] In contrast to the Legal Aid model, the social structure of LSPs was more fluid internally and had less distinct boundaries from externally proliferating activism.

In its reform goals, Legal Services represented a sharp break from the Legal Aid precedent; in the resources used in its reform stategies, Legal

Services was diffusely integrated into a social-movement milieu. In sum, there was a strong link in Legal Services between historical discontinuity in purpose and continuity with contemporaneous external changes. The dualistic character of Legal Services inverted the qualities that had been traditional in Legal Aid societies. On the one hand, Legal Aid leaders had overstated a lack of historical change, proclaiming a continuity in purpose with predecessors reaching back to the 1880s. On the other hand, Legal Aid had been isolated from outcroppings of activism in the legal profession. When U.S. lawyers from time to time became prominent in the pursuit of equal justice through defending political dissidents, representing labor organizers, and promoting civil rights causes, they had no discernible impact on, nor did they draw any significant resources from, the work of Legal Aid.[4]

LSPS quickly distinguished themselves from Legal Aid societies through multiple associations with external activism. The location of Legal Services in a broad movement for social change was reflected in the structure of programs; in the perspectives brought in by staff; and in early controversies over aggressive advocacy. This chapter is organized as a review of each of these supports from the larger social movement for the distinctive characteristics of Legal Services. The objective is to begin a consideration of the conditions for the persistence in Legal Services of an impetus toward social change even after the disintegration of the originating social movement.

Two caveats are in order. First, if the break from the precedent of Legal Aid was sharp, it was not clean. In the next chapter, I qualify the argument of historical discontinuity by noting ways in which LSPS remained subject to constraints on activism that were traditional in Legal Aid societies. In this chapter, I show that many of the ties between activism in Legal Services and broader movements for social change were essentially symbolic and superficial. These observations round out the picture necessary for considering the persistence of reform. The picture is not one of a clear, direct relation between the strength of activism spread generally throughout society and the strength of the impetus in Legal Services toward reform.[5] I eventually argue that reform persisted as a commitment in Legal Services throughout the increasingly conservative seventies in part because (although the activist environment of the sixties was necessary initially to turn legal assistance toward reform) the social movements that surrounded LSPS soon impeded as much as they promoted the advocacy of social reform.

Second, as throughout the text, the discussion is limited primarily to the Chicago experience. For this historical topic this limit is especially severe.

Organizational Structure and Themes of the Sixties

In its geographic layout, the Legal Services program radically departed from the social structure of Legal Aid. Lawyers in the United Charities of Chicago's Legal Aid Bureau had worked primarily out of a single office located downtown in the central business district.[6] In the mid 1960s, the United Charities Legal Aid Bureau became responsible for administering the major Legal Services program in Chicago. The bulk of the United Charities's Legal Services–funded staff was split into sets of three or four and assigned to offices in several of the city's poverty neighborhoods.[7]

In another departure from the Legal Aid tradition, in Legal Services the geographic differentiation was used as a basis for functional specialization. For years, the LAB had maintained a small South Side office at the Mandel Clinic of the University of Chicago Law School, but service case loads carried by the 2 LAB lawyers there were substantially the same as those carried by the 14 or so LAB lawyers located at the downtown office. Similarly, lawyers in the new neighborhood Legal Services offices carried service case loads created largely by walk-in clients. But in addition United Charities created a small, downtown Legal Service unit, initially termed the Appellate and Test Case Division, to handle "significant" cases (Patner 1967). Moreover, independent of the United Charities and its LAB, another OEO Legal Services–funded program, CLC, operated in the city from 1967 to 1972, its 10 to 12 lawyers working out of downtown and neighborhood offices, attending meetings of neighborhood groups, and offering personal services to group leaders in an effort to define an ambiguous mandate ("Community Counsel" 1967).[8]

Uniting the diverse formats for Legal Services work was a folk sociology severely critical of the Legal Aid tradition. In the early national debate, advocates for a Legal Services program justified organizational innovation polemically: for each new structure proposed, they pointed pejoratively to a corresponding weakness in the design of Legal Aid.[9] Legal Aid was portrayed as "bad faith" formally organized. It claimed legitimacy in a passive and therefore democratic responsiveness to client demands. Yet, the critique went, the structure of Legal Aid had subtly influenced felt demands to take a modest, conservative shape. In contrast, Legal Services was to be an existentially aware organization, self-consciously defining itself in interaction with its environment. Emphasizing a new aggressiveness in organizational style, Legal Services leaders couched statements of collective goals in the metaphors of war and the military, and they made ranking and restatement of "priorities" a matter of periodic routine.[10]

Legal Aid's downtown location was said to have domesticated its clientele silently by selecting those whose integration into the city's life independently brought them to its center. Legal Aid's intake process exacerbated this bias. Prospective clients were required to invest hours sitting in a central waiting room before they might receive service. Effectively excluded were those who could not afford to lose either the time or the face, in particular militant group leaders. Legal Services elaborated a contrasting structure. It opened neighborhood offices; intermittently staffed "outposts" in public housing projects; and sent lawyers to sit deferentially to wait for recognition at meetings of community groups.

Legal Aid had been passive in recruiting its staff. Lawyers had been drawn in from announcements displayed at the bar association; by calls made to ex-volunteers at the bureau; and through long-standing referral relations with deans of local law schools. Citing this passivity, critics from Legal Services charged that, when opportunities for far-reaching advocacy walked in, the Legal Aid staff would not see them. As one remedy, the national OEO Office of Legal Services funded fellowships, named after Reginald Heber Smith and colloquially known as "Reggies," to attract top graduates of elite law schools (Smith had graduated from Harvard). The national office also sponsored publications which, in back-page advertisements, functioned as a national job market. Local LSPs sporadically sent recruiters to national law schools. Graduates of national law schools, whose training would not have been focused on local law, presumably would find complex constitutional issues and federal cases more familiar than disputes suited for lower state courts.

Legal Aid had foreclosed its staff's ability to pursue novel lines of advocacy by imposing case loads numbering in the hundreds. In most LSPs, a few lawyers were freed from intake case-load responsibilities at downtown law reform units. The national office created a series of back-up centers specialized by poverty law area and related to major university law schools to operate as think tanks and overseers of major litigation. A few experimental projects such as CLC were given mandates to develop specialized case loads.

Finally, Legal Aid was criticized for letting its past dominate its sense of possibilities. Requests by clients at Legal Aid may have been conservative because poor people had reason to expect that only modest demands would be met. Legal Services would not be trapped by inertia. To stimulate novel demands, press releases on major cases were issued; programs of community education were announced; and, in accordance with OEO regulations, the poor were given seats on the board, with the attendant opportunity to promote an ambience of righteous indignation.

Whatever the validity of this folk sociology (relating organizational structure to felt client demand which I review critically in later chapters), the origins of the critique were not in empirical research. Nor was the theory derived by deductive logic from an articulate sociological jurisprudence of equal justice. It was not at all clear how the structure of Legal Services would "equal" the organizational format for delivering legal service to paying clients. The closest analogue to the neighborhood Legal Services office would be the small private law office in urban neighborhoods, but the lawyers who worked in such settings (Carlin 1962) were among the most disreputable in the bar—hardly the model embraced by advocates of the new program. If the object was to equate the quality of legal service available to the poor with the highest quality service available to the rich, the organizational format as well might have paralleled the corporate law firm, with its hierarchical structure, downtown location, disdain of publicity, and discreet methods of procuring clients.

The new format was less clearly called for by the available facts and philosophy of equal justice than by the broader social movement from which the Legal Services program emerged. "Community" legal counsel, "neighborhood" offices, representation of poor clients on the board, and "community education" all resonated with themes that ran through national social welfare policy in the 1960s: "outreach," "maximum feasible participation," "community control." Before Legal Services was established, citizen participation requirements had been built into War on Poverty programs; Community Action agencies had tried to create new jobs by expanding indigenous ghetto enterprises; and the Peace Corps had popularized an image of the hand-to-hand amelioration of poverty on its native ground.

The trend in social welfare thought was to move the base for the delivery of human services from downtown, the symbolic center of society, to the periphery, where the people in need of service lived. Ideals about law and lawyers had little to do with this thrust. But others of the structural innovations in Legal Services emerged directly from the legal rights movement of the early 1960s. Law reform units, back-up centers, and special efforts to recruit top law graduates reflected formats that had been used with celebrated success by civil rights and civil liberties organizations.[11]

Moynihan (1969) characterized the War on Poverty as the first manifestation of a historical trend toward "professionalized reform" (pp. 21–23), and the Legal Services program is a good illustration. The linkage between Legal Services and the legal rights movement was forged not by the poor but by professionals. Law schools played a notable role in supplying professional advocates of reform. Three experimental programs funded in the early sixties by the Ford Foundation and by the President's Committee on Juvenile Delinquency became models for the Legal Services program: a neighborhood law office, later the Legal Assistance Association, in New Haven; Mobilization for Youth (MFY) in New York's Lower East Side; and the Neighborhood Legal Services Project in Washington, D.C. In his historical account, Johnson (1974) notes the influence in the design of the New Haven project of Yale law professor Joseph Goldstein and students Jean and Edgar Cahn; the role of Monrad Paulson and other Columbia law professors in the design and supervision of the MFY legal unit; and the involvement in the founding of the Washington project of Georgetown law associate dean Kenneth Pye and Howard law professors Patricia Harris and Jeanus Parks.[12] Jerome Carlin, who co-authored one of the early polemics for a new advocacy for the poor while an associate of the Berkeley Center on Law and Society (Carlin and Howard 1965), became the first executive director ("coordinator") of the San Francisco Neighborhood Legal Assistance Foundation. In Chicago, Marshall Patner, who became the head of the Appellate and Test Case Division in the fall of 1966, had worked during the summer of 1965 in a project at the University of Chicago Law School, supervising the writing of briefs by students and arguing dozens of appeals for indigent criminal defendants. Law schools, which were the central stage for the celebration of civil rights and civil liberties test cases, tied the new antipoverty law program into the broader legal rights movement through academic writings (e.g., Reich 1964), but even more through the activism of law students, law teachers, and practicing lawyers on the margins of law faculties.

Staff Ties to Social Movements

In relation to the bar as a whole, Legal Aid's staff had been a unique collection. Legal Aid brought into an integrated working unit lawyers who were not likely to be colleagues anywhere in the profession—a group at once sharing low professional mobility and differing internally by sex, race, ethnicity, and regional origin. Legal Services quickly performed an even more extraordinary integrating function. Its staff cut across vertical as well as horizontal divisions long-standing in the private law market. National samples of the 1967 and 1972 cohorts drawn by the Wisconsin Poverty Research Center show that, in socioeconomic status and educational background, the new poverty lawyers represented a cross-section of the young bar. [On religious backgrounds and parents' political orientation, there were slight differences between the poverty lawyers and young lawyers generally (Erlanger 1978, pp. 259–262; Handler, Hollingsworth, and Erlanger 1978, pp. 145–146).]

Using personnel files, I compared Chicago's Legal Aid staff from 1950 to 1960 (34 lawyers, filling about 13 staff positions at any given time) with its Legal Services staff from 1965 to mid 1973 (141 lawyers, filling about 48 positions). The proportion of women decreased from about 35 percent to about 12 percent. Young lawyers, defined as 30 years of age or less on entry, increased from 59 percent to 83 percent. New, older lawyers—those over 30 but out of law school 3 years or less when hired—declined from 23 percent to 5 percent.

These patterns reflect a marked change toward heterogeneity in alternative professional opportunities. None in Legal Aid had been either on the law review or an honors graduate; only 11 percent were alumni of major national law schools. Of the Legal Services staff, over one-third had been on the law review or had graduated with honors; 25 percent were from major national law schools. The percentage of graduates from local proprietary or Catholic law schools dropped from 50 to 30; the percentage of graduates from nationally prestigious colleges rose from none to 18. Ex-associates of large law firms made up 11 percent of the Legal Services staff; another 7 percent had either clerked for federal judges or taught in national law schools. No lawyer had come to Chicago's LAB with a similar professional background.[13]

Perhaps the most dramatic change was in moral perspective. Some LAB lawyers had had prior social work experience. A few had been students at Northwestern Law School in years when participation in Legal Aid work was a curriculum requirement. But all Legal Aid lawyers, other than an occasional daughter of an upper-middle-class professional family, had, as a dominant motive for entering, a perception that their alternative or prior jobs were less prestigious or less remunerative. Legal Services lawyers brought a historically novel diversity of altruistic, political, and activist themes into the institution. From interviews and personnel files, I found that about one-third of Chicago's Legal Services lawyers had backgrounds in either the Peace Corps, religious social action, ghetto school teaching, civil rights demonstrations, antiwar protests, civil liberties litigation, or volunteer work with community organizations in poverty neighborhoods.

"About one-third" is admittedly vague, but seemingly precise statistics on the question are more misleading. With data from the Wisconsin study's national sample of Legal Services lawyers, Erlanger (1978, p. 261) reports that only about 27 percent had engaged in political activity while in college or law school, and only 14 percent in reform activity (civil rights marches, boycotts, ACLU work). These statistics greatly underrepresent moral activism in the perspectives of early Legal Services lawyers. By its very nature, a rapidly proliferating, symbolically diffuse social movement influences personal perspectives in ways that often do not show up in background indicators.

First, there is the problem of rapid change in moral-political outlook, called "radicalization" in the sixties. The more explosive a social movement, the less valid a description of the current state of moral energies based on a survey of commitments made in earlier times. Erlanger (1978, p. 261) describes a change from 5 percent to 25 percent in prior involvement in reform politics when comparing Legal Services lawyers who graduated before and after (presumably January) 1965. Background statistics on inclinations toward activism among Chicago poverty lawyers who graduated before 1968 would not measure the shock waves of indignation emanating from: the indiscriminate mass arrests of blacks during the riots that followed the assassination of Martin Luther King, Jr., in April 1968; the "police riot" of that summer against antiwar protestors at the Democratic National Convention; and the police brutality in the killing of Black Panther leader Fred Hampton and associates in December 1969. Moreover, whatever their cutoff date, statistics on activism as expressed in the biographies of lawyers before they entered Legal Services neglect changes in consciousness that occurred during careers in the institution.

Social movements are by their nature inchoate symbolic processes.[14] In radicalizing social movements, participants idiosyncratically reinterpret in political terms events they previously had considered morally inconsequential.[15] As the sixties progressed, protests became so varied as to make virtually any anti-establishment attitude a plausible sign of membership; and the symbols of political allegiance became so pervasive that even matters of personal style, such as the length of men's hair, were read as signs of allegiance to "the Movement."[16] If one-third of Legal Services lawyers showed up on standardized indicators of prior activism, many more could have interpreted inherently ambiguous acts as manifesting a spirit in defiance of authority.

Consider the situation of young male law graduates for whom entrance into Legal Services in the late sixties and early seventies held out the promise of a draft deferment. (At one point CLC had about 20 Vista-lawyer "volunteers" in this category.) Some would claim that they would have joined Legal Services even if it had not been a draft dodge, and some did stay after their draft vulnerability passed. Others made no pretense of a moral affinity for the program. (One outspoken, conservative Vista "volunteer" was locally renowned for appearing only occasionally at his South Side office assignment, and then often on his way to Jackson Park with a bag of golf clubs over his shoulder.) Many, probably most, shifted position from day to day. For at least some, for at least some time, the use of Legal Services as a potential draft dodge was an act of war resistance which stimulated a sense of alliance with those opposed to other forms of government authority.

Likewise, the fast-expanding drug and "counter" culture provided a context in which Legal Services lawyers could class themselves at one moment as long-time "outlaws" bitter against the State ("the pigs"); at another moment as self-involved people who had entered a neighborhood office only because its small-scale and informal organization made it unlike "an office," their employment unlike a "straight job."[17] A third set of examples of the emergent malleability of moral-political identity in the sixties comes from the experience of student rebellion. A university student could view himself as a radical by noting his participation in, or just his sympathies with, university sit-ins; but until identified by the school administration as a rebel, he would be free to discount these indicia.

In order further to appreciate the influence of the social movements of the sixties on activism in LSPs, consider trends in the movement itself and their possible reach. From this angle, the rapid politicization of American Catholicism in the sixties appears to have made a discernible contribution to the activist inclinations of Legal Services lawyers. It seems clear that the coincident reformist administrations of the "two Johns," president and pope, significantly mobilized moral activism among Catholic university students in the early sixties; but the precise nature and extent of influence also seems intrinsically unmeasurable.[18]

A few of my interviewees claimed a direct, if ironic, positive influence of their Catholic backgrounds on their entry into Legal Services.

> *Coming here continued your previous direction?* Sure. You recall, I'm an ex-seminarian. You see, in the sixties, many people like myself entered the seminary because we had a social service emphasis. We

> thought this was a way to start a social service career. But we found that the church wasn't the way; it was too conservative. And I continued in this direction in Legal Aid when many of my friends went into straight jobs. So they're jealous of me because I didn't cop out.

But the Catholic poverty lawyers I interviewed usually suggested at most an indirect, arguable relation.[19] Several Jewish lawyers in the Chicago programs indicated that their relatives simply would not take seriously their commitment to poverty law, asking repeatedly, "When will you get a real job?" When asked whether they had faced a similar disbelief from relatives, three Catholic Legal Services lawyers found the question hard to understand. Their relatives had hoped they would become priests and viewed their current work "as another vocation."

In many ways, a significant support to the recruitment of a Legal Services staff bent on social change was the great and uncertain promise of the surrounding social movement. About a dozen neighborhood-office lawyers came in from stints in the Peace Corps. By working in a small office in a Puerto Rican or Mexican-American neighborhood, some could build on community development experiences in poverty areas of Spanish-speaking countries. But perhaps as important, the uncertain future of the Legal Services program in its early years was attractive as a way of continuing to defer the fateful choice of a long-range career.

For others, OEO's initially radical optimism was similarly attractive for inviting an uncertain personal commitment. The War on Poverty promised so much, so vaguely, that one could readily justify becoming a "neighborhood poverty lawyer" not as a definitive career choice but as a challenge of exploration. The supervisor of the East Garfield office in the early 1970s recalled:

> I'd worked in Washington during each summer of law school . . . the first summer with Head Start, then as a program assistant to the director of legal services. I just fell into it. *When you first thought of going to Head Start, was this part of a longer, previous interest in this kind of thing?* It was that I wanted to see how this kind of government worked. You remember the way they talked about what they'd do, don't you? They were getting all the brightest people and all there, and they were going to end all these forms of poverty. I remember reading an article in *Harper's* at the time, where this guy said how they were going to achieve all these goals, and I remember I felt I just didn't understand the guy: how was he going to do this?

One more observation will complete the picture of the extent to which early Legal Services lawyers brought altruistic or activist perspectives into the institution. Some who had no background in activism perceived a protean character in the Legal Services program, such that the act of entry itself signified a commitment to activism. The location of Legal Services at the crossroads of numerous, unpredictable social movements was particularly important to those who came in from "straight" law practices. The perspective brought by these lawyers is worth extra attention because, in the development of the Chicago programs at least, they played disproportionately influential roles. (In 1974, the director and the two deputy directors of the then-unified Chicago Legal Services program all shared this background.)

I interviewed eight lawyers who had worked for firms, either as associates in large firms or partners in small firms. All but one indicated that events unrelated to political or moral issues had unexpectedly disengaged them from careers in private practice. One learned from partners that he "had no future in the firm." Another lost an implicit sense of security when a fatherly head of the real estate department was replaced by a hostile successor. Not all had been adjudged losers in private practice. One had recently become a partner but had then encountered uncertainty and conflict when older partners unexpectedly retired and the other young partners struggled to divide the firm's clients. For some, events in personal histories were the central turning points for a disengagement from private practice. One fellow realized after the break-up of his marriage that he no longer had to take for granted the economic necessity of continuing in a large firm.

Such amoral, apolitical catalysts disposed some lawyers from private firms to consider an exit or at least an excursion from traditional career lines. The initially dynamic image of Legal Services made it possible then to see joining it as a way of overcoming the trauma of leaving what had been a prestigious or prosperous job, although taking this view required effort. It was not obvious that there was sufficient promise in the new enterprise to recruit a group of lawyers with whom one could identify. Confidence that one was in fact beginning an activist involvement had to be built up on the spot, and collectively.

> Howell [CLC's director] wrote a fascinating ad about working with community and action groups. The ad was ambiguous: I didn't know if the position was for staff lawyer or retained counsel. I'd hoped it would be retained counsel, so I could be billing them and stay with the firm. I interviewed with Howell and he said, no, it was a staff position. He

> sent me interesting materials on what they'd been doing; *it read like the newspaper headlines*. This was "OEO." I'd known nothing about it. I hadn't done any Legal Services work. Legal Aid had no interest for me. I'd never go to Legal Aid, I thought. But CLC was not Legal Aid, and Howell emphasized the differences. I was also impressed that Howell had left Isham [a prestigious corporate law firm]. I wasn't the only one, and he was five years older than me. There was a three-week lag between the time I decided and the time I came. It was a time of terrible depression; the only time in my life that I felt like that. It was awful. "Why did you do a silly thing like that?" I'd ask myself. . . . I've always been happy I changed, ever since I got with CLC. Everyone in CLC was happy then; it seemed to me, anyway. *They were in the news all the time*. It was only much later that I realized that when Howell was trying to convince me to take the job, he was trying to convince himself too. (emphasis supplied)

External Sources of Reform Initiatives

The Legal Services Program was quickly and generally taken as a fundamental departure from Legal Aid's ideal of procedural justice. That "poverty lawyers" were up to something radically new was dramatized before mass audiences in a national wave of political attacks on local programs and on their overall legislative structure. Battles ranged from classic class struggles, most notably the opposition by conservative California Republicans to the association between California Rural Legal Assistance and the United Farm Workers union (Bennett and Reynoso 1972); to counterculture issues unique to the times, such as the attack by Texas Representative Collins on the Dallas Legal Services program for representing, against an obscenity charge, the publisher of an "underground" paper who printed a picture of a nude male leading a march to save miniskirts from lower hemlines.

The attacks were usually phrased as objections that nonindigents were being represented, that prohibited criminal-defense representation was being provided, or that undue emphasis was being given to law reform. Mayors led the attack in Chicago, Camden, and Daytona Beach. Senators Gurney of Florida, Tower of Texas, and Murphy of California mobilized indignation. Governors attempted to block federal funds for programs in California, Connecticut, Arizona, Missouri, Louisiana, and South Dakota. Attempts to impose constraints took various forms: regional and national administrators in the Legal Services bureaucracy were "pressured"; "contacts" were tapped to get White House support; restrictive legislation was offered in Congress.[20] Local and national newspapers took positions on the issues, and a rhetorical high point in the public debate was achieved when Vice-president Spiro Agnew (1972) raised the specter of "a federally funded system manned by ideological vigilantes, who owe their allegiance not to a client, not to the citizens of a particular state or locality and not to the elected representatives of the people, but only to a concept of social reform" (p. 931).

The charge that Legal Services's novel direction was a product of an autonomous elite of radical program lawyers was a gross distortion. The distortion was not in the charge of radicalism or elitism but in that of being an autonomous source of social conflict. Some have been concerned to protest that the program's lawyers were not all that radical or elite in education and social class background;[21] but relative to the staff at Legal Aid, they were. Seen within U.S. political history, the Legal Services program was far from being autonomous, however; it was used as a template on which deeply embedded political conflicts were displaced. What was really under attack was the package of compromises and commitments made in the early 1960s by and for the political strength of liberal Democrats.

Social movements of the sixties promoted the development of reform activity in Legal Services: by issuing a call for an expanded conception of advocacy on behalf of the poor; by illustrating, through public-interest law suits, how the call might be answered; and by supplying Legal Services with lawyers whose backgrounds in private practice suggested aggressive adversarial strategies. Other supports came from the development of militancy among groups that became clients at Legal Services and from personal ties between Legal Services lawyers and independent political movements.

The Call to Expanded Advocacy

The antipoverty, social-justice goal was hardly an invention of legal assistance lawyers, but a part of the Great Society designed by President Johnson and funded by the national Congress. Even the American Bar Association—clearly not in the vanguard—threw its organizational prestige behind the idea of using federal funds to pay lawyers to fight a War on Poverty (Johnson 1974, pp. 49–64).[22] Legislative and executive support for a new advocacy promoting economic equality extended far beyond the funding of LSPS. Regulations promulgated by the U.S. Department of Housing and Urban Development (HUD), itself a product of the sixties, supplied the legal basis for suits constraining the discretion of public housing officials.[23] Influenced by Ralph Nader and the new consumerism, Congress passed laws such as the Truth in Lending Act, which created a sanction of damages for failures to make required disclosures in financing. State legislatures proliferated a series of requirements for retail-sales installment contracts, providing poverty lawyers with a wealth of purely technical defenses of the sort long eschewed in Legal Aid.[24]

Perhaps the most consistently controversial activity of Legal Services lawyers was the representation of community groups; yet here the antecedent support of the national polity was most clearly crucial. Many community groups were shaped or fueled by legislative and executive inducements. The "maximum feasible participation" requirement in the Community Action Program within the OEO was specifically directed at the poor. Others of the inducements, however, were not. Health advocacy organizers among the poor were animated by U.S. Department of Health, Education, and Welfare (HEW) funds and regulations that would support "health-planning organizations" located not in Washington but locally and governed by a board with a majority of "consumers," whether poor or middle class. Some community organizations in poverty areas tried to become real estate developers by capitalizing on Federal Housing Administration programs for rent and home-ownership subsidies aimed at "low- and moderate-income" families. The animus against poverty lawyers thus carried with it a threat to renege on commitments previously made not only to the poor but to broader constituencies as well.

Political attacks on poverty lawyers functioned as a subtle scapegoating. Legal Services lawyers often were ahead of the poor and the population as a whole in their reform objectives. But so were many other professional altruists, in government and in philanthropically supported public-interest practices, who were, historically, ahead of the poverty lawyers. The move to expand the general conception of the rights of the poor was induced by a broader legal rights movement, and it was attacked as such. Many conservative opponents of Legal Services also attacked the judicial elite that, through opinions and speeches, had issued calls for what became the anti-poverty thrust of the Legal Services Program.

In a series of cases that were already operating as powerful national symbols while LSPs were recruiting their first staffs—in *Brown, Miranda*-and-*Escobedo, Gault,* and *Gideon*—the Supreme Court had brought whole new populations and institutions under the governance of legal process. The law of the courts had become the leading official force for transcending divisions in rights between races, between the state and the criminally accused, between adult and juvenile criminal defendants, and between poor and rich faced with the criminal process. Unimpeachable spokesmen for the legal profession's mission reflected this national experience as they pleaded for a new advocacy for the poor. In an article entitled "The Responsibilities of the Legal Profession," published in the *American Bar Association Journal* in February 1968, Supreme Court Justice Brennan reviewed the myriad social divisions of the sixties and reached for inspirational cadences to outline a constructive lawyer's role.

> Society's overriding concern today is with providing freedom and equality of rights and opportunities, in a realistic and not merely formal sense, to all the people of this nation: justice, equal and practical, to the poor, to the members of minority groups, to the criminally accused, to the displaced persons of the technological revolution, to alienated youth, to the urban masses, to the unrepresented consumers—to all, in short, who do not partake of the abundance of American life. . . . It seems to me unquestionable that the lawyer in America is uniquely situated to play a creative role in American social progress. Indeed, I would make bold to suggest that the success with which he responds to the challenges of what is plainly a new era of crisis and promise in the life of our nation may prove decisive in determining the outcome of the social experiments on which we are embarked (pp. 122, 121).

Public-interest Law Suits Show the Way

A role for lawyers for the poor as advocates promoting social justice was invented before the formation of Legal Services, and in many respects it was first mobilized outside the new, specialized programs. The natural history of *King* v. *Smith,* the Supreme Court decision that launched the field of welfare law, shows the dependence of that field on the civil liberties and civil rights movements. The case was the first to invalidate a state restriction on Aid to Families with Dependent Children (AFDC) eligibility as inconsistent with the Social Security Act. At issue was Alabama's "substitute father" regulation, a creation of Governor George Wallace through his welfare director Ruben King, which denied payments to children otherwise eligible if their mother was found to "cohabit" with any man. Mrs. Smith's problems started to become a case when she told her story to Donald Jellinek, a northern lawyer working in Selma for the Lawyer's Constitutional Defense Committee, the legal arm of the southern civil rights movement. The case was promoted into a Supreme Court decision by Martin Garbus, the first codirector, with Edward Sparer, of the Center on Social Welfare Policy and Law at Columbia University. *King* was tied to the civil liberties movement through the personal backgrounds of the center's directors. Garbus was recruited by Sparer, whom he had met two years before while defending people subpoenaed by New York State's Un-American Activities Committee.[25]

In Illinois, the *Jack Spring* decision overturned both centuries-old common law and an interpretation of a statute that had held in Illinois for 100 years when it announced that tenants could defend against eviction for nonpayment of rent by arguing the landlord's failure to make repairs.[26] The tenant's attorney was Gilbert Cornfield, a Chicago labor lawyer with a reputation for the support of Left causes. In public housing, the *Thorpe* case (see note 23) was created by a classic civil rights alliance between northern white and southern black lawyers. After receiving notice of eviction, Joyce Thorpe turned to Moses C. Burt, Jr., a local Durham lawyer who graduated college and law school from the all-black North Carolina College at Durham. After the lower state court proceeding, the case was taken over by Jack Greenberg and others at the NAACP Legal Defense Fund in Manhattan.

From 1965 to 1972, when Legal Services lawyers in Chicago participated in potentially far-reaching reform cases, they usually did so with other advocates in the legal rights movement, either directly by working with outside co-counsel or indirectly by advancing strategies simultaneously promoted elsewhere. They litigated reform issues generally recognized as ripe for judicial scrutiny.

> *During a year as a Reggie in the United Charities program, Robert Bennett put together a successful attack on the constitutionality of the Illinois one-year residency requirement for welfare[27] but was beaten to the Supreme Court by Connecticut, Pennsylvania, and District of Columbia cases.[28]*

Legal Services lawyers entered *ad hoc* alliances with public interest lawyers.

> *During her year in the Appellate and Test Case Division, Susan Grossman joined with Marshall Patner, then in the public-interest firm Patner and Karaganis, and with Chicago ACLU lawyer Sybille Fritzsche in a successful challenge to the Illinois antiabortion statute.[29]*

Legal Services's antipoverty litigation was sometimes fed by new developments in academic research coming from the general faculties of universities.

> *With the Lawyers Committee for Civil Rights under Law, and drawing on studies by researchers at MIT and at the Northwestern University*

Center for Urban Affairs, Stan Bass and others at CLC began a suit charging the board of education with racial and economic discrimination ("gerrymandering") in the allocation of funds to students.[30]

In the early years, Chicago's Legal Services lawyers were often associated with locally newsworthy legal rights campaigns, but usually from the periphery. In the saga of the Contract Buyers League—an attempt to renegotiate exploitative home-buying agreements entered into by hundreds of unsuspecting blacks—Legal Services lawyers played the minor role of defending against evictions in state court, while William Ming, Jr., and others from the city's premier black law firm, McCoy, Ming, and Black, along with Albert Jenner and Thomas Sullivan and others from Jenner and Block, pursued affirmative class-action suits in federal court.[31] CLC lawyers contributed bits of library research for early stages of the *Gautreaux* litigation, a series of cases which proved racial discrimination in the selection of sites for public housing and which generated years of intense publicity as the plaintiffs and judge searched for an effective remedy.[32] Alexander Polikoff led the legal strategy, first from a corporate law firm, Schiff, Hardin, and later from the public-interest law firm Businessmen for the Public Interest. CLC lawyers played a variety of support roles for TWO (The Woodlawn Organization). TWO became a continuing national story after Charles Silberman characterized it in 1964 as: "the first successful attempt anywhere in the United States to mobilize the residents of a Negro slum into a large and effective organization . . . the most important and the most impressive experiment affecting Negroes anywhere in the United States" (p. 207). But, whether assisting TWO in defining procedures for an electoral challenge to machine-selected slates of Model Cities community representatives, reviewing the organization's fiscal structure in anticipation of an IRS review, or advising on land buying for a housing development project, Legal Services lawyers remained behind the scenes and well behind TWO's in-house counsel, E. Duke McNeil.

The "Movement" Recruits Aggressive Lawyers

A multifaceted political movement to use legal procedures to fight poverty encouraged the impetus in Legal Services toward structural social change, and the work of public-interest lawyers provided a guiding model. In addition, as indicated earlier, the surrounding, protean social movement was a necessary condition for the recruitment of a number of lawyers from private law practice who came to have disproportionate influence on the development of Legal Services. Several in this group brought strategies of advocacy unprecedented in Legal Aid but traditional in the legal services enjoyed by wealthy individuals and major corporations.

Two ex-associates of large Chicago law firms, Kenneth Howell (from what was then Isham, Lincoln, and Beale) and Sheldon Roodman (from what was then Mayer, Friedlich) took over CLC in the early seventies. They gave it an emphasis on "impact," as distinct from "test-case," litigation. Roodman brought a series of federal class-action suits to speed the state's processing of public assistance applications.[33] To determine whether the public-aid department was complying with deadlines, Roodman periodically reviewed computer print-outs reporting dates of both application and official decision. Legal assistance lawyers in Chicago had never before attempted to control the administration of public assistance on so general a scale.

The economic impact of these suits was presumed by the poverty lawyers to be great. A difference of a month or two in the start of the average grant would make a significant difference in the total state outlay. Yet the legal theory used—an assertion of nonconformity between the state bureaucracy's practices and the governing federal regulations—was regarded as "simple." It was an argument that might be expected from lawyers who, having represented large institutional clients, would be well aware that such entities as government agencies, universities, or business corporations are likely to be out of compliance with scores of legal requirements at any given time.

In Roodman's cases, any gain to the poor would be roughly equivalent to the cost to the state. Howell spiked this recipe for advocacy by adding as a target regulatory requirements that would be costly to an adversary to obey but beneficial to the poor only indirectly, through strategic twists. Howell had been in a corporate law firm, litigating on behalf of People's Gas, just before he entered Legal Services. (He was also a prominent member of the Chicago Ethical Society; and the combination in his biography of business experience, nonsectarian moral philosophy, and social activism was symbolic of the reemergence of the forces that had created the reform-oriented Bureau of Justice in the 1880s.) Like any corporate litigator, Howell's private practice had focused on the control of timing. Because of the political and economic costs of delay, publicly aired controversy alone is often enough to kill a proposed utility rate increase, a new series of bonds, or a legislator's bill. The strategic twists came from the knowledge that the nature and merit of an objection often is less important materially than the effects of the process of adjudication.

Howell's first success came in November 1971. Earlier in the fall, Governor Richard Ogilvie had announced a series of measures to lower the state's costs for providing health and welfare benefits to the poor. Senator Charles Percy was to introduce a bill to increase the federal share. Ogilvie himself ordered the elimination of over $6 million in one month's state reimbursements for public assistance paid by Cook County, purportedly to encourage the county to channel recipients from state to state-and-federally subsidized programs. A figure of $30 million was the projected state gain from another gubernatorial decision, a cutback in Illinois's Medicaid coverage for drug and physician services provided outside of hospitalization, most notably eye and dental care. CLC lawyers attacked this last move.

It was clear even on the publicly visible record that CLC's lawyers had determined to attempt to stop the cuts before they were aware of a potentially viable legal ground. The first move, a motion for a temporary restraining order filed the day the cuts went into effect, was based on the state's failure to obtain HEW approval as required by the Social Security Act.[34] Predictably, this deficiency was remedied the next morning, after the state advised HEW, which had already expressed a position favorable to the cuts, that a formal act of approval was necessary. Howell then discovered what the newspapers termed, and what CLC lawyers privately considered, a "law technicality": a statutory requirement for a "utilization review" by HEW (a process which would entail a series of public hearings over a period of weeks) before it could properly approve the cuts ("Law Technicality" 1971). Voluminous briefs and a fact-finding trial held off the cutbacks for months, until the politics of the state's welfare budget had shifted sufficiently for the director of public aid to announce that improvements in the department's fiscal status enabled it to afford the $30 million after all ("Medicaid Benefits Restored" 1972).

CLC lawyers began to pursue an array of such trouble-making, clout-creating, strategies.

A bank located in a community with a sizeable poverty population is trying to move to a more middle-class site. It might be possible to throw a "monkey wrench" into the necessary administrative review process by dressing up arguments about insensitivity to the community. Bank officials concerned with the administrative and public relations costs of a delayed move might then agree to hire a number of minorities.

Cook County Hospital is coming up for a periodic accreditation review. A threat to stimulate embarrassing news stories on "consumer complaints" might soften the hospital's stance against placing representatives of the poor on governing councils.

> *Perhaps new commitments for the construction of housing for the poor can be obtained if protests can delay governmental approval of the sale to developers of lakeshore air rights owned by the Illinois Central Railroad.*
>
> *Perhaps Com Ed will modify its proposed rate increase if representatives of the poor formally intervene in the necessary rate review proceeding to insist on an elaborate cost study.*

If CLC could successfully cause itself to be reckoned with in these particulars, it might acquire a reputation ("presence," it was called, in one annual report) that would cause it to be consulted, or at least listened to, in advance of policy changes by major institutions in the city.

Militancy in Client Groups

When Legal Services lawyers in Chicago were associated with controversial social activism, they were more often caught up in—than initiating—the drama. The militancy of community groups in the sixties typically had much larger dimensions and deeper roots than any involvement developed by poverty lawyers. The Cook County Democratic organization, headed by Chicago's Mayor Richard J. Daley, led resistance to autonomous community power. Even before the implementation of the War on Poverty in 1963 and 1964, Daley had sacrificed millions of dollars for juvenile delinquency programs by refusing to meet requirements for citizen participation (Greenstone and Peterson 1973, pp. 22, 273). In a series of increasingly loud protests dating back to the mid 1950s, community groups in Chicago had mobilized against Urban Renewal plans (Wilson 1966, p. 409). In 1968 and 1969, organizations in several poor neighborhoods (LPPAC, the Lawndale People's Political Action Coalition, on the West Side; TWO and KOCO, the Kenwood-Oakland Community Organization, on the South; the Uptown Coalition led by the Rev. Charles Geary on the North Side) attacked the city's Urban Renewal and Model Cities plans for neglecting community interests. It was only against this extensive background that CLC could make its first significant contribution to community organizations in poverty areas: a report on the inactivity of the citizen advisory committees set up by the city to fulfill federal requirements for citizen participation. The report was widely used by community organizations to make their case, providing CLC with quick recognition among its potential clientele as an ally of militant protest (Fish 1973, p. 235).

As movements of organized protest among the poor developed into sit-in demonstrations and street confrontations in the late sixties, Legal Services lawyers developed a variety of marginal assisting roles. Students for a Democratic Society (SDS) organizers worked in Uptown between 1964 and 1967, then left, as the group they promoted most directly, JOIN, spawned other groups and disintegrated. One of JOIN's successors was the Young Patriots, a group of Appalachian white youths that came to resemble the Black Panthers as it attempted to transform its image from outlaw gang into indigenous representative of the whole community (Gitlin and Hollander 1970). A free health clinic promoted by the group was opposed by the city's public health department for lacking a license. The ensuing conflict gave Legal Services lawyers an opportunity to argue unequal treatment (the city did not require licenses of for-profit clinics) and to garner widespread publicity.

Politicoeconomic trends on a macro level appear to have been behind an unprecedented wave of activism by welfare recipients. Although litigation against such restrictions as residency and man-in-the-house rules has generally been considered a significant contributor to the "welfare explosion" (cf. Piven and Cloward 1971, pp. 306–320; and Handler 1978, p. 74), a staggering increase in the number of welfare recipients had begun well before Legal Services began striking down eligibility limitations.[35] The leading students of the welfare rights movement point to the contributions of: an early decision in the Kennedy administration to woo minority-group constituencies with economic inducements rather than a civil rights act; Community Action programs which functioned less as service deliverers than as channels for protest; the urban riots of the mid 1960s; and the strategy recipients pursued of aggressively demonstrating at public assistance offices (Piven and Cloward 1979, pp. 264–361). Whatever the precise measure of the impact of litigation in encouraging rights-consciousness among recipients and on magnifying welfare as a public issue, the movement as a whole conferred significance on otherwise modest acts of legal assistance. Sit-in protests by recipients, for example, provided Legal Services lawyers with the opportunity to play controversial roles simply by explaining trespass laws.

Ties to Independent Political Movements

However tenuous, the ties between poverty lawyers and the new militancy of urban community organizations marked a break from the Legal Aid tradition. Another novel tie between poverty lawyers and contemporaneous movements for social change came about through "latent" roles—personal relationships that were formally autonomous from work in Legal Services.[36]

An independent political movement in Chicago gained strength in the sixties. Many Legal Services lawyers identified with it through off-hours campaigning and social contacts, not through client contacts at work. The constituents of the independent political organizations (IPO and IVI, the Independent Precinct Organization and the Independent Voters of Illinois) were, after all, primarily middle class, located in the wards of Aldermen Leon DePres in Hyde Park, and Bill Singer and Dick Simpson on the Near North Side, not in the neighborhoods of poverty law offices.[37] Legal Services lawyers were also represented in professional activities opposed to patronage control of public offices. The Chicago Council of Lawyers, a new professional association created as a rival to the Chicago Bar Association (CBA), began promulgating recommendations against the election of judicial candidates selected by "the machine" and deemed qualified by the CBA. In 1972, no Legal Aid lawyer was on the council, but the president was an ex–Reginald Heber Smith fellow; one of the vice-presidents was a current Legal Services lawyer, and 7 of the 21 board members were, had been, or later became Legal Services lawyers.[38]

An Exaggerated Image

In Chicago, an image of Legal Services lawyers as a force for social change was more conferred than earned. Establishment politicians demanded "radical" enemies in order to lend a manageable interpretation to the crises of the times. A clear example occurred in early 1968. A group of black parents petitioned the board of education to remove the principal and assistant principal of the Crown School, alleging racism throughout its administration. The group had requested help in documenting grievances from a lawyer who was known within CLC to be its most conservative member. (He was the one who, in discussions on role definition, would review *ad nauseam* the frustrating necessity of waiting for community groups to decide on courses of action). The controversy began to receive extensive news coverage when the principal reported that his life had been threatened. A few weeks later, and two weeks after the riots following the assassination of Martin Luther King, Jr., Congressman Roman Pucinski, an outspoken conservative ally of Mayor Daley, was prompted by school administration officials to call for the termination of the CLC Vista-lawyer program. He explained:

> I don't think the Federal government should be financing a program that brings more turmoil to the city. I want to determine, rather to ascertain, whether there is any cause and effect between the work of the program and when the west side went up in flames. ("Cut Off Vista" 1968)

On the one hand, a style of conservative representation could become politically controversial because of the heightened sensitivities of the Democratic machine in Chicago in the sixties.[39] On the other hand, many Legal Services lawyers were seeking ways of conferring broad significance on their work, and the reputation of the Daley administration offered distinctively rich possibilities. A proposal for a crosstown expressway, a highway that would link the Loop and Midway Airport at the cost of displacing tens of thousands of residents, was known to be "dear to the mayor's heart." A suit that could block the plan would profit all opponents of the machine. CLC lawyers could feel they were part of a broader political movement when assisting Chicago's public housing tenants to gain governing power in the administration of their projects. The grievances were distinctly local, literally domestic: elevators did not work; children were falling out of unscreened windows and being burned by uninsulated heating pipes; security was awful.[40] None of the demands necessarily carried implications for reform in the city beyond public housing, itself a notoriously segregated institution. Yet CLC lawyers saw political significance in an emergent tenants' organization, Chicago Housing Tenants Organization (CHTO) on the perception that the city administration would feel threatened by any demonstration of independent organizational power. A stock election day news story in Chicago showed public housing managers threatening tenants with eviction if they did not vote the party line. An independent organization representing 100,000 public housing tenants might afford what advocates of the legal rights movement have termed a "sense of efficacy and entitlement,"[41] a spirit fatal to "the machine's" demand for deference.

The significance of such strategies was largely an internal perception. Compared to the experience of other LSPs, especially California Rural Legal Assistance and New York City's MFY, Chicago's early poverty lawyers were virtually untouched by public attack from politicians. As I describe later, the Daley organization formally and quietly controlled the major Legal Services program in the city, the United Charities program, until mid 1970. Chicago's Legal Services lawyers were at times associated with events that became historic signs of insurgence and oppression, but in unanticipated and peripheral ways.

Lawyers from CLC and from United Charities Legal Services turned out in large numbers in response to the mass arrests made during the riots of the summer of 1967 and during the "Martin Luther King riots" in the spring of 1968. While the CBA acceded to an officially encouraged high bail policy and to rebuffs by the chief judge of their offers to provide defense representation, poverty lawyers joined with other nonestablishment lawyers to attack the city's procedures in litigation, and they interviewed incarcerated defendants in preparation for bail applications. [They have been credited with supplying a modicum of administrative rationality in a context in which "the system" willfully broke down: parents were unable to verify through court officials whether and where their children might be incarcerated, in some instances for days (Balbus 1973, pp. 171–172, 184).] Later in the summer of 1968, during the riots at the Democratic nominating convention, poverty lawyers documented instances of police brutality, again playing roles that were minor in view of the public significance of the events but dramatic within Legal Services for encouraging an antiestablishment, pro-"Movement" spirit.

The Origins and Fate of Reform

To the extent the impetus for reform in Legal Services and the overall movement for reform in the sixties were positively related, Legal Services got much more than it gave: the new program received much more support for its break from the Legal Aid tradition than it contributed to the insurgent force of the wider movement. This review of early external supports forms a basis for my assessment of the ability of LSPs to sustain an impetus toward reform after the disintegration of the movements of the sixties.

The context of a protean social movement was indispensable for the shift from Legal Aid's passive stance to a more aggressive posture of expanding recognition of the rights of the poor. An aura of an undefined potential for significant change was essential to draw into Legal Services a number of lawyers from "straight" careers who brought a strategy of using legal technicalities for leverage to enhance the bargaining power of the poor. Many young, recent law graduates who came with educational backgrounds that had been virtually unrepresented in Legal Aid were drawn to Legal Services by its perceived affinity to war resistance, the civil rights movement, the Peace Corps, the counterculture, university student rebellion, anti-"machine" politics, and religious social activism. The combination of an activist Supreme Court, legislatures that had been influenced by Naderism, executives who were devising regulations to elaborate the War on Poverty, and the earlier success of public-interest lawyers in civil rights litigation invited—almost demanded—an expanded conception of the rights of the poor.

Parallel Great Society programs and new commitments of funds to old urban renewal programs aided reform activity by Legal Services lawyers even to the point of creating new abuses and adversaries to attack. Many of the most intense early clashes between Legal Services lawyers and politicians arose not from direct attacks on traditional establishment structures but over battles for control of other remedial programs such as Model Cities. Adversaries promoted a "reform," even a "radical," significance for Legal Services work by occasionally raising to the level of front-page controversy tasks of advocacy which, seen outside of the social-movement context, would appear to be quite modest.

There are two common views of the fate of the reform impetus in Legal Services in the seventies. One points to Legal Services as the single healthy survivor among the institutional innovations of the War on Poverty. The other perceives a destruction of the spirit of reform and a return to the passivity of Legal Aid after the Nixon election victory of 1972 and the dismantling of the OEO. There is a sense in which both are correct. In the late seventies, LSPs did not draw the political fire that progressively heated the institution up to 1973. But the lowered profile of Legal Services was not due to a decrease in the institution's commitment to reform. Legal Services lost a militant public image in large part because its initial reputation for insurgency was less earned than conferred: an aspect of militancy was evoked through associations, many symbolic or peripheral, with external pressures for social change that then became dormant.

In fact, the internal capacities of LSPs for mounting the sort of reform strategies that originally brought controversy substantially increased in the 1970s. In addition, the impetus for reform, although symbolically muted, became independent of a supporting social-movement context. I build further toward these points by arguing in the following chapters that, after the Legal Aid tradition had been broken by the dynamics of the sixties, politically neutral standards of professional quality became autonomous sources for an impetus toward reform, both in the careers of Legal Services lawyers and in battles for organizational control against proponents of the philosophy of Legal Aid.

Chapter 5

Legal Services Programs and the Sixties: Tension and Independence

As had been the case in the late nineteenth century, the expansion of the principle of equal justice in the 1960s depended on a widespread outburst in U.S. society of critical, reformist energies. The features which distinguished LSPs from the Legal Aid tradition—neighborhood offices, board seats for poverty community representatives, a staff with activist and elite educational backgrounds, militant groups as clients—followed directly from themes of the sixties. But the overall relation between the activist impulse in Legal Services and the broader social movement was not that simple. An organizational capacity for reform was not created by the direct incorporation of external pressures for social change into new structures. At the start, the distinctive features of LSPs were effective much more as symbols than as direct facilitators of legal activism.

The distinctive design of LSPs was essentially a symbolic departure in two basic ways. Through political compromises made by administrative leaders, the structure of the new LSPs was often little more than a thin overlay on the old Legal Aid format; this was generally recognized by participants at the time. It was not generally recognized, however, that the new organizational design itself reflected a faulty folk sociology. It had been assumed that if militant, progressive forces in the larger social movement were to characterize the practice of poverty law, Legal Services would have to discover conducive organizational structures. The call was for a revised arrangement of the relation of lawyers and clients, and for a staff with unprecedented moral concerns and professional competence. But evidence soon mounted that the structures specifically designed to bring into LSPs external pressures for reform were not operating as expected. In fact, as I repeatedly emphasize, the structures tying Legal Services into the larger movement as often appeared to block reform as to promote it.

The following review of early tensions between themes of social change in the sixties and the capacity for reform in Legal Services balances the portrait of complementarity presented in the last chapter. It also continues to develop the account of the unexpected, somewhat ironic process by which Legal Services's capacity for reform became autonomous from the sixties. I have already shown that many of the ties between Legal Services and the sixties were largely symbols. The distinctive structural features of LSPs were symbols sufficiently powerful, however, that they recruited into the institution people who eventually built a capacity to sustain reform, often by working around the very structures that had been designed to help promote reform.

The chapter begins by noting initial constraints on Chicago's Legal Services lawyers that were created by political and administrative compromises of the War on Poverty's spirit of social change. Then it analyzes the unwarranted assumptions on which the design of LSPs was expected to promote the advocacy of reform. A third section follows the unanticipated career of CLC, a local LSP originated to give representation to controversial community groups, which was transformed informally into a reform litigation agency. CLC's career was an early clue to the source and nature of the institution's new, self-generating inclination toward reform.

Compromises of the War on Poverty

Legal Services formally was an arm of the antipoverty program, but its mission never was to alter social-class relations. For one thing, the antipoverty program as a whole was not that radical. Even on a rhetorical level, the antipoverty banner was a classic liberal compromise. At first glance, the "war" certainly appeared resolute, but the failure to specify the enemy signaled political bad faith. It was a call for radical improvement in the status of the poor without a simultaneous commitment to reduce the superior status of the well-to-do.

The policy of citizen participation in antipoverty programs was novel and controversial, but the fundamental structural commitment was conservative:[1] virtually all components of the War on Poverty segregated the poor to specialized ameliorative settings. In the early 1960s there was no measurable commitment to cross-class public day care; to a national cross-class health system; or to a negative taxation system that would remove the stigma of poverty by blurring the line between "welfare" and earned income to the extent that tax subsidies had already blurred this line for the wealthy.

Similarly, none of the proponents of the Legal Services program defined "equal justice" as requiring an across-the-board reorganization of citizens' access to lawyers. All tacitly agreed (there is no reported debate on the question) to strive toward equality in the legal system through separate law offices for the poor and nonpoor. Occasionally there was disagreement over the quantitative measure of poverty (the income limit), but never over the assertion that only "the poor" should receive "free" legal services. Advocates for Legal Services differed among themselves primarily on the choice of a format for assisting the poor, especially on the balance to be established between "full-service" neighborhood offices and law reform think tanks (Johnson 1974, pp. 34–35).

That the proponents of a Legal Services program were virtually all lawyers indicated the limited penetration by the more radical movements of the sixties. Indeed, the early leaders of the national office of Legal Services had as one of their top concerns the achievement of independence from the rest of the OEO. They wanted to remove LSPs from the political storms of the Community Action Program. They also wanted a *lawyer's* institution, one dedicated to values which would symbolize the honorific concern of lawyers for moral principles. The two objectives were congenial. Resistance to OEO control could be rationalized as a requirement of professional ethics: domination by nonlawyer bureaucratic superiors appeared to violate the sanctity of the lawyer–client relationship. In the planning for Legal Services and later in the battle against a drive to increase OEO control by bringing LSPs under regional administration, program activists forged an alliance with the nationally organized bar. This was a type of interest-group ally unique to Legal Services within the War on Poverty; no other antipoverty program could draw on analogous clout to resist a loss of autonomy within OEO (Johnson 1974, pp. 36–70).

In the negotiations between activists for Legal Services and leaders of the organized bar, a sense of crisis impelled both sides to a quick accommodation. In 1965, advocates for Legal Services recalled that the overnight creation of the War on Poverty had been made possible by the temporary, extraordinary latitude given President Johnson in the shock waves following the Kennedy assassination. They sensed in the brewing controversies over citizen participation that congressional consent for the development of Legal Services might suddenly disappear. Because it was a national institution, Legal Aid offered a unique apparatus for quick implementation. Presumably a withdrawal of legislative support would be less likely if it would entail the destruction of already established offices. Thus the Legal Services administrative leadership favored independent groups of activists in places where they arose quickly, but elsewhere it made grants to existing Legal Aid programs.

For its part, the organized bar, particularly as represented by American Bar Association President Lewis Powell, felt that federal government action to support expanded legal assistance to the poor was imminent. American Bar Association leaders recalled that the American Medical Association's uncompromising opposition to "socialized medicine" had placed the AMA on the sidelines during the shaping of the Medicare and Medicaid programs. Without ceremony, the ABA leadership abandoned its tradition of decrying as socialistic the idea of government subsidy for Legal Aid. So long as the structure of LSPs would segregate the poor to a specialized caste of lawyers for service, it would leave the bulk of the profession unaffected.[2]

In Chicago, Legal Services began as a transparent overlay on the traditional Legal Aid format. The first grant of Legal Services funds in the city was administered by the LAB of United Charities. The director of the LAB became the top executive of an expanded legal staff, while remaining formally subordinate to the executive director of United Charities, a social worker. A veteran of the LAB staff was selected to lead the neighborhood-office operation. Neighborhood lawyers initially were instructed to call the downtown LAB supervisors for everyday professional advice. The Legal Aid Committee of United Charities remained formally subordinate to the United Charities Board, which became the final policy-review body for the integrated Legal Aid–Legal Services organization. OEO Legal Services policies mandated representation for the poor on governing boards, but the Legal Aid Committee initially continued with its corporate law firm makeup, later providing token representation for the poor. The United Charities Board, to which the Legal Aid Committee formally was subordinate, made no structural commitment to enfranchise the poor.

Chicago also illustrated some of the political forces behind the compromise of a reform impetus for Legal Services. Legal Services in Chicago was subordinate not only to the LAB, which itself was subordinate to the United Charities, but also to the Chicago Committee for Urban Opportunity (CCUO), Mayor Daley's vehicle for bringing antipoverty funds into the city. In OEO language, United Charities was a "delegate agency" of CCUO; CCUO was the direct "grantee" of OEO Legal Services. Mayor Daley, acting through his appointed CCUO head, Deton Brooks, made the receipt of Legal Services funds at United Charities contingent on an agreement to limit both suits against the city and the representation of community groups.

These restrictions made Chicago famous among observers of Legal Services as an example of a politically compromised program.[3] CCUO was famous in its own right among OEO watchers. From conservative Minnesota Republican Congressman Albert Quie (Donovan 1967, p. 67) to social scientists performing nationwide studies (Greenstone and Peterson 1973, p. 19), observers judged the CCUO as the single CAP (OEO Citizen Action Program) with the greatest degree of establishment domination and the least citizen participation. With his direct line into the White House, Mayor Daley had an unexcelled ability to flaunt citizen participation requirements without fear of sanction by OEO (Moynihan 1969, p. 145). Brooks, previously an administrator in the Cook County Public Aid Department, was an unabashed defender of the Daley Machine who had himself received national publicity as a black opponent of civil rights leaders (Greenstone and Peterson 1973, p. 160).

The affiliation with the CCUO shut Chicago's Legal Services lawyers off from militant community groups. TWO's leadership had fought Brooks publicly, characterizing CCUO as a "colonial power" at one point in an unsuccessful effort to go around CCUO to Washington for direct CAP funding (Fish 1973, pp. 88–89). United Charities Neighborhood Legal Services offices were housed in CCUO Urban Progress Centers. When the Montrose Urban Progress Center opened, SDS-influenced community groups in Uptown protested what they termed a "colonial invasion" (Gitlin and Hollander 1970, p. xxix).

Conservative forces blocked the importation into Legal Services of the most controversial themes of the sixties. When two Reginald Heber Smith fellows developed an ongoing representation relation with the Black Panthers and other militant community figures, they could have been forced out either by national Legal Services restrictions on criminal representation or by the local exclusion of client groups not acceptable to CCUO. When they acceded to the inevitable and resigned to develop People's Law Office on Halsted Street, Legal Services lost contact with the most politically challenging demands by the poor in Chicago for legal assistance.[4]

Theory of Organization

The isolation of Legal Services from external forces for social change was not solely the product of political compromise. Structural features of Legal Services that were specifically designed to link it with broader activist energies did not work out as expected. The format for LSPs had been justified on the basis of a folk sociology that seriously misread the social forces of the institution. By placing representatives of newly militant community groups on the boards of local programs, OEO Legal Services did not necessarily promote militant legal strategies for the poor. Often the effect was the opposite. What many community group leaders valued most was not reform strategies that would have long-term and far-reaching benefits but immediate service for individual clients in their neighborhoods. Like the urban political leaders who employed traditional patronage strategies, new poverty community leaders were trying to build personal allegiances and membership in their organizations by displaying control over the allocation of government social services.[5]

Questionable empirical assumptions also underlay the case for the organizational format of the neighborhood office. A study of three cities containing both downtown Legal Aid and neighborhood Legal Services offices found relatively little difference in clientele (Fisher and Ivie 1971). Expectations of neighborhood Legal Services lawyers that their new organizational setting would call out demands for militant antipoverty action were disappointed on a mass basis. The typical client continued to request personal assistance in an immediate crisis.

Even the priority on selecting staff with activist backgrounds proved at best ambivalent for sustaining the reform impetus. Demoralization was often most rapid among Legal Services lawyers who previously had been active in other parts of the legal rights movement. The lawyer next quoted lasted less than two years in the 47th Street office:

> In law school I did better grade-wise and got a good junior-year job. It was with . . . *the* prominent firm to get a job with from [his law school]. . . . I worked under [a famous trial lawyer, doing *pro bono* work] in [a famous] marijuana sales case. That was very rewarding. I had feelings of grandeur, that I can save the world, that kind of thing. . . . At that time, I thought that I was on my way to becoming a top-flight lawyer. And still, with my friends, when I get drunk, I think of that case and my feelings at that time. That case affected the lives of 800–1000 people. It was very exciting. We were testifying before the legislature and other government bodies—the crime commission. . . . I get drunk, and it bothers me that that could be the high point of my legal career.

So it was for lawyers with elite educational backgrounds and for those with experience in private firms: the social-movement context made it possible to draw them in, but their prior experience often spurred the process of demoralization. The following lawyer, one of several who had worked for prestigious law firms, left Legal Services after six months in a neighborhood office. She specifically noted the neighborhood location as a problem.

> I had worked in a superior-quality organization, a firm that just didn't make compromises in the quality of the work it would put out, and I missed that in legal aid [*sic*]. It's just not done there. . . . Really, what led me to leave was the constant intake, and no time for quality work because of it. If you had to go to court downtown, you wasted half a day—the time it took to get there [from the neighborhood office] was just too great.

Insofar as advocates of reform expected that the Legal Services' staff would draw on the surrounding social movement for activist motivation, this expectation also was frequently disappointed. The counterculture theme in the sixties induced several neighborhood lawyers to retreat into isolating spiritual journeys and to perceive the institution as irrelevant to social progress. The Legal Services career of a supervisor of the North Avenue office was described by two co-workers as a progression suggestive of the panels in a Jules Feiffer cartoon.

> He worked for a conservative firm in town for three years. He was getting right into that: moved to the suburbs, bought a house, had a wife and child. Then he came to legal aid [*sic*]. He bought a three-story flat, moved into the city with his wife and child, and then he got increasingly alienated from work. You could see it happen gradually: his hair got longer and longer, his clothes more and more sloppy. Finally he left, went West, to a town 50 miles north of San Francisco, bought a boat and is going out with other people, learning to be a fisherman.
>
> [In his last year] he was getting so involved in mind-expanding experience, all his excitement—all the excitement that infused him—came from outside the office and had nothing to do with the job. He was proud of having the best food coop. That was the kind of thing that excited him. He had worked his way up to Legal Services, and that was his big interest and excitement. Near the end he was at the point where he'd get on his bike at the end of the day with a joint in his mouth. We were all getting rather concerned about him. We took him aside and asked him if he realized that he was jeopardizing his legal career by doing that; he could be more discreet. . . . *How did he explain*

what he was going through, and his relation to the office? It got very tiring after a while for us. He'd get into the whole bag of how we are all part of the problem here, not the solution. We weren't solving anything, but the opposite. Like if we beat a deficiency judgment, then the client would take the money and partake in Consumer America.

Group Representation

The folk sociology underlying the distinctive structural features of LSPs was thus not proving out. Although for many observers, an effective legal strategy to alter the social-class position of the poor would seem to depend on alliances with indigenous community organizations,[6] there was a failure to anticipate how the lawyers who would have to implement the mandate would experience it. Here too, the fact that Legal Services was surrounded by a protean social movement often hindered more than facilitated the mobilization of reform.

Lawyers in CLC and some in United Charities Neighborhood Legal Services perceived a vague, "high-priority" directive to "work with" community groups. Reflecting their diverse backgrounds and the multiple ties between Legal Services and movements in other institutions, the lawyers gave diverse interpretations to this mandate. For a new lawyer at CLC, it seemed natural "to head up an economic development team. I had the corporate law background, so I was to set up franchises, businesses." A lawyer who had taught in a ghetto school and who expected to pursue a graduate degree in education at some later date specialized in community work in a Puerto Rican neighborhood office. He became increasingly involved with an experimental, community-controlled school and eventually left to put full time into the project. In the Mexican neighborhood office, an ex-seminarian who was also an ex–Latin American Peace Corps volunteer put together his experiences in altruism and took on the mission of being (in a colleague's phrase) "padre to the pueblo."

Organization leaders continuously failed in their efforts to direct the staff's initiatives with community groups. From the start and for about six years, the neighborhood office staff was generally chastised for not making contacts with groups. Meanwhile, at the Appellate and Test Case Division, a lawyer who had been hired to develop law-making litigation functioned instead as a lawyer for groups. Using contacts he had established with tenant unions during law school, he devoted virtually all of his time to rent-strike negotiations.

Staff lawyers appeared ready to justify as within their mandate virtually any involvement with groups of neighborhood residents, and administrators at downtown headquarters had no yardstick to measure results. A lawyer in a West Side office who had been a Catholic college basketball star saw his mission as the arrangement of a basketball schedule between Catholic and black high school teams. In a letter written when he resigned (under pressure), he explained that, although his work had not generated cases, did "not make the headlines," and was not "capable of being accurately evaluated . . . in statistics," he had been able to

> agree [with local "blacks"] on long-range goals for the West Side—the development of community and individual responsibility, pride and hope for the future. . . . We are confident that in our own quiet way we have had an effect on the community that will someday have far-reaching consequences [although] it will not surprise us if we do not see the results in our lifetime.

LSP leaders shared in a general failure to grasp the social reality of community lawyering. Critics and proponents alike misrepresented the work of legal advocacy for community groups, the former by accusing poverty lawyers of crossing a nonexistent line separating lawyers from organizers, the latter by drawing romantic analogies to lawyers in the labor union movement. Sympathetic commentators contributed to the confusion by charging that vague statements by the national leadership of Legal Services on priorities and proprieties were responsible for exposing the staff to political attack (Hannon 1969, Blumenthal and Soler 1971). In fact, the line between representing and organizing is inherently vague; the distinction cannot be made clear by matching precise regulatory language with firm leadership resolve. Nor, apart from isolated exceptions such as Cesar Chavez's United Farm Workers, did the community groups with which poverty lawyers worked have any semblance of the labor union movement's power to withhold something of value.[7]

The distinction betweeen representing an organization as a lawyer and organizing it as an activist does not cut clearly, whether applied to poverty or corporate law. The services performed by lawyers on behalf of organizations frequently are indistinguishable from roles played by nonlawyers in offices for public relations, labor relations, lobbying, and business planning. In-house corporate counsel often become executives or directors after their intimate participation in the business has made the change little more than a formality.

The distinction between lawyering and directing the development of organizations was especially artificial when applied to poverty lawyers. Lawyers cannot work for an organization without working through the medium of particular individuals who claim the right to represent the entity. If struggles for internal control are in progress, any advice the lawyer gives will have the strategic character of advice given to a particular faction. If the advice influences the ability of one side to prevail, the lawyer's representation will literally have had an organizing effect.

For systematic reasons also, the groups with which poverty lawyers worked were embroiled recurrently in internal struggles for dominance. Most based their existence on the very fact of being organized. Some were issue centered—opposed to the construction of a highway, a college, or block busting. Others were formed in response to legislative provisions for citizen participation in the planning or administration of such social welfare programs as Urban Renewal, manpower training, and health maintenance. Some groups consisted of those who shared a source of government income or services, for example, from public aid, public housing, or public schools. Others focused on a class relation in the private economy: tenant unions, migrant councils, or associations of minority employees. All had as their chief strength the image of being representative—the symbols of collective unity. Their resources for power were basically protests and public-pressure campaigns, or the formal status of being "community representatives" within a preestablished administrative scheme.

The fact that symbols of representation were their central power resource gave organizations of the poor distinctive tendencies toward internal struggle. Whoever could achieve recognition externally as the group's representative would have a claim to the group's bargaining power. Poverty lawyers sometimes were drawn into internal conflicts simply by associating with a member with leadership aspirations, inasmuch as the appearance of having counsel itself helped the member make his symbolic case! Legal Services lawyers were also drawn into organizing struggles simply by responding to requests for individual service. In poor people's organizations, an official's ability to direct legal services to clients can build a personal following.

If the folk sociology underlying the presumed line between lawyering and organizing was misconceived by critics, an equally serious error was made by advocates who anticipated an effective community counsel role. Legal Services lawyers won a major victory by forcing the Daley Machine into Model Cities elections in which machine candidates ran against slates supported by indigenous organizations. Then they watched the machine win overwhelmingly. In the late sixties, the Uptown neighborhood office enjoyed a reputation for developing the most successful relationship with community groups. But in the words of the office's departing supervisor, by 1972 the community context had become hopeless—Uptown had become "a mental ward," a "dumping ground" for state mental hospitals.[8] By 1971, only two of CLC's four neighborhood offices were related to viable, indigenous groups: the KOCO office was in disarray (Fish 1973, p. 286), and the West Side continued to be a vast territory unoccupied by professionals. Welfare rights organizations were strong in Chicago for a couple of years. But by the time a local Legal Services lawyer had won judicial recognition of recipients' rights to "fair hearings," professional insiders to the welfare rights movement were concluding that the groups could not mobilize their members to implement the new rights.[9] In Chicago, few militant poverty-area community groups survived into the seventies. TWO was the one community organization that survived, even thrived, during the early seventies, but Woodlawn virtually vanished. The area around East 63rd Street, where the Legal Services office stood, was abandoned by great numbers. In an increasingly popular analogy, Woodlawn's streets of vacant tenements were compared unfavorably to postwar, bombed-out European cities (Fish 1973, p. 309).

Community organizations were too weak to provide Legal Services lawyers with significant reform roles; and conversely, poverty lawyers contributed little of significance to the development of strong, militant community organizations. Two historically emergent themes in the careers of community organizations pitted their organizational interests in promoting reform against those of Legal Services lawyers. First, in the mid and late sixties, new groups carved out a role by selling a message of distrust of outside, white institutions. "Black power" communicated the message across the country. In Chicago, the theme was given the gloss of Saul Alinsky's organizing philosophy. Even within the more moderate groups which Alinsky influenced (such as TWO and OBA, Organization for a Better Austin), the basic policy was to keep lawyers at a distance. In the more extreme groups, such as the West Side Organization, leaders were self-professed "criminals" and whites were "devils" (Ellis 1969).

The second relevant trend among community organizations was toward a federated format. OBA, TWO, and NCO (Northwest Community Organization) were all umbrella organizations containing sometimes dozens of smaller organizations, each with its own leaders, emphases, and informally recalled history. Hunter (1974, pp. 156–170) has argued (not quite in the following words) that urban community groups in the sixties acted in an institutional environment that encouraged the rise of a federated structure. Community organizations traditionally had been narrow-issue vehicles focused on the preservation of local values, sufficiently small that leaders could maintain direct contact with most members. Federated organizations developed to speak in the interest of community change, on behalf of numerous collective members, and to outside powers, most often to governmental agencies such as the police, the board of education, and the department of urban renewal. The boundaries of community areas that were used by major urban bureaucracies to organize their personnel and resource commitments called out parallel lines of organization among residents. As government agencies and a few large private institutions (e.g., Sears on the West Side, the University of Chicago on the South Side) became involved in negotiations with community representatives, the latter began to reflect in their structure the bureaucratic (as in TWO's specialized subgroups to promote housing, social welfare, and employment), professionalized (with lawyers to draft agreements, organizers with full-time jobs, and public relations officers capable of media slick), hierarchical character of their counterparts across the bargaining table.

Poverty lawyers risked being tossed out by political infighting as leaders jockeyed for dominance in emergent federated hierarchies. Just as they saw some relief in sight in a new consolidation, Legal Services lawyers often were displaced by professional advisers hired by a new umbrella group. For a West Side neighborhood supervisory lawyer, the experience was one of working for 18 months to negotiate a consensus among smaller groups so that a grant proposal on behalf of the health needs of the West Side's "Mile Square" community could be submitted to a federal agency, only to be subsequently displaced by a lawyer hired with an earmarked portion of the grant.

The Career of Community Legal Counsel

In the form of special-interest, closely held, locally oriented groups, community organizations of the indigent were thus too weak to sustain significant representative roles for Legal Services lawyers. As federated organizations, their legal needs were too great. With few exceptions, then, Legal Services lawyers did not fulfill assignments to represent community groups in the ways that their advocates and detractors had anticipated. An illustrative case of the unanticipated results is the career of Chicago's Community

Legal Counsel. This small Legal Services program was transformed in an unplanned direction as its dozen lawyers, one by one, encountered conflicts between the interests of their careers and the interests of their organizational clientele.

CLC lawyers turned away from involvements with groups and became impact litigators. So long as they remained subordinate to the organizational interests of their group clients, they were pressured to compromise potentially far-reaching cases. Group leaders often wished to concede litigable issues as a means of promoting bargaining on extrinsic issues. [This inconsistency between the careers of lawyers and of poor people's organizations has been analyzed extensively by intimate observers of welfare rights organizations (Wexler 1970, p. 1054).] Organizers were concerned primarily with convincing potential members that joining was personally beneficial. Class-action suits undercut the organizer's strategy by suggesting that only the lawyer was essential; they increased benefits for all in a given abstract category, whether organization members or not. As welfare litigators won what organizers saw as "stunning victories,"[10] welfare organizations lost members in droves (Handler 1978, pp. 161–162).

In the typical career of the community poverty lawyer, the early stages of establishing relations with the group were highly motivating. The negotiation of access and the acquisition of an understanding of informal social networks provided involving, personally taxing demands. Next, the knowledge and personal relations previously established were turned into resources for mounting group projects. But then it became necessary for the lawyer to go backward in his development in order to maintain a constant relation with the group. If the group changed leadership, the lawyer risked being identified with a discredited faction and ejected. If the leadership remained constant, the value of the relationship to the lawyer often eroded anyway. As the lawyer's contacts in the community widened and as the relationship between the lawyer and the group grew more intimate, the lawyer received more and more requests for routine legal assistance. It became progressively more difficult for many community lawyers to resist requests from leaders to give preferential personal service to sponsored clients. Sufficient rapport had been established that community leaders could call through the switchboard by asking for the lawyer by first name. At this stage in the relationship, it would have been offensive for secretaries to use standard screening devices to buffer the lawyer.

By shifting to impact litigation, CLC lawyers solved a host of career problems. Each had become caught up with community personalities and events which were crucial to maintaining a viable role with clients but which had become impractical and tedious to share with others back in the office. Litigation improved the lawyers' visibility to peers and to superiors. Weeks spent in negotiations were less reviewable than a day's efforts in drafting a brief. Other lawyers did not need to have a personal acquaintance with the facts or personalities involved to discuss a "case."

If it had been unclear to the lawyer himself whether he was making a contribution to the group, this too was resolved by the shift to impact litigation. In litigation, the lawyer would be clearly indispensable. Also, for those who had been concerned that they might be stepping over the line between lawyering and organizing, litigation promised optimal legitimacy: if the courts accepted one's work, no critic could claim superior authority to question its propriety. Success in working with a group had carried the risk that the group would become ineligible for a poverty lawyer's assistance; the organization's career could be advanced only by limiting the poverty lawyer's. In contrast, one could try to build a progression in judicial victories; each adjudicated success might become the basis for a new range of litigation strategies. A drive for such crescive experience, the very essence of the career phenomenon, turned CLC's lawyers from community counseling to impact litigation.

Planned and Unanticipated Supports for Reform

Few activist poverty community groups survived the decline of the general "Movement" of the sixties. Their chief product was not a tangible good nor even an internal service to members but the representation of the poor to outsiders. Their fate was severely contingent on external demands for that symbolic work.

The fate of the Legal Services Program, more particularly the fate of its impetus toward reform, has not followed the history of the social movements of the sixties. Why not? In a sense the explanation is that the issue has been stated with a misleading chronological emphasis. The character that originally distinguished Legal Services from Legal Aid survived through the seventies because even during the sixties it had become substantially independent of the surrounding movement.

The history of the Legal Services Program contradicts expectations about organizational development that have become sociological clichés. We should expect a positive relationship between the strengths of social movements and those of the organizations they precipitate. But from the start of the Legal Services Program, forces in the general movement for social change were compromising inclinations of the new poverty lawyers toward reform. We should expect the structure of organizations to turn them gradually from activist beginnings to conservative ends. But the distinctive organizational features of LSPs neither initially worked as anticipated to promote activism nor became insurmountable bureaucratic barriers. Instead, the overall process of institutional development was more complex.

The ferment of the sixties was a necessary precondition for a break in the institution's history from the narrow mission of Legal Aid. (Neither legal philosophy nor the ABA had been making major moves in that direction.) But although Legal Services was designed to promote reform, political compromises hedged on commitments. Moreover, the theory of organizational design used to structure stimuli for reform was based on a faulty sociology. (There had to be *some* new theory of organization. If the Legal Services Program was to depart radically from the Legal Aid tradition, the organization would have to be designed very differently.) As a result, the distinctive features of Legal Services were primarily symbols of a radically new institutional direction. They did become effective, but only indirectly, by conveying an image of radically new possibilities for reform. (Remember the quote in the last chapter from the CLC lawyer who would not have gone into Legal Aid but who came to Legal Services because, from the outside, from reading the newspapers, CLC seemed somehow associated with all the facets of the new activism.) Legal Services attracted people who ultimately built a capacity for reform, though often by working around the structural novelties designed to help them.[11]

Chapter 6

Becoming a Poverty Lawyer

Legal Services lawyers have shared an emphasis on "involvement" that sharply distinguishes them from those at Legal Aid. Whereas Legal Aid lawyers characteristically had perceived the job as having explicit career value either in itself or as a stepping stone to private practice, Legal Services lawyers typically have ridiculed career considerations. Many have had more prestigious offers. Others, as I have indicated, have discounted motives of occupational mobility with moral, political, and countercultural ideologies.

Not all Legal Services lawyers have abjured a long-range, explicitly careerist perspective. In Chicago, a handful made themselves known as "liberals" who had been destined for permanent careers in "this type of work" since college or earlier. But the overwhelming majority of entrants have come with the demand—extraordinary in the history of this institution although not among young professionals generally[1]—that the workplace continuously engage them in order to retain them.

In chapter 3, I offered a theory of the Legal Aid lawyer's career in order to show how the day-in-court interpretation of the requirements of equal justice was embodied in a personal working perspective. Here, I explain how the new poverty lawyers have constructed their distinctive working perspective. It is primarily through the pursuit of involvement that Legal Services lawyers have made themselves vehicles for reforming the structure of poverty.

It is crucial to recognize that what follows is not directly a theory of the persistence among legal assistance lawyers of a drive toward reform, but an attempt to explain the conditions for the persistence of their personal involvement. Part of the analysis holds that reform activities have functioned systematically as a means of maintaining involvement, not the other way around. Over the last 15 years, reform activity has remained a sought-after, essential condition for making work in LSPs intrinsically compelling, even while the societal meaning of poverty law reform—the implications for altering the structure of poverty—may have changed significantly. By understanding that poverty lawyers have gravitated toward reform activities as a necessary means to making work stay attractive, not necessarily as a preconceived goal or an overriding career motive, it is easier to appreciate the historical change in the nature of poverty law reform described in the last chapter.

The Theory in Brief

The lawyers quoted below only occasionally refer specifically to experiencing involvement. This is to be expected. In its most general form, involvement is achieved by a complementary fascination with the object of attachment and an appreciation of the self that emerges in response to it.[2] When asked, people explain involving experiences by describing what they have been doing as interesting, demanding, challenging, intriguing. At its most dramatic, involvement can be a proving of the self; at its least euphoric, the discovery of disturbing truths about the self; in an unpretentious form, fun. Generally, an involved person is learning something about the world and, implicitly, about the possibilities of the self. But the focus on the self is necessarily implicit, because the essence of the experience of involvement is an immersion in something outside the self.[3] Legal assistance lawyers are more likely to talk about involvement indirectly and in the negative, when they are detached and worried about a lack of what they often call "personal growth."

A description of involvement suggests its first condition: to consider something complex, important, or significant.[4] Often within a year, or by two years at most, legal assistance lawyers find that their everyday work, in the form in which it is defined and presented to them through client intake, has lost its novelty. If they are to discover a continuing source of personal growth, they must redefine the problems of the poor so that they are significant to people beyond the local social environment.

As in any modern organization, some poverty lawyers enact roles that are separate from the organization's distinctive frontline work, performing backstage tasks that have pretensions of long-range, institution-building significance. They may be involved in training programs; personnel relations and union negotiations; or projects that innovate ways to coordinate and evaluate staff. My business here is only with the distinctive frontline work of LSPs, the legal representation of the poor. The staff has a limited set of options for expanding the significance of civil legal advocacy for indigents. These consist of various styles of reform litigation that can make cases literally more interesting by implicating the interests of socially distant parties.

If responsibility for litigation is diffused through a hierarchy or monopolized at its top, a significant case may not be a personal challenge for many of the participating lawyers. A second condition for involvement is to experience *personally* a significant task. Legal Services lawyers have often had to meet this condition innovatively by seizing control over reform litigation.

Not only does the local environment at legal assistance assert that the problems of the poor are routine; it insists that they should be left that way. Put another way, the practical barriers to involvement have moral aspects. As a third condition for remaining involved while on the institution's front line, poverty lawyers must fabricate a culture with which they reinterpret pressures toward the routine and motivate themselves to transcend the proximate social environment.

This chapter is based on about 75 loosely structured interviews and on observations made over an 18-month period in 1972 and 1973. The evidence is a variety of qualitative indicators: (1) signs of the coexistence of involvement and the explanatory conditions; (2) reports showing a simultaneous disinterest or detachment from the job and an absence of one of the explanatory conditions; and, especially important for processual verification, (3) accounts of the development (or loss) of involvement as lawyers begin (or stop participating in) reform litigation, experiencing independent responsibilities for reform litigation, or producing a culture of significance.

Making Cases Significant

Legal assistance lawyers have attempted to make their work significant to audiences beyond their proximate social environment through a variety of reform strategies. These include using class actions; bringing law reform cases, which illuminate doctrinal issues for a broad legal community; representing militants whose actions are symbolic to supporters and opponents; and coordinating complaints into campaigns to put notorious merchants out of business. The common methodology is to redefine an individual client's problem as it has been narrowly defined by an adversary so that it impinges upon greater interests. These strategies raise the stakes for Legal Services practice, with the result that work experience literally becomes more challenging.

Reform activities can radically transform the social structure of the poverty lawyer's everyday work world. A case may come into the office as a dispute between one poor person and a retail-store credit manager, the latter represented in municipal court by a lawyer from the lowest stratum of the bar. It may go out as a class-action suit brought on behalf of thousands of poor people; before federal appellate judges who speak to a system of lower courts; against top state and federal officials who are covered closely by news media and who are represented by corporate law firms.

Reform litigation can remove each of the limitations imposed by the proximate social environment on the development of cumulative meaning in everyday work (see chapter 1). When poverty lawyers rest a case on an argument over the "facts" of an individual dispute (did the tenant receive notion of eviction? did the salesman misstate the price?), they often must take the double risk that the client will not show up in court and, if he does show up, that he will change his story. But in class-action suits, clients who disappear can be replaced with other clients. In a test case, by the time the appeal has begun, the facts typically have become "frozen"; the lawyer may not need any further performance from the client in order to pursue the litigation. Significant cases usually last longer than clients in the lawyer's career. It is common for successful class-action suits to motivate both sides to litigate issues of procedure and compliance up and down judicial hierarchies for years.

That the maintenance of involvement in Legal Services depends on participation in reform litigation is indicated by differences in rate of turnover by organizational position. Rates of turnover have been consistently higher in neighborhood offices, where lawyers must respond to requests by individual clients to handle their problems, than in "downtown" positions, where lawyers are expected to concentrate on reform litigation. In the neighborhood offices of the Chicago Legal Services program from 1966 to 1974, only about one-third of the 99 lawyers remained more than two years. During this period, CLC operated independently of the larger institution. After 1969, CLC turned its emphasis to reform litigation. Over three-quarters of the 10 or more lawyers who began working for CLC in 1969 or thereafter remained more than two years. By 1974, the CLC leadership had taken over Chicago Legal Services, and several new reform litigation positions were created. In 1980, in this organization, now called the Legal Assistance Foundation, there were about 13 reform litigation leaders, and 10 had tenures in Legal Services of at least seven years.[5]

These statistics may be misleading because turnover, or leaving an organization's payroll, does not always signify a change in involvement in work. More convincing are reports of the experiences of lawyers as they began participating in reform litigation. I interviewed a lawyer working in the Family Division of the LAB:

> *Are there some cases that you've had that have been more memorable than others?* Yes, my free-transcript case. That's where I changed the law. *How did that come about?* I took a crappy case and developed a side issue from it. [The issue is a free transcript for appeals in divorce cases for "paupers." The Legal Aid director has spoken of L.'s success with great pride, emphasizing to me how excited L. was over handling the case—the most excited he'd ever seen L. in his work.] It was my first appeal in 5½ years [at Legal Aid.] [L. describes the case in detail and with an enthusiasm that exceeds his response to any other topic I've raised in this two-hour interview.]

Even more telling are accounts in which involvement is seen to fluctuate with periods of participation in reform litigation.

> I'd always been concerned with professional growth, that there wasn't any on this job. Then it seemed from time to time something would happen to give me renewed hope. . . . From the [client] interviews, some things came up that developed into appeals. Like this case against the debt-pooling outfit. It's a class-action. It's not like the kind of trivia you usually get. . . . We've been working nights and weekends on it. We've done a lot of work on it. We put in a 55-page complaint. . . . I got in with A. [another lawyer] on [this] case, and later into the voter's rights case [on the provision of election instructions in Spanish in voting booths]. I did the brief in support of the TRO [temporary restraining order], and the direct examination in federal court. For the first time, I felt that the Spanish-speaking people felt that I was doing something useful. Oh, you always get individual signs of gratitude, from individual cases. But we got a lot of response from people not directly involved.

Achieving Autonomy

Experiences of personal growth in significant litigation are sometimes so emphatic as to suggest what might be termed a status rush: a heady sense of unusually rapid career development. The following quotations show an appreciation of unusual opportunities resulting from the relative absence of organizational structure between the lawyer and significant work. They celebrate the view that poverty lawyers can take more responsibility for matters of greater public controversy, with less internal constraint, in higher courts and at a younger age, than can their peers elsewhere.[6]

Denotations of the status more rapidly gained in Legal Services vary with previous experience and law school reference groups. But, significantly, the perception of superior opportunity was common across such variations. Lawyers with prior experience in prestigious corporate law firms noted their enjoyment of a previously unavailable professional freedom.

> "I like being a lawyer, even on stuff that may seem terribly dull to a layman, but a lot of that [corporate law firm] stuff is simply inherently dull. Nobody could make, have, any fun out of it. A case involving, for example, the setting of rates for a water company . . . which we tried over about a four-month period . . . and all it is is just a question of accounting, cost study, and it's dull. This thing is more fun not only because of the work [who and what you are representing] but also because I can do whatever the hell I want to here. And if I think some case is going to be boring, some matter uninteresting, I really don't have to do it."

Similarly, recent graduates saw their poverty litigation experience as extraordinary relative to the opportunities their law school peers were finding.

> One day we were going down to Springfield to argue a Supreme Court of Illinois case. I said, let's go over the arguments that you [a more experienced and older Legal Services lawyer] will make. He said, "What do you mean, I'll make? You'll do the oral argument." I said, "But you could do it better." I'd just been admitted a month before. I was just 24 years old. My friends hadn't even made it to traffic court yet. He said, "Don't worry, they won't listen anyway." After I was out [of Legal Services], friends would call me all the time on how to do things. I'd been in every court from the municipal court to the Supreme Court; I'd been in the newspapers and on TV. I knew I could do anything that I wanted.

When leaders did not give young lawyers control over major cases, the social structure of client intake enabled the subordinates to grab and hold it. Several of the most consistent law reform litigators fought program leaders for control of their "big" cases. Reflecting on these struggles, one leader pointed to the freedom the staff lawyer derived from his everyday, unmediated contact with clients:

"There are people [in Legal Services] who have no business trying the kinds of lawsuits we try. And if they get into it, the only way I can deal with it is ignore it, or else I have to take over the case, handle it myself, or forget about it. Because if I got into the details I'd go wild. *Could you flesh that out? What kinds of things shouldn't they be handling?* They really shouldn't be handling any kind of suit. You see, most of these, they're tougher cases than most lawyers get in private practice. When I was in private practice for eight years, I never, in my law firm—60 lawyers—in the course of the four, five years I was there—I know we couldn't have had more than one case in the U.S. Supreme Court. I mean, this office has had, in 2½ years—this office, with one-third the number of lawyers—has had at least half a dozen. And they're all novel issues; they're the kind of cases that have to be extremely carefully researched, briefed; and they require far more intellectual ability than the average lawsuit. And we have people in this office who, in my judgment, are simply incapable of doing that. They're lousy lawyers for that kind of thing, but that's what they see as the reason they're in here . . . The odd nature of this business, it's totally different from private practice, in that in private practice the work comes in from the top. If it's my client, I'm the senior man. The client comes to me and tells me what the problem is. I have the client contact; I know what the client wants; I go to the meetings with the client; you work for me. In this business, the client comes in on the bottom. You know what the client wants."

Numerous resources for case control follow from initial client contact. Knowing "what the client wants," the subordinate can invoke the sanctity given by professional canons to the attorney–client relation and thereby resist superiors on the grounds that their directions violate the client's wishes. With client contact, the subordinate is in at the start of a case, and an extra act is necessary to inform a superior of it. If the cooperation of the client is needed at various points in the litigation, the superior who would be involved must rely on the subordinate, but not necessarily vice versa.

A neighborhood lawyer who successfully resisted the "rip-off" of his major cases by higher-ups pointed to his direct contact with clients as a crucial resource:

We were supposed to check with the Appellate Division, but we took the attitude that we'd do it anyway. In one class-action, we threatened to sue for our jobs if we were interfered with, on the grounds that they were violating the canons on lawyer–client relations. . . . [In one

> case the leader] filed an unverified complaint [without a client's signature] Friday. I filed a verified complaint Monday. There was no question of who filed first; his wasn't verified. I always had the clients. He withdrew before Judge C. It was embarrassing for him. But he deserved it. It was a shitty thing for him to do. *What was your protection against the leader taking the case earlier?* [He] couldn't take it because I had the file. Possession is nine-tenths of the law. That's why I always keep the papers in my files. If someone wants to come in and copy them, fine. But I keep a complete file. I had the clients and the facts.

Every poverty lawyer I have interviewed who had had an ongoing personal responsibility for reform litigation recalled at least one troublesome struggle for case control. For each, the maintenance of involvement required some work to achieve autonomy. In the early years of the United Charities Legal Services program, neighborhood-office lawyers had to defy their downtown superiors and risk being fired in order to want to remain. CLC's lawyers were all highly tuned to detect proprietary infringements and irresponsibly seized control. After 1966, young lawyers began entering the traditional United Charities LAB with expectations of involvement. They found it necessary to reshape the received definitions of their "desks" in order to achieve direct control over reform cases. Their problem was the opposite of the neighborhood-office lawyer's; whereas the latter feared a loss of control after beginning a suit, activist LAB lawyers attacked the specialization and screens in the LAB's highly organized intake process.

Two consumer lawyers, fearing that Legal Aid interviewers were sending away significant cases, secured a rule that required the lawyers' prior consent. The rule was accepted by their supervisor, even though she recognized the embarrassing implication: she was included in its subordinating reach. A recent law graduate who had entered the LAB expressly to prepare for a move to a neighborhood office recalled using various strategies to achieve autonomy on his "desk."

> I forced that desk to get into interesting issues. It had been a nonlitigating desk, but it was the greatest vehicle for litigation. But there were all these limits: $300 maximum recovery; no punitive damages; and class actions were hard to bring off. I had to work on [LAB officials] for changes in these rules. . . . *What changes did you press for, and which did you get?* Changes in the type of case. For example, they had a rule—or no rule that you wouldn't take a case if it was worth less than

> $50. I got that [prohibition] in. I wouldn't take any plaintiff's case for less than $50. I had to scream and yell for that, but I finally convinced [the officials]. . . . I started to take different kinds of cases: the first employment discrimination that had been taken off that desk. . . . I was getting into utility cases, which was supposed to be J.'s area. But I'd write it up so that I'd get it.

In short, the maintenance of involvement on the front lines of legal assistance work required a struggle for autonomy in the control of significant cases that was quite independent of variations in the organizational structuring of the work process. Achieving autonomy required organizational conflict—conflict within the context typical of Chicago's LSPs in the early seventies, a context of relatively unmediated contact between staff lawyers and clients—conflict as well within the formally and hierarchically controlled intake process characteristic of the LAB.

Elaborating a Culture of Significance

The third condition of involvement is the symbolic transformation of moral pressures toward routine into themes of transcending significance. Whether in neighborhood offices or in downtown reform positions, Chicago's poverty lawyers experienced similar moral pressures in reform litigation. Individual clients often did not appreciate the interests of the larger and more indirectly involved clientele. Judges sometimes threatened to render their preparation worthless, refusing an open-minded hearing. Opposing counsel typically failed to prepare themselves. A culture of significance should thus be expected in both the neighborhood and downtown Legal Services offices, but there is one aspect of the theory of involvement that is especially relevant to the neighborhood setting.

Downtown lawyers in LSPs characteristically have been relieved from intake responsibilities. In contrast, neighborhood staff lawyers have faced a routinely discouraging environment. They have had a special need to resist local pressures in order to retain a perspective on significance. In the neighborhood offices that I studied, a staff of three to five lawyers was average. The maintenance of peer relations that could provide a collective forum for the expression of a transcendent culture was an uncommon and unstable achievement.

Neighborhood lawyers who described themselves as demoralized spoke as isolated individuals. One was discouraged by a supervisor who identified with the local professional environment.

> I [would] frequently . . . talk about leaving. A. [his office supervisor] would always say, "you're doing all right, fine. You're too hard on yourself." . . . She would say, "You get good pay, you're a good lawyer, things aren't going badly." Her competence is different from mine, in terms of what she'd be satisfied with. I combine law reform with top quality. She emphasizes top quality but isn't that oriented to changes in the system. She has accepted the court system as it is, and most of the statutes she works with. She tries to win the cases on the facts. She gets along fine, fits right in with the p.i. [personal injury] bar.

Disenchantment with the job was related to an absence of a shared culture of reform. Conversely, career interviews showed the quick development of involvement when a collegial relation that expressed this culture was struck up. The supervisor of one office emphasized the impetus he received from the supervisor of another office on a jointly handled case.

> One of my problems . . . is that I can't sustain B.'s rage, a rage in self-righteous terms. . . . You must dehumanize the opposition, identify yourself completely with the client, and believe completely that the other side is really bad. You must be brutal, unrelenting. B. is good at this; he can sustain a tremendous indignation and energy. . . . *How did this Credit Systems case develop?* A year and a half ago, I had a case through intake. . . . I knew the defenses if we'd be sued, so I just sat on it. Then I talked to people in other offices, to B. and C., and they had clients who had problems with Credit Systems too, so we decided to file a class action.

Entering and leaving a collective culture of significance was closely related to the rise and decline of involvement. From 1966 to 1974, there were six dyads containing lawyers who maintained an involvement in reform litigation during careers of two or more years in Chicago's neighborhood offices. The members of each of these pairs shared "latent culture" (Becker and Geer 1960), background characteristics formally irrelevant to their jobs, which they drew on to form close friendships. One pair had been college fraternity brothers. Another two fellows had been on the law review together. Another couple had in common a small-town midwestern upbringing, a background rare in the staff as a whole. Two long-time bachelors made another pair. In these offices, new members frequently were brought in through their prior relations with current members. Those who failed to join the collective spirit risked being forced out. The dyads created rich, internal symbolic environments autonomous from the cultural worlds neighborhood lawyers were invited to enter through intake. Indeed the lawyers in five of the pairs broke down the distinction between "job" and "personal life," regularly seeing each other and talking about work after hours and outside of the office. In each of these pairs, when one member moved out of the office, the other soon left as well.[7]

Significantly, the members of the dyads did not always practice together on litigation. They helped each other sustain a posture; they did not necessarily help one another with professional tasks. In some of the pairs, one supplied technical knowledge, the other moral outrage. The professionally dominant member might go to the other to have everyday frustrations comically transformed or simply to find a good audience. To make sense, in the neighborhood office, of expressing a view that cases had far-reaching implications, one had to find someone who would appear to be an intelligent, willing listener.[8] Otherwise, the expression of the reform perspective in this setting literally would be crazy.[9]

How does the culture of significance work to sustain involvement? How does it transform definitions of the legal assistance lawyer's work from the expectations of routine that are presented by the local environment into a transcendent perspective of significance? At least three themes in the culture can be isolated.

The first theme is that problems that would otherwise mean frustration can be transformed into resources for reform. Every instance of significant litigation expresses this theme. Individuals who have suffered a harm that legal assistance lawyers previously had been unable to remedy are cast as representatives of others in a judicial drama that promises to turn moral discouragement into exemplary reform. Reform litigation contains a paradoxical principle. Its excellence depends on the depths of misery of its beneficiaries. Poverty lawyers may extend this irony to frustrations at the periphery of litigation and to problems for which a litigated solution is unlikely or even irrelevant.

The everyday exposure to pitiful clients may be seen as a "goldmine." Clients whose multitude of severe problems makes them an inexhaustible source of significant cases may be celebrated as "great" or "beautiful"; their pathetic appearance will enhance their value as representatives of other beneficiaries who would appear to be less in need. Similarly, the greater the number of people harmed by an adversary, the more significant the case will be and the more worthwhile the lawyer's efforts on it.

> [While I am interviewing A. in his office, B. comes in and asks] "How do you find out if a property is FHA financed?" [B. has a client whose rent has been raised. The financing information may indicate some way to gain leverage over the owner. A., realizing it will not be easy to get the information, wonders if the effort will be worthwhile. He asks]: "One client, or the whole building?" [B. laughs]: "Oh, there are hundreds of people in this building."

By expecting cases to be handled according to their routines, judges, adversaries, and opposing counsel imply that the interests at stake are insignificant. Given the right perspective, the more outrageous these pressures, the more easily they can be transformed into resources for reform. A stupid decision by a state judge may be taken as an occasion for mounting a general attack on the lower court systems. To this end, an otherwise unremarkable issue for appeal may be phrased as an indictment:

> [From CLC activity reports] A. and I presented a motion on [misdemeanor defendant's] behalf to obtain a free transcript of the proceedings for appeal. The motion was based on the U.S. Supreme Court case of *Williams* v. *Oklahoma City,* which is directly in point. Magistrate Jankowski denied the motion because the U.S. Supreme Court's interpretation of the U.S. Constitution is not the law of Illinois, and he will follow the law of Illinois. We then went to Judge Lahowski and asked him to reverse Jankowski. He refused to make any decision and said the magistrates could use their own discretion. [In a subsequent report]: The question to be reviewed [in the U.S. Supreme Court] and which Magistrate Jankowski and the Illinois Supreme Court needs the U.S. Supreme Court to answer is: "Whether the decision of the U.S. Supreme Court in *Williams* . . . is applicable in the State of Illinois and binding on the Circuit Court of Cook County." [This was celebrated by its inclusion in numerous reports, which were circulated through the organization.]

In the same spirit, unethical behavior by opposing counsel may be made a basis for a disbarment effort. Deceitful and harassing methods of collection may be described in a counterclaim for punitive damages that is added to the defense of a debt suit. And "incompetent" representation by an opposing counsel which makes "unnecessary" work for the poverty lawyer may be argued as a basis for charging the adversary with the costs and attorneys fees of the litigation. Each of these responses takes an instance of initially frustrating adversarial conduct and, by making an example of it, turns it into a resource for reform or extraordinary punishment. That success may not materialize, and that the poverty lawyers may be fully aware of that likelihood, serves to augment rather than diminish the quality of these actions as a cultural technique for sustaining involvement. The goal is to illustrate the extremes to which an uncompromising posture can be taken.

Threats to involvement may come from internal as well as external sources. A lawyer in a sometimes internally divided office noted the value for peer cohesion of battles with downtown over case control.

> *What was the relation with downtown from your office?* A. would call up and defend the other party. Like he did with D. [a supervisor in a different office], he did with me. D. would say, "We should have the freedom that CLC does, to represent groups." D. was getting stopped on, or questioned about, routine things like injunctions against landlords. A. wanted to know, did he really have to do that; couldn't he do it a quieter way. It was, seriously, almost to the point of A. saying, do you have to do significant things? I went into that nursing home, with the newsmen behind me, taking pictures, and that led to a CBA investigation. Sure enough, A. had me downtown, asking me to explain it, why did I have to do that. B. [supervisor] would just tell them to go to hell. That was one thing that held us together.

Dramatic instances of unbending militance in the face of restraints received extensive collegial review. Several versions circulated of the following demonstration of involvement under fire.

> Another hilarious scene: King got assassinated, . . . I remember it got real quiet. I went outside, and you could hear a pin drop. The next day they started rioting in the morning. I was in the office with L. and G. [two staff lawyers]. L. was having a big controversy with this guy who represented some models, and I remember hearing L. say, "Fuck you, you son of a bitch," and he hung up. And oh, about a minute later C. [the opposing counsel] calls back, and they engage in more heated debate, and L. ends it again with, "Oh fuck you, you son of a bitch," and hangs up again. Two minutes later A. [director] calls up. C. had called him. They used to do that all the time, report us to the higher ups, and A. would never back us up. So A. calls back and he'd just hear L.'s end of it, and they engage in a heated debate on it, and L. hangs up on him. A. had apparently said, 'you're fired,'

> and L. had said, "You can keep your goddamn job." Wham. [Laughs] It didn't bother him. He was working; he was writing a brief or something. And these calls would come in—"fuck you, you son of a bitch"—and he'd keep writing. The guy's really composed. It's just remarkable. He's really composed. Then A. calls back again. Then he unfires him. Then he fires him again. And while all this is going on, they're burning down the West Side. Incredible. You hear gunfire out there [laugh].[10]

With practical and with purely symbolic devices, poverty lawyers must intensify their involvement in order to sustain it. They must fold more and more frustrations into efforts for reform, actually increasing their work to avoid sacrificing its significance. A second cultural theme is that the lawyers may distance themselves from pressures toward routine with incredulous outrage and humorous ridicule. These techniques can be used to sustain an impetus toward reform in the face of an infinite number of frustrations.

By expressing incredulity at judicial or adversarial conduct, a lawyer can assume a posture of righteous superiority. Incredulity implies the disruption of naïveté, but its use is not limited to new or inexperienced lawyers. On the contrary, it can be practiced most effectively by experienced lawyers. The emphatic assertion that behavior is extraordinarily improper requires confident assumptions about what is ordinary and proper. Performing one's first professional expression of incredulity with flawless self-confidence is a significant status passage in the career of a poverty lawyer.

Most acts of incredulity are performed on the basis of an elaborate tacit context and with great economy. They are difficult to illustrate briefly. One lawyer may raise an eyebrow, point to a sentence in a pleading or opinion, or interject a phrase in the course of a long description of a court scene, and he will expect a comrade to "read in" the background which would make the denoted behavior recognizable as an "unbelievable" misstatement of facts or law by an adversary or as an indication of prejudice by a judge.

Incredulity guards a perspective on significance cautiously. By refusing to expect the identity that others expect of them, poverty lawyers take care not to assume it. Various ridiculing devices are also used to set oneself off from the person others expect. One lawyer cast his frequent opposing counsel in the characters of Snow White's dwarfs and gave them roles in allegorical comedy routines he borrowed from the professional comedian, George Carlin. Many mimicked adversaries, judges, and clients to resist identification:

> [Jim gets off the phone with an opposing counsel, laughs, and says], "Hey Jimmy, [chewing an imaginary cigar], whaddayasay we make a deal?"

The functional value of ridicule was articulated for me by a consumer protection litigator who enjoyed an unexcelled reputation for venting outrage. Each of the six or so times I had been in his office, I had witnessed mocking activities. He would describe angrily the conduct of an adversary to another staff lawyer, who would supply heavy sarcasm and transform the atmosphere to one of ridicule. The two had apparently been doing variations on this ritual virtually every day for over four years.

> The main way we work together . . . his main virtue and the main virtue of the job to me, is that it lends itself to a lot of laughs. It's like reading a good novel—very humorous—that exposes human frailties, foibles, idiocies, human greed. It's a wonderful position to observe all this in: co-workers, clients, judges, opposing counsel, people working for the schlock companies. But most people don't appreciate it to the full if they don't have a sense of humor. Our clients, they're of course not to be laughed out of the office, but there's an opportunity for a lot of laughs. And we are able to laugh at it . . . the collection lawyers, a bunch of phonies, going in for sham continuances, the threats they use, making fools of themselves in court, shouting at us for the benefit of their client, making facetious arguments before judges, posturing. I love it all. It's like one of those British movie comedies, or like a sarcastic Dickens novel. Or Alice in Wonderland. Honestly, I really love this job.

Mimicry and ridicule do more than just establish distance from their targets. They lend special significance to confrontations with demeaning expectations. Those who would frustrate the poverty lawyer's purposes are cast as representatives of types and made unwitting participants in moral dramas. The poverty lawyers thereby transport themselves from the everyday routine of legal assistance into naturalistic comedies and classic satirical novels.

A final theme in the culture of significance exploits the possibilities for irony in the reform litigator's work. Rich contrasts may be drawn between the abstract, promissory stature of reform suits and their immediate implications for concrete clients. A theme of the absurd simultaneously portrays futility and promotes involvement. The portrayal responds to discouragement by tacitly affirming a transcendent spirit. An accomplished act of describing absurdity paradoxically presumes the rationality, meaningfulness, and value of its own creation. It denies absurdity by celebrating it.

Litigation specialists who work from downtown offices removed from client contact may appreciate the pretentiousness of their posture when clients break through:

> [Over coffee, A. tells B. of recent events in his relations with a janitor who works in some federally subsidized apartment buildings. A. describes the owners as dealing with the buildings in plantation style. A boiler went out; thousands were without heat. While the janitor's requests for aid went unanswered, the landlord's wife called from the suburbs and requested that he come clean her rugs in preparation for a party "because you did such a great job the last time." He refused in order to try to fix the boiler and was fired. This becomes background for A.'s next story. A. has told the janitor to call before coming to his office. The janitor walked in without calling. A. quotes himself]: "I told you, you must call first. I'm a lawyer, I'm busy, I have all this work, lots of other clients; you're not the only one." [The janitor], a 6 foot, 6 inch black man, with his head hung low, says: "I'm real sorry, Mr. A. I'll never do it again. I know you're a busy man, but the only thing is, I've been out of work now, with no money, and my kids are in the hospital, and my wife is sick too. But I know that's no excuse; I should call first."

In the same vein, A. describes his relations with a black lady who moved into a white section of a racially bifurcated ward.

> White neighbors surround her house with shotguns; bottles are thrown through the windows. [A. fantasizes a conversation]: "We've got an important civil rights principle here. You go back to that house. Put your kids in the closet if you must, and I'll sit downtown and write an important brief on this."[11]

A final example shows how poverty lawyers can create a culture for involvement by appreciating dearly a client whose personal struggles cast their own as insignificant. By dwelling on the pathos of the client, the lawyers can celebrate their work as an absurd yet therefore heroic attempt to achieve significant results with makeshift means against apparently hopeless odds.

[Cl. comes in, and A. introduces him to me as "the third-largest manufacturer of cornhusk brooms in Chicago." Cl. is an old man, without teeth, who mumbles with a heavy black accent. His clothes are crumpled and dirty: an old beret; pants which were once part of a suit but are now thread-worn work clothes. He has huge fingers that appear extremely arthritic. A. later tells me that that's from the bones breaking repeatedly when working machines.]

[They talk about corporate business forms and financing. I'm wondering: This man owns a business? A. later tells me that his brooms are of excellent quality and much desired, but by a decreasing number of people. He had a chance to make or break himself for good a few years ago when a deal with Sears was in the works, but he couldn't meet their volume. Some time ago A. and B., another staff lawyer, worked on his case. He defaulted on a $10,000 loan from the Small Business Administration (SBA) and is now *persona non grata* there. He's been literally keeping his business going on shoestrings and other waste materials.]

[A. is determined he can keep him going by pursuing credit under the right facade. Cl. and A. talk about a legal shell that will disguise Cl.'s control enough so that he can get credit, but not so much that it will pass control to the friend whose credit reputation will be the key to the scheme.]

[B. comes in, and now both he and A. have great fun with Cl.] B.: I was over around your place the other week, and the wreckers were there, working next door. And the construction guy said to me, pointing to your place, "We could take the ball and go over there next."

Cl.: They ought to. It's a terrible building.

A.: That's not a rough neighborhood, is it Cl.?

Cl.: It's getting rougher. I've got to move. They did [this and this] to me. It's getting too rough for me.

[They all laugh. It's been incredible for years that he could stay there, given the crime and economic dangers. When Cl. says he's moving, B. asks if he can move his equipment without it falling apart in the move. This occasions laughter from A. and B., and, after a pause, from Cl.]

B.: How's your rooster?

Cl.: Fine.

[Then A. recounts] when [Cl.] defaulted on the SBA loan, IRS men were sent out to padlock his building and equipment. From fear of the neighborhood, they were constantly looking over their shoulders. One said, "I've got to get out of here, this place is too rough for me." Then they got inside and found that [Cl.] has chickens around that eat the droppings from the corn that goes into the brooms. And he has a rooster there. It is ferocious and it attacked one of the IRS men as he was trying to padlock [Cl.'s] equipment.

[On Cl.'s way out, B. and then A. repeat]: Whatever you do, don't send anything into SBA with your name on it. It'll be thrown right out again. They've got your file, and when they see your name, they'll check their files and will pull out your old one. So if you send anything to the SBA, don't put your name on it. Put your friend's, else it will come right back at you. [A. and B. laugh again and again at this.]

The Culture and Fate of Reform

The poverty lawyer's culture of significance does not appear to reflect values specific to a poverty law practice. Irrespective of the social status of their clientele, lawyers may be found claiming professional superiority by using incredulous outrage to depict judicial stupidity and adversarial venality. Nor does the poverty lawyer distinguish himself in the profession by fighting for autonomous control of significant cases. One would expect the same from aggressive lawyers in the most materially grasping practices. Lawyers in legal assistance programs who channel their energies into reform litigation may do so not from any philosophic commitment to social change but in pursuit of challenges traditionally valued in the profession. In sum, the conditions that sustain the experience of involvement while representing the poor have no *necessary* relation to the principled mission of the institution of civil legal assistance.

One implication is that the impetus toward reform in the Legal Services' staff has *always* been independent of the social movements of the sixties. If values and cultural perspectives that are shared throughout the legal profession were sufficient bases for maintaining staff commitment to reform in the sixties, it should not be surprising to see a continuity of commitment in the relatively quiescent seventies. Put another way, the requirements for involvement in legal assistance work include no particular philosophy of social reform or equal justice. Thus, the same mechanisms and experiences of involvement may continue into the eighties, even if the substantive content and intensity of reform changes.

Chapter 7

Personal Careers and the Persistence of Group Character

Within a few years of their creation in the mid 1960s, Legal Services programs generally eclipsed Legal Aid societies in numbers and in public visibility. But there was not as decisive a change in the philosophy actually governing the work of legal assistance lawyers. In the late sixties, young lawyers did begin to bring expectations of involvement and strategies of reform into Legal Aid societies, but they did not always predominate. Many lawyers also approached jobs in LSPs with concerns for long-range career development, adopting routines of service that had been traditional in Legal Aid agencies.

What has influenced the balance established between the two philosophies in given legal assistance organizations? National politics and local leadership policies have not been determinative. The national leadership of Legal Services was inconstant on the issue during the political turmoils that surrounded the OEO. In the late seventies, after the transfer out of OEO, the leaders of the new national Legal Services Corporation adopted a consistent policy, but it was to leave the question of philosophic balance to forces at the local program level. In turn, local program leadership, originally extensively recruited from outside the institution, has more recently been drawn increasingly from the ranks of the LSPs. Thus, to investigate the contingencies of the relative influence of the two philosophies, it is necessary to examine implications of staff perspectives themselves.

In this chapter I begin a contrast between the ways in which the personal career perspectives historically associated with Legal Aid and Legal Services organizations influence the character of legal assistance work generally. The extent to which the two perspectives will come to characterize legal assistance work at any given time cannot be determined simply by predicting the number of staff lawyers who will then represent each perspective. The matter of personal influence on collective character is more subtle; a collectivity is something greater than the sum of its parts.[1] The perspective taken by a given staff member conditions the ability of other members to tie their separate lines of participation into collective themes.[2]

I consider the collective influence of personal career perspectives along two dimensions. First, there is an organizational sense in which legal assistance lawyers may develop continuities that transcend their individually generated lines of action. All organizations face problems in creating continuous lines of action running over discontinuities in the tenures of members and among the roles played by current members. Taking an internal look at a legal assistance office, one can examine its degree of organizational continuity: to what extent are there continuities in the work of staff lawyers who occupy different positions in the organization or who have been members at different times in the organization's history? To the extent a legal assistance lawyer contributes to the organizational continuity of his philosophy, he promotes its collective existence.

In a familiar form, the issue of organizational continuity appears as the problem of succession.[3] Does the collective character of a legal assistance office survive changes in membership? When a lawyer leaves, are his efforts picked up and made useful either by a replacement or by a colleague who remains? In a more general form, organizational continuity is a matter of whether the work of members is coordinated during their shared tenures. Do individual lines of action complement or cancel each other?

Second, a collective identity may also exist in an institutional sense. Here, the reference is to the fitting together of members' behavior, not with each other directly but with external audiences and constituencies. All organizations depend for their existence on a recognition of their role in a receptive political and legal framework, on the prior shaping of their recruits by various socialization process, on external markets for products, and so on. A collectivity becomes "institutionalized" to the extent that powerful audiences—say, a specialized constituency of alumni or investors, plus a well-established interest group, and a federal governmental agency—make commitments to sustain it. A collectivity grows as an institution when it secures a qualitatively enlarged mandate, that is, when those who would be recruits, buyers, patrons, or political allies appreciate an expanded version of the organization's mission.

Personal careers in organizations can affect a collectivity's institutional fate in several ways that are illustrated in the case at hand. In the course of their tenures in given offices, legal assistance lawyers may devise tools that broaden the capacities of others to engage in similar activities. Moving on after participating in a given program, their work in their new affiliations may continue to contribute to their former organization. In these patterns, staff members expand the reach of their philosophies in the collective domain. Other patterns can be seen in relations between competing legal assistance organizations. By affecting whether their organization will take over, defer to, or eclipse another agency,[4] staff lawyers influence the extent to which their personal perspective on legal assistance work will become the collectively governing philosophy.

Each of the two major types of personal career perspective on legal assistance work makes unique contributions to the collective persistence of its interpretation of equal justice; and each also makes demands for personal career development that uniquely restrict the continuity of its philosophy in the actions of others. Legal assistance lawyers may not expressly choose either the type of career they desire or the extent to which they care to make their own institutional philosophy generally influential; yet they make these choices every day. They do so, as do members of all groups, by constantly negotiating a series of tensions between personal and collective interests.

There is the tension between private interests and the encroachment of organizational demands. At one extreme, members may struggle throughout the workday to keep occupational concerns outside of personal experience. Poignant studies have described workers on assembly lines engaged in widespread, cooperative efforts to obliterate their experience of the definitions of themselves made by mechanical divisions of labor. Toward this phenomenological end, they may use banter, improvise competitions, or mark off the daily schedule into periods for coffee or "banana time" (Roy 1959/60).[5] At the other extreme, proselytizing organizations threaten to put all aspects of the personal lives of members into the service of collective interests (Selznick 1952, Coser 1974). Legal Aid lawyers, in coping with routine, and Legal Services lawyers, in pursuit of involvement, have rarely arrived at either extreme; but they have deviated from the mean in opposite directions. Thus, in chapter 6, there were the dyads of poverty lawyers whose occupational culture regularly ran without break into "off-hours"; and in chapter 3, a Legal Aid lawyer who hit on the coping device of humming a tune to himself in the face of an adversary's abuse.

The question, How much of personal life will the member allow to be penetrated by organizational concerns? has an inverse side: To what extent is organizational activity privately appropriated by the member?[6] Members may enter the organization already fully trained at their own expense, produce while on staff for the benefit of the group without requiring further educational assistance, and leave without removing anything of value created during their tenure. Or they may enter wholly untrained, require continuous training by the group to be useful to it, and when they leave, take every idea of value produced during their tenure. Here too, Legal Aid and Legal Services lawyers have struck quite different balances between the interests of personal careers and collective continuity.

All groups must also define some sort of trade-off between personal career and collective continuity on matters of reciprocal moral commitment. At one extreme, the group makes no commitment to retain the member at any time that his contribution to the collectivity is less than its outlay to him, and members continue to contribute to the group after they leave its payroll. At the other extreme, the group makes a commitment to retain members even after they cease producing for it, while departed members go on to work against the interests of the organization. Again, Legal Services and Legal Aid lawyers have shaped contrasting perspectives in these terms.

To sum up the different trade-offs, Legal Aid lawyers have promoted the organizational continuity of their offices while contributing little to institutionalize Legal Aid's collective, day-in-court mission. The inverse trade-off with collective persistence has been struck by lawyers who have employed the career perspective historically distinguishing Legal Services lawyers. They have succeeded in expanding the resources available to implement a drive to reform the structure of poverty, while failing to sustain integrated programs within given offices.[7] This chapter and the next two are organized around the two dimensions of collective persistence. I consider first the relation between the two career perspectives and organizational continuity, and then I contrast the implications for institutional dominance. The latter discussion turns directly into chapter 8, which describes an aborted process of organizational merger between Chicago's Legal Aid and Legal Services offices. Chapter 9 reviews changes in LSPs since the sixties on the issues of organizational continuity and the institutionalization of poverty law reform.

Organizational Continuity

The stepping-stone perspective is common among lawyers in public institutions. In low-level government tax offices (Spector 1972), high-level regulatory agencies, the offices of public defenders (Platt and Pollock 1974) and public prosecutors, and in Legal Aid, lawyers have often worked expressly to gain marketable knowledge and employment contacts for mobility to external positions.

A frequently noted aspect of this career perspective is its potential to take on an immoral taint (Alschuler 1968, p. 111; cf. Kuh 1961, pp. 175–190; Caplan 1970, pp. 206–210). In many public law offices, the stepping-stone career is recognized and even legitimated. Organizations formally concerned with one set of purposes invite amoral affiliations by people whose lives are headed in opposite directions. Thus, in full recognition of the fact, prosecuting organizations give training to future defense attorneys; regulatory agencies advance the aspirations of lawyers who will serve the regulated; and Legal Aid lawyers traditionally learned and left to take the other side as collection lawyers. Each of these institutions takes the risk that its alumni may subsequently use knowledge of internal procedures against the organization. Members with stepping-stone perspectives are also suspect during their tenure because it is understood that moral dedication is not the basis for their conformity; allegiances may reverse before membership is relinquished.[8]

In the transition from Legal Aid to Legal Services, the change in the bargain struck between collective and personal interests was dramatized by the emergence of a new type of deviance. The older type was in full bloom shortly before the Legal Services program began: five of the young lawyers in the Chicago LAB (about half of the nonpermanent staff) were fired when their superiors detected a conspiracy to funnel clients through the office's intake process to a private law office. Shortly after the Legal Services program was implemented, leaders were confronted with lawyers who, instead of violating the institution's purpose by exporting the organization's clients for private exploitation, imported clients and openly retained cases in defiance of their superiors. In one incident, when a neighborhood lawyer was transferring to another Legal Services project, the head of the Appellate Division unsuccessfully attempted to stop him from taking out cases that official wanted to litigate.[9] In another conflict, two Reggies assigned to the downtown Legal Services office were terminated for their involvement in the representation of black and Latin radicals in criminal matters. Deviance, previously secretive, became righteous defiance. Legal Aid lawyers had abandoned the institution's purposes before leaving the organization; now Legal Services lawyers began leaving the organization without ending their involvement in the institution.

Involvement, when it is the dominant perspective guiding members' careers, provides an organization with extraordinary resources. To the extent members can justify their affiliation through self-discovery or the experience of "personal growth," an organization can compensate for any uncompetitive market position it may have in the material benefits it offers, in the extent to which it assists members' subsequent careers, or in job security. If members experience a progressive development of the quality of their work, they may abjure calculating perspectives on long-range careers and free the institution from amoral, suspect forms of self-interest. At the same time, members' involvement places an organization in its weakest state, for participation that depends on personal growth is literally the most selfish form of affiliation. When members premise their careers in an organization on a process of self-discovery through exploring possibilities in work, they impede collective continuity.

Weaknesses in the organizational integration of LSPs can be seen from three standpoints, those of leader, member, and independent observer. Leadership in Legal Services faces two ongoing staff problems. The first is presented by lower echelon lawyers who begin significant litigation and retain control against superordinate will. The second is presented by lawyers who respond to clients' pressures for involvement in personal problems by abandoning litigation, and sometimes adversarial representation in general, in favor of counseling. The problems for exercising control from above can be highlighted by asking why leaders hesitate to fire both types of intractable staff lawyers.

Reform litigators can afford to voice disdain for job tenure because they know they are especially costly to fire. Reform litigation can build a reputation for a Legal Services program. Appellate victories provide leaders with evidence of "quality professional work" that is automatically communicated throughout the national Legal Services network and beyond to a larger professional audience. It is much more difficult for leaders to demonstrate the overall quality of a program's individual service work.

As for firing staff lawyers who stray into what leaders may pejoratively label "social work," the perspectives of leaders on their own careers often gives them pause. In interviews, some Chicago LSP leaders reported that they could not understand neighborhood lawyers who seemed content with routine practices. Having committed themselves to Legal Services for only so long as they found it interesting, these leaders felt they lacked the *bona fides* to deny to others the opportunity to prove an incomprehensible dedication. Because they themselves were professedly pursuing a selfish involvement, the superordinates restrained their inclinations to dismiss mediocre lawyers who appeared altruistically committed to a lifetime of service to the poor.

Leaders in Legal Services must deal with ongoing ideological struggles among staff lawyers. In pursuit of an involving interest in work, each new cohort insists on confronting old policy questions anew. An observer of a Legal Services program in the late seventies could hear arguments which were first played out in the mid 1960s. The issues might be stated as individual client service versus antipoverty litigation, responsiveness versus reform, or accountability to the expressed demands of the poor versus responsibility for shaping public recognition of the rights of the poor. Such debates may be personally fresh to the advocates, but they are redundant in the history of the collectivity. Insisting that they be personally convinced of a moral justification for their membership, staff lawyers have often resisted previously settled, hierarchically imposed program emphases. Collective agreements on priorities have often failed to continue for long. Recognizing the difficulties of formalized command, and involved in their own projects of innovating methods of governance, Legal Services leaders have experimented with a variety of approaches to consensus, from episodic retreats to everyday procedures for democratic decision making.

Members perceive organizational discontinuities when they complain about "ripped off" cases, "failure of communication," and a lack of training. The transformation of cases into materials for involvement brought a novel organizational problem: conflict over proprietary rights in cases. The traditional interest of lawyers in Legal Aid in shifting parts of heavy case loads to others remained, but now a case might also be something worth fighting to retain.

Calls for more "communication" also became common. There was a new sensitivity to problems of "duplication" owing to lack of communication. Staff lawyers complained of similar research being performed on the same problem by different lawyers working for different clients. In a way, legal assistance organizations had always been uniquely vulnerable to problems of duplication. In private law firms, identical research by different lawyers for different clients is a path to collective prosperity: the more duplication, the more "billable hours." In legal assistance, duplication has no compensating benefits.

Yet I found no evidence that Legal Aid lawyers had ever been exercised over a lack of communication. The reason the problem of duplication arose with the advent of Legal Services was surely not that the new lawyers were duplicating efforts more often. On the contrary, with the new distinctions among appellate, neighborhood, and community group lawyers, and with the various conceptions of institutional mission brought by staff to each of these positions, the work of legal assistance lawyers had become far more differentiated. The problem of duplication arose because of a change in the perspectives of the lawyers—specifically, the new expectation that work should have significance beyond its benefit for the individual client. It was the demand on the capacity to organize legal assistance to the poor that had increased.

In one specific pattern of conflict, poverty lawyers preparing reform litigation became concerned that strategically unwise or substantively unsound suits on the same issues might be brought precipitously by other poverty lawyers, ruining the prospects for all (e.g., Albert 1968, Seid 1969).[10] More generally, heightened expectations for coordination were symbolized by the new title of legal assistance organizations. They were now "programs"; the efforts of staff were supposed to be integrated into a programmatic attack on poverty.

With the introduction of expectations for involvement, training also became a bigger problem. Here too, markedly increased demands on the capacity to organize resulted. Specialized activities—training sessions, training materials, training institutes—emerged in response. Tension between more and less experienced Legal Services lawyers over issues of training has taken two common forms. Reversing the pattern in private practice, the novice in legal assistance makes the initial client contact and then brings questions to a superordinate. On the one hand, senior poverty lawyers, searching for specific factual situations and novel issues to litigate, have feared that junior lawyers would fail to ask questions when they should and therefore send away clients with significant cases. On the other hand, senior litigators typically have disparaged the role of in-house teacher supporting the intake routine; the learning needs of novices often have been at odds with the maintenance of involvement by the more experienced lawyers.

The career structure in the Chicago LAB from 1955 to 1965 avoided training problems. Senior lawyers did not look for significant cases in the work of new lawyers. Instead, a hierarchy of supervisors taught daily, supplying similar advice on questions brought from intake interviews by cycles of new lawyers. Supervisors, by remaining to develop permanent Legal Aid careers while the "rotating" lawyers turned over, thus protected organizational continuity.

In addition to the phenomena perceptible from the positions of leaders and subordinate members, other organizational discontinuities can be detected from the observer's vantage point. These are phenomena that may exist even though no one in the organization perceives them. Consider the problems of succession. New members may not realize that predecessors left work in a preparatory or unfinished state. Succession is a literal test of collective identity, a test of whether the relations between members can be arranged to establish continuity in lines of action over changes of membership. Despite comparable rates of tenure in Legal Aid and Legal Services, turnover emerged as a major problem in Legal Services because expectations for involvement exacerbated problems of succession.[11]

Comparing lengths of tenure of lawyers in Chicago's Legal Aid and Legal Services organizations up to 1974, both groups had medians at around two years. The rotating-lawyer half of the Legal Aid staff was officially limited to a maximum of two years, but many did not last that long. Legal Services lawyers, to whom no formal maximum has applied, had a median stay of about 24 months.[12] In Legal Aid, the unexpected exit of a staff lawyer increased the burdens on supervisors considerably, as the abandoned case load demanded immediate attention. By monitoring the size of case loads and the boundaries of "desks," however, supervisors insured that unanticipated staff departures would not become "disasters." In Legal Services, when neighborhood lawyers have left, those who have picked up the abandoned case loads have often found files in the wastebasket, in unintelligible disarray, or full of what they have viewed as "junk" cases and potential "malpractice" suits.

It was a sign of organizational strength that Legal Aid's supervisors automatically and immediately found their burdens for managing active case loads increased when disinterested staff lawyers left prematurely. In Legal Services the problem of unfinished work frequently has not even been detected; when detected, it has frequently been ignored. Entering from a variety of professional and altruistic backgrounds, and making their backgrounds relevant in pursuit of involvement, Legal Services lawyers have given widely divergent meanings to personal growth. Cases thought significant by the lawyers who brought them have often seemed unchallenging, too challenging, or morally uncompelling to successors. Cases have often been left unprosecuted after preliminary barriers in lower courts have been surmounted; after sought-after appellate remands to lower courts have been obtained; or even after "final" victories have been won in courts of last resort, at the point when implementation requires ongoing surveillance of an adversary's compliance out of court. Campaigns to reform a public bureaucracy through a series of cases have lost their momentum when their initiators have left. Legal weapons innovated by one poverty lawyer to build a position of dominance in handling a specialized case load have often remained unused by the next.

Succession has sometimes taken on crisis proportions in LSPs. Exiting lawyers have taken large chunks of the organization with them. The departure of neighborhood lawyers who had been involved with community groups has frequently occasioned waves of protest over the selection of replacement staff thought less sensitive to the neighborhood. Some offices have been shut down as a means to peace. Upon the exits of Chicago neighborhood supervisors who had been involved in constructing "radical" neighborhood offices or in innovating "communal" styles of office governance, almost everyone else in their offices had turned over—lawyers, paraprofessionals, and secretaries.

These mass departures are dramatic examples of a more generally valid principle. Sociologists should not be surprised to see that, on the front lines of legal assistance work, where reform is a necessary condition for involvement, there are systematic inconsistencies between involvement and continuous collective action. Repeatedly, research in other occupational settings has found that the process of collective experimentation at reforming working conditions itself accounts for the extraordinary involvement of initial cohorts in new projects.[13] Subsequent cohorts, entering an already constituted, successfully routinized scene, fail to sustain, much less build upon, the earlier intensity of performance.

Institutional Capacity

Although organizational continuity has been damaged by turnover in Legal Services more than in Legal Aid, the departure of members from given offices has had an opposite effect on institutional capacity. When lawyers left Legal Aid societies, they left the institution. In contrast, by opening private offices in poverty neighborhoods, by moving to positions with reform litigation opportunities in law school clinics, or by taking jobs in other LSPs or in the national Legal Services administrative network, Legal Services lawyers have often made their exits continuations, not departures, in spirit. After having enjoyed what they considered extraordinary personal growth, many reform litigators have anticipated that more prestigious and more remunerative jobs would be more confining and thus a step back in their personal careers. In the process of maintaining involvement, members may have an unusually powerful disruptive effect on an organization, but their way of participating in the institution may have an unusually powerful adhesive effect on them.

Whereas Legal Aid was effective in preserving the contributions of its members within the organization, Legal Services has been much more effective at retaining experience in the institution. Movement to "straight" law practice was relatively rare among lawyers leaving the Chicago LSPs, and movement to other Legal Aid societies was virtually absent among ex-LAB lawyers.[14] This difference was produced through a difference in the way collective purpose penetrated private life during membership. On the one hand, Legal Aid's lawyers made differences in their personal backgrounds (including differences in race, ethnicity, and regional origin that traditionally separated lawyers in the private profession) irrelevant at the work site. Legal Services lawyers, on the other hand, built on different background experiences to implement colorfully diverse interpretations of the collective mandate. By the same token, Legal Services lawyers had relatively more in common by virtue of the very fact that personal perspectives were not clearly separated from participation in the collectivity. Legal Services lawyers were less likely to leave the institution when they ended membership in a given organization because they were less likely to leave the institution when they left the office every day.

The structure of Legal Aid societies made the job basically a nine-to-five activity. Clients were channeled from the central office's open door through a multistage interview process to staff lawyers; clients were not supposed to be acquired or retained in off hours. Legal Aid's passive definition of clients' rights meant that, when overtime was spent, it was spent in the office, putting a volume of files in shape, not at home writing briefs. Since little could be done on the job outside of the office, one of the common career problems faced by Legal Aid lawyers was to learn how to leave worries about clients at the office. After work, the staff turned to private lives in which their status as Legal Aid lawyers had little perceptible daily relevance.

In Legal Services, the pursuit of involvement in work led naturally to the involvement of work in "private" life. In various ways, staff lawyers took up organizational activities after hours: attending meetings of community organizations; socializing with newspaper writers who might prove useful for strategic press releases and with "spies" in government agencies who might reveal administrative procedures and plans; casually reading the daily paper with an eye out for policy changes that might be opposed. The practical requirements of reform litigation further blurred the line between personal and organizational time. Almost by definition, unprecedented cases are not amenable to standardized time boundaries; they present special difficulties for defining "sufficient" preparation. For neighborhood lawyers, off-hours socializing was almost a necessity to sustain involvement. It was essential to create a collective culture of significance that would resist and transform immediate pressures toward the routine. Peer relations sufficiently strong to transcend local pressures would almost inevitably merge "work" and "personal life."

Just as in one respect members build institutional capacity by contributing to an organization's collective purpose when they are outside of its offices, in a second respect, they develop that capacity when action they take to promote their own work has a positive spillover on the work of colleagues. Struggles among poverty lawyers over significant cases have often been signs both of organizational discontinuities and of institutional continuities. The appellate victories of a Chicago consumer-rights lawyer, locally famous for his insulting manner toward less knowledgeable colleagues, were incorporated into standard pleadings and became routinely available to novices throughout the program. After her migration to an out-of-state Legal Services program, a lawyer who had found her Chicago supervisor uncomfortably dominating in joint work picked up his class action pleadings and extended them to clients in the new jurisdiction. A major Supreme Court decision won by a renegade lawyer in the Chicago program was frequently cited as authority in suits brought by colleagues who had opposed his power to control significant litigation.

In a third respect, members' careers may have implications for expanding their collective domain in competitions to control a shared institution. The superiority of Legal Services lawyers on this dimension was demonstrated in the history of interorganizational relations. The national pattern was for LSPs to eclipse Legal Aid societies. In general, Legal Aid societies either have been absorbed by LSPs or have operated with a shrunken jurisdiction over parts of individual service work, especially domestic relations and bankruptcy, that are regarded by independent Legal Services organizations as routine and insignificant. Members of LSPs have displaced members of Legal Aid organizations in law school clinics, in bar association committees, and in the National Legal Aid and Defenders Association (NLADA).

The larger staff size and financial resources of Legal Services suggest an overwhelming influence in domains shared with Legal Aid. In the early 1960s, 400 lawyers were employed nationally by Legal Aid organizations on a combined budget of less than $4 million (Brownell 1961, p. 68). By the early seventies, over 2000 lawyers were employed on a Legal Services budget of $70 million.[15] Yet the incapacity of Legal Aid lawyers to shape the development of LSPs has not been a direct result of inferior numbers, as can be seen in the Chicago experience.[16]

In Chicago, Legal Aid was related organizationally to Legal Services from its start in 1965. Legal Aid having been a bureau of United Charities of Chicago for 50 years, it was this "family service agency" which administered the initial OEO Legal Services grant in Chicago. At first, despite the numerical imbalances, senior Legal Aid personnel officially led the Legal Services staff. By 1971, the new poverty lawyers had established substantial internal autonomy. First professional and then administrative control of the neighborhood offices passed from a senior Legal Aid lawyer to a lawyer who had entered Legal Services from a major law firm in 1968 to head the law reform unit. CLC, the small Legal Services project initiated in Chicago independently of United Charities in 1967, then began a "merger" with United Charities Legal Aid/Legal Services. The merger triggered many battles between Legal Aid and Legal Services staff and supporters. In 1972, lawyers from CLC assumed leadership of all the Legal Services–funded staff positions, and for a few months they also held formal authority over the LAB. Then in 1973, the LAB and the LSPs were severed. Their relationship then stabilized in a new form. The LSPs, which soon had four times the staff and budget of Legal Aid, were completely integrated into a new entity called the Legal Assistance Foundation. The LAB shrank slightly and continued as a part of United Charities.

Underlying the formal changes in organizational relations was a radical difference between the Legal Aid and Legal Services staffs in their capacities for institutional leadership. The features of the Legal Aid lawyer's career perspective that had contributed to the bureau's organizational strength became sources of weakness in the struggle with Legal Services. Conversely, the perspective on involvement characteristic of Legal Services lawyers impeded their internal organization but provided strategic resources for eclipsing the influence of Legal Aid in the collective environment. The next chapter is a detailed analysis of these resources as seen in the seven-year process of negotiation between Chicago's Legal Aid and Legal Services programs.

Chapter 8

Legal Services Programs Eclipse Legal Aid

During a decade of conflict starting with the creation of Legal Services in 1965, one consistent imbalance of strategic advantage derived from the different meanings of conflict in the Legal Aid and Legal Services career perspectives. To Legal Aid lawyers, the process of organizational change was consistently demoralizing. For those who saw themselves as permanent staff, internal conflict was a direct threat. For those who expected to use Legal Aid as a stepping-stone, battles over control of the organization were irrelevant; they felt pressured by colleagues to express insincere loyalties. In contrast, Legal Services lawyers often took conflict with Legal Aid as a further basis for involvement. They easily fit conflicts with Legal Aid into an everyday perspective on institutional reform.

Another advantage enjoyed by Legal Services lawyers followed from their lesser social distance from clients and lawyers on boards of directors. Through their work with community organizations of the poor, Legal Services lawyers forged unique common interests with client representatives. Through reform litigation, poverty lawyers made their professional environment one with which board lawyers from large firms could personally identify. Legal Services lawyers established the priority of litigation for social, political, and economic reform by tapping the commitments to professionalism held by powerful members of the private bar.

In treating the decade of struggle in the Chicago legal assistance programs, my aim is not to explain discrete changes in the forms of interorganizational relations so much as to demonstrate the continuous advantages in the Legal Services perspective for defining the shared domain. There are two related reasons for attempting to explain aspects of the process rather than its formal products. First, my research was limited to Chicago, and the goal of generalization suggests taking as the unit of analysis recurrent strategies of conflict rather than isolated formal changes. Second, the process has not ended. Informally, struggles between lawyers with the two career perspectives persist within many LSPs.

To present a coherent view of the process of organizational change, the chapter is organized chronologically rather than analytically (i.e., by strategic resource). As the history develops, however, the ways in which the two career perspectives were related into a strategic balance that tipped decisively toward the side of reform becomes increasingly explicit.

Conflicts between Legal Aid and Legal Services lawyers in Chicago can be divided into two periods, 1965–1971 and 1971–1974. The second period began with the announcement of a process to merge the legal assistance programs of the United Charities of Chicago (UCC) with Community Legal Counsel. The merger became a vehicle for bringing long-standing, subterranean staff pressures into formal decisions on organizational development. To set the background for the unexpectedly rapid takeover by CLC in the formal merger, I first review the progress that Legal Services lawyers had already made informally within the framework of United Charities.

The Early Years: Legal Services Lawyers Move toward Independence within UCC

UCC responded to the prospect of a federally funded Legal Services program in the mid 1960s with unenthusiastic professions of an obligation to step forward (UCC's character as a family-service agency housing the LAB is described in chapter 2). No other course would protect its monopoly. In 1964, NLADA downplayed the need for expanding legal assistance to the poor and waved charges of unethical practice at suggestions of independent alternatives. The strategy was to bolster the demand that Legal Aid organizations be the central vehicle for what NLADA then gingerly called the "so-called" War on Poverty. Chicago's Legal Aid leaders backed NLADA's policy statements and, after they decided to participate in the federal program, stressed to their constituents that the decision to create a new federal program was, after all, out of their hands (United Charities of Chicago 1965*b*, 1965*d*).

If the organizational framework of UCC did not augur well for aggressive poverty lawyering in Chicago, many observers saw worse omens in the initial format. United Charities began participating in the Legal Services program as a subordinate of the Chicago Committee on Urban Opportunity. The CCUO was, as noted earlier, created by Mayor Daley to control the city's allotment of OEO funds (see chapter 5). Neighborhood Legal Services lawyers were to be professionally accountable to UCC Legal Aid, but they would be physically located in CCUO Urban Progress Centers (UPCs) and would receive clients through a screening process managed by CCUO personnel.

The Daley Machine quickly made blunt demands for political control. In the first few months of operation, Arthur Young, director of the LAB, was contacted by William Zipperman, a city corporation counsel speaking on behalf of the mayor. Zipperman was worried about potential suits by Legal Services lawyers against the city, about the extension of a legal voice to community organizations, and about excessively permissive income eligibility standards. Most of all, the city's lawyer was worried about

> the political implications of establishing law offices in the pockets of poverty because of the effect he believes it may have upon the local practicing lawyer. He indicated that some lawyers . . . are quite concerned with the establishment of neighborhood offices. There is some feeling it seems about this—it may have political overtones since these are the people who are the voice of the neighborhood and [*sic*] the Democratic party loses them they may lose their control. (United Charities of Chicago 1965*a*)

UCC LAB acceded to the pressure in various ways. It declared a policy to transfer to the downtown LAB office all cases which might turn into suits against the city. UCC passed up the opportunity to run the Legal Services program in a more independent format. At one point, UCC had a choice to relate to CCUO as a delegate agency or as a provider of services on contracts which would be reviewed directly by the city's Aldermanic Council. UCC weighed the alternatives and leaned toward the latter. Under the Economic Opportunity Act, the delegate agency structure would require UCC to pay a 10 percent "local share" of the program's cost. The contract alternative would shift the burden of the local share to the city, which might be induced to participate if UCC made a "contribution" to help CCUO meet its 10 percent obligation. When presenting this plan to a board committee, UCC's executive director, Robert F. Nelson, and Legal Aid Director Young gave reassurances about CCUO control: "We think it is safe to say that the relationship of the Legal Aid Bureau and the United Charities to the Chicago Committee on Urban Opportunity is much better in Chicago than similar relationships in most major cities" (United Charities of Chicago 1965*c*).

In early negotiations with CCUO, Young offered the assurance that as to "Scope and content: Basically legal services will be provided in the traditional way." He suggested as the sole note of novelty that "since many people in the poverty areas find themselves overwhelmed in debt, [we] plan to have financial counselling available both before and after debt involvement." On the issue of "resident participation," he stated that "by the nature of legal services, it is not anticipated that the residents will participate in the program except as they are served and as they take advantage of counselling and other aids leading to prevention of legal entanglement" (United Charities of Chicago 1965*e*).

From the start, UCC LAB had to be pushed continuously by Legal Services leaders to adopt new qualitative dimensions. The refusal to incorporate residents other than as clients appeared to fly in the face of OEO requirements for citizen participation. At the end of 1965, the new national director of OEO Legal Services, Clinton Bamberger, personally pressed UCC LAB "to consider a method of involving the poor for advisory purposes and including them in the policy making structure" (United Charities of Chicago 1965*f*).

> Early in 1966 the Office of Economic Opportunity at the federal and regional level criticized the Chicago plan and said it could not continue:
>
> A. They did not like the contract plan with the City. . . .
> B. They indicated our plan was not comprehensive and should include new features.
>
> A new plan was submitted which accomplished the following:
>
> A. Changed the plan from a contract to sponsorship basis, thus making United Charities responsible for ten percent sponsor share. . . .
> B. Extended the program as follows:
>   1. Put service in seven Poverty Centers and outposts rather than three.
>   2. Created a special unit at the Juvenile Court.
>   3. Created a small Trial and Appellate Division.
>   (United Charities of Chicago 1966)

The expansions, though still short on some OEO Legal Services priorities such as community representation,[1] were made reluctantly:

> The Executive Director [of UCC, Nelson] has substantial doubts that the expanded program should be submitted, since in his estimation the agency would need to find somewhere between $45,000 and $55,000 of cash as a sponsor share. He hesitates, however [*sic*] to rule out submission of the program, since other large cities are submitting programs of this size and the Office of Economic Opportunity has in the past questioned why Chicago, through the Legal Aid Bureau, is not attempting to more adequately meet the need. (United Charities of Chicago 1966)

Legal Aid intended to operate without a basic change in mission, as though there had been no fundamental change in the institution's environment; and this was reflected in personnel decisions. Without making a search outside the organization, leadership was drawn from the Legal Aid staff. The implicit assumption was that Legal Services would be an extension of Legal Aid. Young, the director of the LAB for the previous decade and a Legal Aid lawyer for 30 years, continued as the director of the LAB as it expanded to implement the OEO Legal Services program. He remained subordinate in form and practice to Nelson, the executive director of UCC, who in 1965 was a social worker with almost 20 years' experience and political strength in the post. A lawyer with 20 years of experience in the LAB was moved from a domestic-relations supervisory position to administer the Legal Services program.

The first break in the pattern of promoting from within was made to fill the top position in the new Appellate and Test Case Division. This unit was created in 1967 in response to pressure for a reform emphasis from the national office of OEO Legal Services. Its first leader, Marshall Patner, had once been an associate in a large law firm and had just been running a criminal law reform project at the University of Chicago Law School.

As UCC LAB reached out to control Legal Services, it committed the LAB to remain essentially unchanged for the long-range future. The movements of LAB lawyers into Legal Services positions and subsequent retirements created a set of vacancies in the LAB supervisory hierarchy. They were filled in accordance with the traditionally observed seniority principle. Four lawyers, each with over 10 years' experience in the LAB, moved up. Burton Terry became the new head of the downtown intake operation, the old LAB. Another LAB staff veteran became overseer of a new set of OEO-funded, law-student intake interviewers. By 1970, two other senior LAB lawyers had moved into the supervisory positions at the top of the LAB's Economic and Family Divisions.

The concept of leadership advanced for the neighborhood offices by career Legal Aid lawyers extended traditional patterns in Legal Aid. Stress was placed on centrally controlled administrative routines to govern matters of physical and formal organization. Initially it appeared that the character of the old downtown LAB unit would not be altered at all in the process. No LAB lawyer moved to the neighborhood offices; none worked regularly with the new Legal Services staff on professional matters. New neighborhood lawyers were simply assigned for two weeks to be interviewers in the downtown LAB operation. There, in repeated daily trips to LAB officials for advice, they were to learn what a welcoming memo described as "the procedures and philosophy of United Charities."

Conflict immediately developed between the new neighborhood lawyers and their Legal Aid leaders. Many of the new lawyers quickly declared their independence by bolting for neighborhood assignments before completing training at the LAB. In interviews, many remembered the LAB severely, as a unit run by "formula people" adept at turning prospective clients away at first contact, without service and with false hopes for receiving service elsewhere. Once in the neighborhood office, the new lawyer saw the director, Young, primarily through memoranda which seemed to waver inconsistently between recitals of UCC LAB eligibility restrictions and referral procedures and exhortations to OEO program priorities. The administrative lawyer in charge of the neighborhood program neither represented clients nor provided training. He was seen in neighborhood offices primarily when he appeared with office supplies. Neighborhood lawyers ridiculed him as "the guy who brings my toilet paper."

In the face of a rapidly changing institutional environment, LAB leaders remained passive and the direction of leadership became ambiguous. They initially expected to extend their traditional philosophy to the neighborhood offices but, when OEO Legal Services pressed, they dutifully asserted that community contact and structural reform were priorities. CCUO simultaneously demanded that lawyers be assigned to new UPCs as they were developed. The resulting spread of the staff over multiple offices diluted the strength of each to order the growing list of official goals. Neighborhood offices that were budgeted for three or four lawyers often had only one or two recently admitted lawyers on staff. Neighborhood lawyers uniformly recalled overwhelming case loads and a constant threat of "chaos."

In 1968, the Legal Services–funded staff began to organize challenges to Legal Aid's authority. At one point, LAB leaders contemplated as a solution to the problem of neighborhood overload that the neighborhood offices become interviewing stations and refer downtown, to the LAB, all cases requiring court work. The one neighborhood office that had distinguished itself by initiating reform litigation, East Garfield, blasted a response: downtown LAB lawyers would sell out clients by settling good cases; only incompetents would accept the dull job the plan envisioned for the neighborhood.

A larger group of neighborhood lawyers soon presented 21 militant "requests." After charging a "lack of leadership, direction and planning from the top," they demanded procedures for staff recruitment and assignment, official priorities for case load control, improvements in staff salaries, and, to insure insult, a commercial delivery service to replace the neighborhood program director. Three months later, citing a lack of response, the staff threatened to strike, air grievances at a press conference, and press for a CBA investigation of the UCC LAB leadership. In another effort, a group of the neighborhood-office supervisory lawyers sought to create a decision-making body of their own. In an informally circulated memo, they minced no words: "There exists *no structure* for making policy decisions. Worse, there exists no *democratic* organ for decision making that would allow all to participate in this process. This fault may have been acceptable prior to expansion but it is not now."

LAB's leaders first ignored the attacks, then offered contradictory policies. As staff pressures began to grow, Young responded in a memo that sought to downplay tensions: "There has been some concern expressed . . . as . . . to the . . . overwhelming caseload [*sic*] and the probable continuation of this situation for some time . . . as between . . . law reform and direct services the former would take precedence" (United Charities of Chicago, 1968*a*). Six months later, with the staff threatening revolt, Young confronted the conflict directly, reversing his earlier policy statement in the process:

> It would appear that there is a voice, of a vocal minority at least, that the Legal Aid Bureau has no direction or if it has, this has not been communicated to the staff of the neighborhood offices. Although I am of the firm opinion that the purposes of the Legal Aid Bureau have been set out heretofore in written memoranda, oral presentations and in copies of various bulletins from the Office of Economic Opportunity, etc., it may be that because these pronouncements were met with "laughter and cynical disregard" that . . . there are some who may not know what we are trying to accomplish. Our first and original function, of course, is to provide direct services. . . . Our second purpose is to provide legal services in such a manner that the condition of the poor may be modified, changed or altered in such a fashion that they will be helped out of their condition of poverty. . . . For several months now we have been wrestling with the problem of case load and have been unable to come to any satisfactory conclusion. (United Charities of Chicago 1968*b*)

While LAB leadership was failing to provide leadership, the Legal Services staff made progress in redirecting the institution. They won a major victory for expanding their mandate by pressing to sever the relationship with CCUO. The relationship had been a daily irritant to neighborhood lawyers. CCUO personnel would object when representatives of unapproved community groups came in. A screening process run by UPC personnel required prospective clients to complete a lengthy questionnaire which required the applicant to declare whether or not his birth was legitimate, to describe conflict between his parents, and to describe why he left school (one multiple-choice answer for the latter: "School said too slow"). In early 1969, UCC leaders followed the staff's lead and included in the work program submitted to the OEO Office of Legal Services a commitment to represent community groups and a proposal to move out of the UPCs.

CCUO then cut off funding. Once again, UCC had to put a price on principle. UCC had advanced its own funds to finance the Legal Services program in previous months, expecting to receive a backdated OEO grant through CCUO, as in previous years. The risks were substantial, but there was also significant new encouragement for defying CCUO. OEO Legal Services officials had informally approved the new work program. There was also a new national administration, which meant that UCC could use its strong local Republican ties to cut the Daley organization out of the path of OEO Legal Services funds to Chicago. UCC chose, however, not to risk its resources by making the move for direct funding. UCC struck out the proposal to leave the UPCs and formally ordered the staff not to represent community groups. OEO Legal Services then forced a crisis by declaring the revised work program unacceptable.

Pressure from the Legal Services staff made UCC's decision-making process a series of wide-open public events. The staff took the cue from the national OEO Legal Services office and demanded that UCC seek direct funding from OEO. To add force, the staff petitioned the UCC Board and the CBA, which had a formal role in governing UCC's legal assistance operations, and threatened mass resignation. In the course of the year, UCC and CBA committees moved from concession to CCUO, to resounding expressions of principle, and then to a personal lobbying of OEO officials in Washington for direct funding.[2]

Internal Weakening of Legal Aid

The moral bargain between the institution of civil legal assistance and the organized legal profession was fundamentally renegotiated in the transition from Legal Aid to Legal Services. Legal Aid lawyers had contributed a risk-free measure of honor to the elite of the private bar by performing its altruistic dirty work. Bar leaders considered actual work at Legal Aid to be beneath their professional competence; they served personally by sitting on quiet supervisory committees (see chapter 3). Legal Services lawyers, many of whom enjoyed expressing their moral distaste for large corporate firms, were nonetheless drawing on moral credit from precisely that source for protection against establishment interests adversely affected by reform activism. In a series of controversies across the country, senior partners of prominent firms put their prestige up against congressional, gubernatorial, and mayoral attempts to restrict the rights of Legal Services lawyers to sue the government, represent militant groups, and file reform litigation.[3]

Thus even before the formal merger process in Chicago, Legal Services lawyers had reversed Legal Aid's relationship with its most powerful interest-group ally. Another weakness in Legal Aid had already emerged: the dramatic contrast in the meaning of internal conflict to the two staffs. Whereas conflict with Legal Aid brought an extraordinary cohesion to the usually fragmented Legal Services staff, in the previously cohesive Legal Aid staff, conflicts with Legal Services created deep, unprecedented divisions. Legal Aid not only failed to lead Legal Services; the attempt led to disintegration within Legal Aid. Put conversely, Legal Services lawyers not only moved toward independence; they subtly undermined Legal Aid's institutional foundations.

By 1971, the original director of the neighborhood offices had been demoted. He was replaced by Gordon H. S. Scott, who had entered Legal Services in 1969 from a well-known conservative corporate law firm, Kirkland and Ellis, to head the Appellate Division. In an early attack on United Charities's influence, Scott dismantled an allegedly useless statistical department staffed by UCC employees. A change on the level of personal influence facilitated these changes. Young, the overall UCC Legal Aid/Legal Services director, began to take advice from Scott and others in the Appellate Division.

To most of the senior Legal Aid staff, Young's deference to Appellate Division "hot shots," "superstars," and "boy wonders," who were often self-consciously elitist, was galling and demoralizing. Further divisions erupted within the overall senior Legal Aid staff as Young began evaluating them with new criteria. In his annual evaluations of LAB supervisory personnel, complaints began to appear about a paucity of appeals and "interesting" cases.

Similar criticism perked up from below. A serious internal threat to the integrity of the senior LAB staff informally developed as young lawyers in the lowest formal slots in the LAB increasingly manifested Legal Services perspectives. Several had come from jobs in the LSPs, and others were on their way to them. Many developed interests in reform litigation and abjured concern for the place of the job in their long-range careers. The new career perspectives of young LAB lawyers undercut part of the original justification for maintaining a senior Legal Aid staff.

The rotating lawyer system adopted by the LAB in the 1950s had, by forcing turnover after two years, created training responsibilities and salary increases for the senior staff. When the UCC LAB took on the Legal Services program, the rotating lawyer system was abandoned; yet at the same time, new commitments were made to preserve the LAB's supervisory structure. Senior staff were moved to positions of leadership on the Legal Services side. Resources brought to the LAB by OEO Legal Services enabled the LAB's supervisory lawyers to drop or drastically reduce their own case loads and to become more exclusively administrators.

While commitments to the LAB supervisory structure increased, professional supervisory responsibilities in the LAB were becoming increasingly unnecessary. By 1972, five of the six staff lawyers in the LAB Family Division had over five years' experience in Legal Aid. Neither they nor their supervisors thought they required much professional supervision. In the Economic Division, several young lawyers turned their desks toward significant litigation and developed interests in staying longer than had the rotating lawyers, also making supervision less necessary. Moreover, their reform activities afforded experience with courts and cases superior in professional prestige to the legal practice of their formal supervisors. Many, feeling they had grown beyond their Legal Aid superiors, assumed a right to operate autonomously in reform litigation. A few turned for professional advice and colleagueship to lawyers on the Legal Services side.

In addition to these internal implications, the Legal Services program disrupted the historically reliable support that Legal Aid had enjoyed from external constituencies. First, as previously described, in battles to achieve their own independence, such as in the struggle against CCUO, the Legal Services staff voiced strident criticism of Legal Aid to private lawyers sitting on the United Charities's and the bar association's Legal Aid Committees. But in addition, by administering the Legal Services program, Legal Aid had unexpectedly invited unprecedented, harsh criticisms from a wholly new source, the OEO Office of Legal Services. In a report that gave decisive support to one of Scott's attacks on UCC, OEO evaluators characterized the statistical system as overly expensive and largely superfluous. Later, OEO Legal Services evaluators judged the LAB supervisory hierarchy in much the same terms.

Most profoundly, the very existence of Legal Services began to threaten private financial support for Legal Aid. Although the downtown LAB did not take up the broad Legal Services mandate for reform and community group representation, the Legal Services side did display a mandate that covered all of Legal Aid's work. Legal Services funds in Chicago soon doubled those supplied through charitable channels to the LAB. The resulting danger was not merely theoretical. In 1967, the UCC Executive Committee was

> shocked to see that the Community Fund Priorities Committee had decided that legal services to the poor were basically a governmental responsibility and that the Committee recommended that the Community Funds [*sic*] support of Legal Aid Bureau be continued only at its present level without further increases to offset the effect of inflation on salaries or other expense items. (United Charities of Chicago 1967)

Then there were the political risks brought to UCC Legal Aid by its Legal Services lawyers. Controversial poverty litigation made UCC Legal Aid vulnerable to a loss of support from traditional contributors. The UCC Legal Aid Committee did not attempt to review routine cases to insure professional quality, nor did it initiate or otherwise promote specific reform cases. But staff director Young was required to bring potentially controversial cases for review before filing. This politically selective review process was justified as an ethically defensible imposition of purely professional standards. Activist Legal Services lawyers scoffed at the claim of political neutrality. UCC LAB officials persisted with the defense anyway, apparently trying to convince themselves. The biased social structure of the review process was Legal Aid's way of embracing professionalism while preserving the loyalties of conservative constituents. This is how Young would defend UCC Legal Aid against charges by

> "the more vociferous members of the OEO staff who feel that the United Charities is an establishment agency . . . [that doesn't] want to make too much waves. . . . The record is absolutely different from that. I don't think that there's been one lawsuit that's . . . ever been curtailed. You see, we operate with, instead of a board of directors, a Legal Aid Committee. And I've had a number of chairmen of the LAC, some from the establishment law firms, the prestigious law firms and even the most conservative; the only question I've ever been asked [is] Is your lawsuit valid, have you got precedent, do you know what you're doing? And if I could say yes, well then there was never any question about

> it. And I always felt . . . You know, another criticism . . . by the staff is, "What the hell do you have to go to the board for? Why can't you determine what cases we ought to handle? My response to that is, I don't go to the board necessarily to get them to approve a certain case, but if I'm going to make waves, a lot of waves . . . I feel I get better support when I call up the chairman of our [UC] board or the Legal Aid Committee and say Bob, or Ted, or Joe, or whoever it is and say, We're filing this suit. When that case breaks in the newspaper the next day, and somebody calls this guy up, he can say, Yeah, I know, I know they were going to file that suit. . . . I can't remember which suit it was, but I got a call at my house one night, Saturday at 11 o'clock, from the then-director of United Charities, who got a call from the then-president of United Charities, who was at a cocktail party someplace; and apparently the president of United Charities and the chief editor of one of the city newspapers . . . the editor of the newspaper said—I forget, I don't even know what the case was about at the moment—You guys have done so and so and so and so and I'm going to write an editorial in my newspaper against you, whereupon the president of United Charities [Board] got real upset and called the director of United Charities, who called me, and I said, Well, I'll look into it. It turned out nothing happened, but you see if you don't tell these people these things then they can't answer and it puts them in a bad position."

If the bias was usually implicit, extreme risks to contributions to United Charities provoked explicit restraints. The following reproduces the entire minutes of a 1970 Legal Aid Committee meeting:

> The meeting concerned certain proposed litigation, to be filed in the federal court, to challenge the constitutionality of the Illinois Anti-Abortion statute. Legal Aid Bureau attorneys had worked up the case in cooperation with the American Civil Liberties Union. The purpose of the meeting was to determine whether a Smith Fellow assigned to Legal Aid Bureau's OEO Program should be identified as a Legal Aid Bureau attorney in representing an eligible plaintiff in the proposed suit.
>
> The questions primarily discussed concerned (1) the legal basis for the action (2) the special interest of the poor in the litigation, and (3) whether income from contributions would be adversely affected if United Charities became identified with the institution of the action.
>
> After discussion, the Committee seemed reasonably satisfied as to

> points (1) and (2). However, the Committee was concerned about adverse reaction from its supporters if United Charities (or the Legal Aid Bureau) were identified as a moving force in the institution of the litigation.
>
> It was finally decided that the Legal Aid Bureau should intervene at a later date, to represent the interests of the poor, but that the Bureau should not be identified in the commencement of the action. (United Charities of Chicago 1970*b*)

Legal Aid was thus threatened at every level of its organizational existence. The senior staff was exposed to direct criticism. The rationale for their superior hierarchical positions was undermined. Financial supports were shaken. Even the daily environment for Legal Aid practice became less comfortable. Legal Services lawyers were offending opposing counsel and courts by refusing to be "reasonable." Senior Legal Aid lawyers, sensitive to local professional opinion to the extent of suffering embarrassment when respect was withheld, felt obliged to apologize to opposing counsel and to judges for the abrasive styles of their young colleagues. Collection lawyers in particular complained to Young that neighborhood lawyers did not settle cases senior Legal Aid lawyers would have settled. The following field note reflects the disruption of support for Legal Aid in one of its local professional environments.

> *The head of the civil division of the state's attorney's office told me today that Legal Aid–OEO lawyers are the most abrasive as a group that he's ever met. Howell and Scott are especially offensive, one unspeakably so. They even wanted him to investigate affirmatively a countercharge against the cops every time he drops a charge for resisting arrest. And after talking about working together on a suit against a third party, after he said he'd have to check with the attorney general first, Legal Services filed without checking back, suing him. In contrast, he knows the "old guard well." They were of low competence, not innovative, but they weren't moralistic. They know that lawyers have to be reasonable, to settle.*

Merger

The idea of a merger between the United Charities programs and CLC was proposed in late summer of 1970 by the director of the OEO Office of Legal Services. By this time, the United Charities LAB dominated its Legal Services program in form only. On the level of informal influence, lawyers expressing the Legal Service career perspective were operating independently, in some respects dominating Legal Aid lawyers. The traditional distance between Legal Aid's board and staff had masked much of the informal shift of power from those in charge of planning for UCC LAB. Although the merger was another stage in an ongoing struggle for institutional dominance, it had special significance because it created opportunities to remove at the board level the disparity between formal and informal power relations. The Legal Services staff ascended in the merged organization with a force and suddenness that stunned United Charities.

Each side understood the origins of the merger in its own terms. Legal Aid's leaders saw Washington's interest as that of a bureaucracy concerned about administrative problems. Why administer two Chicago Legal Services projects instead of one? UCC was being generous in its offer of an organizational home to CLC. CLC, a small program, had no local constituency to provide private funds and could not expect to find a patron in the Nixon administration. The expectation was that UCC, with little impact on itself, would quickly absorb CLC.

UCC's sense of security was evident at the start of merger negotiations. The regional OEO Legal Services office has backed CLC's pressure to make the merged legal assistance organization independent of UCC control. The United Charities Executive Committee considered a response.

> Question was raised as to why we should merge with an organization which has no funds, little in the way of staff and only limited experience. It was concluded that our role now is to clarify the challenge and negotiate to insure the continuity of our program, going to Washington, if necessary, and playing a strong hand. No change in our present operation seems indicated now. (United Charities of Chicago 1970*a*).

A commitment to merge would mean that formal organizational issues would have to be addressed at the board level. To construct an integrated operation of CLC and the UCC law programs, a new collective entity would have to structure a governing board, adopt personnel policies, select an executive director, and fashion a common work program. Initially, UCC resisted conceiving the merger as a process of formally establishing a new organization. It argued that it could expand and continue as it had for six years: by expanding the authority of the LAB director to encompass the Legal Services–paid staff, by operating at the board level through the traditional device of corporate lawyers sitting on the United Charities Legal Aid Committee (LAC), and by extending UCC administrative and personnel policies.

For its part, CLC did not initially have a substantially different understanding of its power relations with UCC. CLC leaders and staff were not at all confident of national support (the Nixon administration seemed, if anything, inclined to seize any opportunity to run reformist elements out of Legal Services), and they could not rely on community groups to protest against a loss of CLC's integrity, even if national leaders would listen. As its annual report had recently announced, CLC had just begun to establish a "presence" in Chicago. CLC had therefore just one bargaining resource for opposing UCC: the argument that the UCC proposal to govern through the UCC LAC would violate national regulations governing LSPs. The Office of Legal Services had long expressed dissatisfaction with UCC's resistance to client representation; new statutory language now appeared to require at least one-third representation of the poor.[4] Although UCC LAC had itself signaled a willingness to include in its membership the requisite community representation, CLC argued nonconformity on the grounds that the LAC would remain a subordinate committee of UCC, which had given no such signal.

By seizing the issue of nonconformity, and by receiving crucial support from OEO Legal Services officials in its interpretation that the UCC board and not the LAC was the proper unit on which to figure representation, CLC found the leverage to transform dramatically the issues and the power balance in the negotiations. The "merger" was suddenly couched not as a relation between little CLC and the much larger United Charities law programs, but as a relation to be worked out between *all* the LSPs and the relatively smaller United Charities LAB. The shift was not generally appreciated. CLC, a small group, spoke alone in formal opposition to United Charities. Most Legal Services lawyers in Chicago were still formally under United Charities authority; representatives of the poor had as yet no independent, official voice.

In early 1972, the CLC staff prepared to move physically into the United Charities office space that housed the LAB and the downtown Legal Services units. The organizational device agreed upon at that time was a corporate shell that was readily at hand, the old Legal Aid Society (LAS). Over 50 years before, in 1919, the LAS had been absorbed by United Charities when the UCC LAB was created. The reappearance of the LAS in 1972 symbolized a reverse historical turn. The LAS (as reviewed in chapter 2) had been created originally in 1905, in a merger between the Bureau of Justice, with its ambience of indignation about social injustice and moral philosophy derived from the Ethical Cultural Society, and the Protective Agency for Women and Children, with its background in the social work leadership of the

Chicago Women's Club. The LAS had operated as a historical intermediary, a vehicle through which legal assistance in Chicago passed out of the reformist posture of the Progressive Era and into a charitable social work home at United Charities Legal Aid. Now the LAS would play a brief role as an intermediary in the ascendance of a reformist leadership in Legal Services over the Legal Aid tradition.

According to an agreement worked out between UCC, OEO Legal Services, and CLC, the directors of the resurrected LAS Board were to be one-third appointed by UCC, one-third representatives of the poor, and another one-third divided between designees of CLC, law schools, and bar associations. UCC was to delegate the administration of all Legal Services funds and staff to the LAS, but UCC was to negotiate a separate contract for the administration of the LAB by LAS. While a permanent director was recruited, the LAS was to be governed by a five-person committee composed of staff leaders from CLC, the UCC LAB, and the UCC Legal Services neighborhood offices.

The Legal Services staff demonstrated strategic superiority in virtually every major issue faced by the LAS Board. At the first LAS Board meeting, the plan to run the LAS staff by a temporary committee was unceremoniously scuttled, and CLC's staff director, Ken Howell, was appointed temporary executive director. Several months later, after two waves of a national search, Howell's appointment was made permanent. In the interim, personnel policies favorable to short-term employees in such matters as the arrangement of pension contributions were adopted over the objections of the senior Legal Aid staff. By early summer of 1973, the power relations of a year before had been turned on their head. Ex-CLC lawyers held virtually all the top staff positions in the LAS program. Responsibilities for the professional supervision of the LAB staff had been partially transferred from senior Legal Aid staff to Legal Services (and ex-CLC) staff. A plan to reorganize the LAB by reducing lawyer positions and dismantling the supervisory hierarchy had been approved at the LAS Board level, *with the unanimous consent of the UCC appointees.*

Strategic Positions

Differences to Legal Aid and Legal Services lawyers in the meaning of institutional change and intraorganizational conflict became increasingly pronounced. Attempts were made by Legal Services lawyers in different organizational positions to mobilize collective pressure at key stages. They involved themselves deeply in the merger; for to many, it was another challenging project in institution building. During the early negotiations, neighborhood Legal Services lawyers made attempts to organize a distinct voice in the merger planning. One CLC lawyer called for a meeting of all staffs involved in order to discuss the idea of unionizing. Joint meetings were called by members of the different Legal Services staffs to consider tactics for securing staff positions on the new board and to petition Washington directly on specific issues. No such initiatives emerged from the LAB staff.[5]

Reform litigators sustained their involvement in the merger process by folding conflicts with UCC into their everyday work perspectives. Over objections by LAB negotiators that the arguments were "unreasonable," Legal Services lawyers developed issues of principle out of details of formal rules. Of major significance was the argument by CLC on UCC's nonconformity with federal requirements for the structure of a Legal Services governing board. This argument paralleled those made in typical poverty law class-action suits, which seek to reform local bureaucracies by citing their violation of federal regulations.

Treating the merger issues in the spirit of their everyday work, Legal Services lawyers celebrated their strategies. They easily extended the culture they had developed to support reform litigation. For fun, outrageous plans of attack were imagined: a welfare rights leader might be induced to present herself for service at the LAB office so that she might explode with indignation when asked for the $1 ("voluntary") registration fee. True to the apprehensions of senior Legal Aid lawyers, Legal Services lawyers relished dramatic scenarios in which they would achieve temporary control, "clean house" and otherwise "shake things up," and then leave the organization, allowing successors to reap the benefits while in absentia they took the blame from UCC. At strategic points in the merger, in order to embarrass UCC with its constituencies in private philanthropy, UCC Legal Services lawyers cunningly leaked stories to newspapers about the ascendance of Legal Services influence in the merged organization. CLC lawyers gaily relived their audacity at showing up uninvited, and to their leader's dismay, at the law offices of a UCC Board lawyer where board-level merger negotiations were being held. A neighborhood lawyer enhanced his reputation among peers by confronting UCC Board representatives and the Legal Aid director with demands for information about the state of merger negotiations and with assertions of bad faith.

For Legal Services lawyers, the most difficult personal moments in the merger process occurred when they encountered attempts by senior LAB lawyers to be reasonable. After the CLC staff moved into the downtown UCC law offices, senior LAB lawyers, in a spirit of cooperation, occasionally brought to their attention cases they, the LAB lawyers, had begun. LAB lawyers were thus unwittingly providing the Legal Services staff with evidence for an argument of Legal Aid's incompetence. Ex-CLC staff lawyers felt pressured either to dissemble or express criticism directly. Their solution continued a pattern established years before by the downtown Legal Services staff when it first entered offices on the same floor with the LAB intake operation. They chose routes to walk through the offices that would minimize daily personal contact with the senior Legal Aid staff.

The merger had the opposite meaning for Legal Aid lawyers. As part of their identification with UCC LAB, senior lawyers traditionally deferred to their director and board on policy matters. They approached the merger with a sense of trust that they would be informed about deliberations at high levels at the appropriate time. As part of their stepping-stone career perspective, a few young Legal Aid lawyers tried to ignore merger issues. They reported in interviews that, because they expected to leave the institution soon anyway, merger crises affecting the Legal Aid staff would only accelerate their exit.

The permanent Legal Aid staff flatly considered the mobilization of Legal Services staff pressure at the board level to be improper. The LAB director recalled that

> before OEO came in, there were full staff meetings monthly. But there wasn't so much staff participation as there is now. The staff didn't participate in running the office as much as they do now. It wasn't a democracy, and no business should be a democracy.

Commenting on a LAS Board meeting at which the Legal Services staff gave their opinions of candidates for executive director, one LAB supervisor recalled that before OEO

> I was never at board meetings. We didn't care. We just did our work. There was nothing like this. United Charities made policy, and that was that. I like that. That's why private industry, and not government, interests me [as an alternative job]. It wouldn't be allowed in private industry—the politicking.

The other LAB supervisor summarized the views of senior Legal Aid staff.

> I guess there's an age difference on the attitudes toward the merger. I don't know what is going to happen, or how it will affect me, but I

> guess whoever is the executive director is the important thing. Now, the young people, some of the staff, have said the staff should have a veto over the executive director. The older people don't go along with that, let me tell you. This should be run like any other large organization. Like at GM you don't see the people on the assembly lines have a veto over the board of directors. My way of looking at it is, if you don't like a place, well you should just leave it, not try to change the structure from within it.

Merger hostilities undercut the professional identification with the local environment that had been the basis of Legal Aid careers. As the power of ex-CLC lawyers grew in the LAS, Legal Aid staff officials began to consider alternative jobs for the first time in their organizational careers. They specifically noted that, apart from the possibility of an undesirable outcome, the uncertainty in the process of the merger was itself demoralizing.

> Let them make the rear wall [of the downtown office] into a law reform unit. That's fine with me, as long as they leave us alone. I just wish they'd end the uncertainty. You keep hearing, x, y, or z will happen; and it doesn't; you don't know if it will; I just wish they'd close this office [the LAB intake] if they're going to.
>
> *Have offers or opportunities come up on occasion and you have given some thought to leaving?* No, you see I've always enjoyed working here. . . . I had the respect of the other people I was working with. . . . So I hadn't really thought about leaving until OEO came in. *Was it the administrative tasks that OEO brought to you that you didn't like?* No, I like that. It was that there were always so many changes. Things were different from what they had been. Maybe people needed a shake-up, but I don't know. *What differences are you referring to?* The changes all the time. Especially since this merger talk started, things are so unsettled. I don't know what they're going to do with the merger, but I just wish they'd go ahead and do it already.

In addition to the different career meanings of intraorganizational conflict to the two groups of lawyers, the Legal Services lawyers were in a more advantageous position for shaping the direction of collective change because of their lesser social distance from the board. In relations with board representatives of the poor, Legal Services lawyers enjoyed unique advantages. CLC appointed to the LAS Board representatives of public housing, welfare, and migrant groups whose organizations CLC lawyers had represented and in some cases formed. Other community representatives on the board spoke for organizations that neighborhood lawyers had been instrumental in creating. Legal Aid lawyers had not worked beyond the boundaries of LAB's intake, and they had not sponsored client representatives for board positions. When the LAS began meeting, the community representatives thus came with background understandings shaped by Legal Services lawyers.

In relations with lawyers on the board as well, the Legal Services staff was separated by a much smaller social distance than was the LAB's staff. For their appointments to the LAS Board, UCC Board lawyers selected not ex–LAB staff lawyers but their own peers, lawyers from business law firms. In contrast, Legal Services lawyers effected the appointment to the board of some private practitioners they knew from school and social life. Among the law firm partners appointed to the LAS Board by CLC were a tennis partner and two law school classmates of Howell. Other lawyers on the LAS Board were designees of law schools in which Legal Services lawyers had taught; an ex–Chicago Legal Services Reggie appointed by the Chicago Council of Lawyers (a local independent bar association several Legal Services lawyers had helped form and on whose board several served); members of civil rights and civil liberties organizations with whom Legal Services staff lawyers had cooperated on cases; and partners of law firms which had hired Legal Services staff lawyers and defended against their suits.

Most important, Legal Services lawyers had a distinctive affinity with business law firm lawyers through the professional stature of reform litigation. Alliances were often formed indirectly and naturally, without the necessity of personal lobbying. As I have tried to demonstrate, the social organization of the legal problems of the poor is such that participation in sophisticated legal work depends on participation in reform litigation. Legal Services lawyers could argue that to raise the professional quality of the institution's work to the maximum would require support for reform activities. By playing on the convergence of professional quality and reform significance, Legal Services lawyers repeatedly transformed politically controversial arguments over support for social change into politically neutral commitments to provide "high-quality" legal services to the poor. They pressed leaders of the private bar to support reform efforts that ran against the latter's own substantive preferences in order not to appear to be abandoning ethical commitments to equal justice. In the Chicago merger, Legal Services lawyers constantly exploited their distinctive opportunity, relative to Legal Aid, to couch policy interests in the values of professionalism.

Policy issues were effectively obscured by issues of professional quality in the selection of an executive director and in deliberations to reorganize the LAB. In considering candidates for executive director, client representatives deferred to the professional evaluations made by lawyers on the LAS Board. By finding candidates from large firms to be the most qualified professionally, board lawyers, as a group, including those with the most conservative reputations from UCC, implicitly preferred candidates who cited reform as the first priority.

As a practical matter, the merger added less than 10 lawyers from CLC to the 55 already in the 7-year-old UCC Legal Aid/Legal Services operation. But "merger" was symbolically, and therefore practically, a fundamental process of organizational change. It triggered, for the first time in Chicago, a formal consideration of the talents required for staff leadership. The merger would produce "the largest Legal Aid program in the country," the LAS Board's Search Committee for an Executive Director kept reminding itself (I sat in on its meetings). Attributes such as administrative skill and diplomacy were discussed, but professional standards were threshold considerations. The choice was clear among applications from CLC Director Howell, with his substantial experience as counsel to public utilities in trial and appellate litigation; Scott, the head of the UCC Legal Services Appellate Division, who had been a legal draftsman with Kirkland and Ellis; and a senior Legal Aid lawyer with 25 years of experience primarily in domestic-relations work. Taking the professional qualifications of the first two as a floor, the third application, from the ranks of the LAB, was dismissed without discussion. There was no need to reach the predictably thorny questions about conceptions of collective mission.

To solicit candidates for the executive director job, board lawyers drew up a list of large-firm lawyers who had personally represented the poor. Those on the list had practiced in civil liberties, civil rights, and other public-interest, class-action litigation, or in the criminal representation of controversial militants, usually through the ACLU or the Lawyer's Committee for Civil Rights. None had worked in Legal Aid. In Chicago, many lawyers from private firms had served individual poor clients at volunteer clinics, but those who had developed widespread reputations for interest in representing the poor had done so in significant reform litigation, not in individual divorce matters.

Legal Aid staff officials sensed the implicit bias in the selection process. When the United Charities appointees on the committee favored the candidacy of a partner from a large corporate law firm who was opposed by some of the Legal Services staff, Legal Aid's senior staff was not comforted.

They anticipated that, like other lawyers who had entered Legal Services from corporate law firms, this fellow would side with the reform litigators out of professional affinity, never develop a long-range identification with the organization, and "just stay long enough to shake things up."

The final blow to the Legal Aid staff came when the United Charities lawyer-appointees joined the rest of the LAS Board in approving a work program that implied a restructuring of the LAB. Under this plan resources would be shifted to reform by effectually replacing most of the LAB supervisory staff with paraprofessionals. An earlier attempt to strike this blow had failed. Months before, Howell, acting as the temporary executive director of the LAS, had announced policy grounds for curtailing the LAB intake operation and reducing resources in domestic-relations work. Heated controversy broke out. Howell then shifted to an argument that the work to be cut was so routine that lawyers were not needed to perform it. The director of the LAB argued in opposition that equal justice requires that lawyers, not paraprofessionals ("sublawyers"), represent the poor. Board lawyers brushed this aside, noting that paraprofessionals were increasingly being used in large firms to handle routine tasks.

The Legal Services staff now put into play a host of the strategic resources they had developed over several years. They had long since reached beyond UCC and the CBA to bring new critical audiences to Legal Aid. Legal Services staff supporters now reminded the LAS Board of a 1971 OEO evaluation of the overall Chicago program which had characterized the LAB's supervisory structure as superfluous. The career perspective of involvement had so infiltrated and weakened the LAB that a young staff lawyer whose desk at the LAB would have been cut in half under the proposed work program wrote to the board that the change would be desirable because at least half of his assigned work was insignificant and dispensable.

Historic tensions within Legal Aid between professional and charitable conceptions of institutional mission reappeared to undermine Legal Aid's integrity. Arthur Young, director of the LAB since the mid fifties, had looked forward to the development of the Legal Services Program. From his long perspective, the new federal effort was a way of implementing a more professional emphasis in the face of the social work forces in United Charities which, with such policies as restrictions on divorces, had compromised ethical requirements to provide a day in court regardless of moral views. Now Young, who had been displaced as staff director without any formal action when Howell was appointed temporary director of the LAS, wrote in support of the plan to dismantle the LAB hierarchy he had helped create.

Young was joined in his policy statement by Gary Palm, the young director of the UCC-supported Mandel Clinic at the University of Chicago Law School. Palm symbolized the change toward activism that had occurred at the clinic since the early sixties, when it had been directed by a long-term LAB staffer. Even the community representatives wanted to define the LAB's work as routine. Jobs might then be transferred to paraprofessionals, who could be hired from the community.

When the LAS Board recommended its plan for the LAB, the UCC staff mobilized their major strategic resource. Top UCC staff officials in the LAB and other departments in UCC petitioned UCC Board committees to refuse to delegate the administration of the LAB to the LAS Board. They argued that Howell, the LAS executive director, had shown his intention to dismantle the LAB intake operation, and even though the present plan did not explicitly go that far, the LAS Board had been unable to control him in the past. The "integrity" of the LAB—its distinctive organizational character—was said to be at stake; and it was. The senior Legal Aid staff embodied the UCC Legal Aid philosophy, and their internal careers were threatened. The special relationship between organizational character and members' careers in Legal Aid finally came into play. The Legal Aid staff successfully tapped the implicit commitment UCC had made to them over the course of their careers as they became increasingly committed to it.

The argument to preserve the independence of the LAB was carried by the United Charities executive director to the UCC LAC, whose members were largely the UCC lawyer-appointees to the LAS. There it lost. The next stage was the UCC Executive Committee, whose members were largely not lawyers and not appointees to the LAS. There it won. The final stage was the full UCC Board. There, according to top UCC staff and board lawyers, it became an internal controversy of "unprecedented" proportions. Members of the UCC Legal Aid and Executive Committees debated the issues, and the full board returned the matter to the executive committee for further consideration. Before the question was again put to the UCC Board, A. Gerald Erickson, the UCC executive director, acted decisively. UCC still had the only formal authority in Chicago to receive a Legal Services grant from OEO. The Chicago Legal Services staff could only be paid if UCC delegated the grant from OEO to the LAS. Erickson threatened to refuse to accept the Legal Services grant from OEO. The LAS Board was prepared to apply to OEO for direct funding, but a delay in funding carried great risks just then. The OEO director at the time was Howard Phillips, an arch-conservative who had been widely publicized as looking for opportunities to scuttle OEO programs. With an anxious eye to Washington, the LAS Board decided to maintain a low profile. It withdrew the proposal to administer the LAB in order to induce UCC to accept the OEO grant routinely.

The Legal Services staff soon returned the name "Legal Aid Society" to UCC and obtained direct funding from OEO. The Legal Aid and Legal Services programs completely "demerged." The Legal Services operation, now called the Legal Assistance Foundation (LAF) of Chicago, had won the struggle for institutional dominance and was prepared to press for more turf in the shared domain. Symbolic of the success of the Legal Services staff, the new president of the LAF Board was a corporate law firm partner who had been a United Charities appointee to the LAS. While United Charities had held the OEO grant, the LAS (i.e., the Legal Services staff) had been blocked from soliciting contributions from traditional supporters of UCC LAB. Now, as UCC Board lawyers had warned UCC, several LAS Board lawyers predicted that their firms would split their annual contributions between the LAB and the LAF. Now also, after UCC LAB had become convinced of the undesirability of its involvement in the federally funded program, and after LAF had obtained direct federal funding without competition, LAF planned an independent approach to the major contributors to LAB at the Community Fund, the bar association, and the large law firms.

Chapter 9

Legal Services in the Seventies: Instability and Reform within a Declining Social Movement

In several respects the history of organized civil legal assistance to the poor displays a cyclical pattern. An early shift from a social-reform orientation to an exclusive emphasis on individual service was reversed decades later. Over 60 years ago, the Chicago Legal Aid Society bridged a transition from the morally indignant legal assistance organizations of the nineteenth century to a passive Legal Aid society. In the early 1970s, the Chicago Legal Aid Society was resurrected from almost-forgotten historical files to play a transient role in the eclipse of Legal Aid's day-in-court philosophy by the anti-poverty orientation of the Legal Services program.

As the collective mission turned away from and then back to reform, the social ecology of legal assistance organizations reversed and then reversed again. The pioneering organizations of the late nineteenth century were created and motivated by widespread activism in the Progressive Movement. Legal Aid societies then operated as isolated symbols of an altruistic philosophy, having relatively little to do with each other, with the work of lawyers elsewhere in the profession, or with national political events affecting the status of the poor. When the Legal Services Program was founded, it was a small part of a general movement for social and racial justice and for broad-scale institutional reform. Major patterns in the internal social structure of legal assistance organizations also turned in one direction and then back again as the institution's mission moved from reform to service to reform. Reminiscent of the staffs of the nineteenth-century organizations, and in sharp contrast with Legal Aid's staff, Legal Services lawyers have been relatively close to the private lawyers on their boards in social origin, professional background and style, and at times in forums for litigation.

Did the institution take another of its cyclical turns in the seventies? Legal

Services programs became cut off from a broad-based, external movement for social change. Poverty lawyers no longer earned frequent political attacks on front pages and in editorials.[1] In the mid seventies, after national legislation had imposed new restrictions and transferred Legal Services from OEO into the new Legal Services Corporation, many analysts concluded that the Nixon administration had successfully gutted the institution's reform capacities.[2] From within the institution, Gary Bellow (1977), a widely respected voice first identified with controversial poverty law initiatives during his days at California Rural Legal Assistance, warned that lawyers for the poor were falling into unimaginative, "routine" practices.[3] Legal Services staff lawyers began to express a concern that the national Legal Services leadership was sacrificing quality goals (i.e., reform) to a campaign to increase the number of Legal Services lawyers ("Counsel to the Poor" 1980, p. 90). Toward the end of the era of the sixties, journalistic accounts portrayed Legal Services lawyers as wrestling with conflicts between their interests in professional self-development and their altruistic goals, without prospect of victory (Starr 1974, p. 31). Legal Services Corporation leaders indicated a similar perception as they announced a need to address a runaway problem of staff turnover (Legal Services Corporation 1977). To the general news-reading public, a wave of strikes by recently unionized Legal Services lawyers may have suggested a turning inward of the aggressive energies for economic justice that had been directed outward and on behalf of clients when Legal Services programs were formed.

In fact, Legal Services programs did not revert to the characteristics of Legal Aid with the passing of the sixties. Neither did they persist without changing fundamentally. In internal social structure, Legal Services programs remained weak organizations. Internal hierarchies did not acquire the strength often thought typical of the organizational aging process. The anarchic tendency present in Legal Services programs from their start was represented in the sixties by struggles against the top for individual autonomy over case control. Internal conflict persisted and led to a mushrooming of staff strikes in the seventies, reflecting a new instability in internal structure that developed with the loosening of anchoring ties to external constituencies as the movements of the sixties declined.

The institutional strength exhibited by Legal Services programs in the sixties—their ability to expand the collective domain by acquiring resources and by enlarging official definitions of the rights of the poor—also grew in the seventies. While political attacks against Legal Services programs faded,[4] the types of litigation that had previously brought politicians to the attack, such as class-action suits against local and state government units, became much more widespread and continuous. Over the decade, poverty reform litigation grew into a more predictable and more sophisticated professional activity. By the time the national elections of 1980 had produced a presidential administration bent on eliminating federal funding for poor people's lawyers, Legal Services programs had proven that their impetus toward reform was self-sustaining and autonomous—clearly capable of surviving the demise of the social movements of the sixties, if not the suddenly powerful conservative politics of the early eighties.

I review first the trend toward internal instability, next the substantial progress made in the seventies toward institutionalizing an impetus toward reform. Then one more issue remains. As poverty law reform strategies matured from their origins in the antipoverty programs of the sixties, they changed in meaning to become a means of legalizing poverty. The dilemma posed for legal activists by the transformation of poverty reform litigation is the subject of the last chapter.

The Outlines of LAB and LAF in 1980

I left field research on the Legal Aid and Legal Services programs in Chicago in 1974, shortly after the merger between the two had ended and the Legal Services staff had formed the LAF to receive the federal grant. The following analysis of subsequent developments is based primarily on informal, irregular interviews with senior LAF lawyers and on organizational documents and publications of LAF and of United Charities.

After making some minor accommodations, LAF and the United Charities LAB agreed tacitly to operate without threatening each other's independence. The most important line of interaction developed on domestic-relations and bankruptcy work. LAF, expelling what its staff considered "shit work," referred many clients with bankruptcy, personal-injury, and family disputes to the LAB. The LAB referred requests for uncontested divorces to an LAF "mill," a unit which, with two lawyers, dissolved 1500 marriages in 1979. Operated by an ex-LAB lawyer, LAF's uncontested divorce unit enabled LAB to sidestep what had long been a bothersome problem: How could United Charities, which for most of this century has held itself out as a family-service agency, justify a machinelike practice of breaking up marriages? How could its lawyers, as professionals bound by an ethic of moral impartiality, defer to a moral prejudice against divorce?

LAB's internal structure survived a conflict-ridden, seven-year experience of running Chicago's major Legal Services program. Three of the four lawyers in staff-leadership positions in 1980 were continuing LAB careers dating from the 1950s. The LAB remained primarily an individual-service operation, although two lawyers (who entered the Economic Division almost 10 years ago, after previously building a close relationship while working in a Legal Services neighborhood office) continued to produce occasionally noteworthy consumer law reform decisions.

LAB's fiscal health weakened in the seventies. A low rate of turnover (in 1980 half the staff had at least 10 years' legal assistance experience) built up budgetary pressure of the sort that led to the creation in the mid 1950s of a staff formally split between permanent and rotating lawyers. In reports to the public, LAB made no effort to define a competence that might distinguish it from LAF and thereby open up novel sources of income. The organization did not keep income even with inflation. From 1972 to 1980, total income rose only from $850,000 to $1 million, well below the inflation rate. During this period, the downtown staff was reduced from about 18 to 16. In fiscal 1979, United Charities was forced to increase its own contributions to the LAB by 50 percent over the 1978 level in order to make up a $100,000 (10 percent) decline in the LAB's annual outside income, a decline caused primarily by a sharp reduction in contributions from the private bar.

The internal social structure of LAB in 1980 did not appear to be well equipped to innovate toward a more prosperous future. Its staff was almost consumed by the attempt to seize the unanticipated opportunity for expansion presented by OEO in the 1960s. One abiding consequence was a freezing of the staff hierarchy for decades, as senior LAB members were promoted in administrative expansions made to govern the Legal Services program. As a result, Legal Aid retained its traditional organizational strength, the ability to fashion a smoothly integrated, stable internal division of labor. But organizational strength remained a counterpoint—to a degree a cause—of institutional weakness.

Conversely, the Legal Services staff, housed in the LAF, continued to expand its collective resources and mission despite the emergence of a new wave of conflicts over internal organization. There have been several lines of development in resources and in priorities. In funding, the Chicago LAF grew dramatically in the 1970s, as did financing for the Legal Services program nationally. In its last year under OEO, the Legal Services program received $100 million from Congress. For 1980, the appropriation for the Legal Services Corporation was $300 million. In Chicago, the 1972 Legal Services grant was about $1.5 million; in 1979, the LAF had a budget of about $3.8 million. During this period, the size of the attorney staff increased from about 55 to about 90 (exclusive of Reggies and Vista lawyers).

Organizational growth meant expansion at the perimeter where staff meets new clients, but even more it meant the elaboration of layers behind the front lines, a building up of the center somewhat more than the periphery. The size of the neighborhood staff almost doubled. The average number of staff lawyers in the 1980 neighborhood offices was between seven and eight, as opposed to between three and four in 1971. But there were seven neighborhood offices in 1980 rather than the eight that existed in 1971. (In response to steady population decline, the Woodlawn office was closed in 1973.) Meanwhile the downtown legal staff more than tripled, from about 10 to about 30. In 1971, a new neighborhood lawyer looking above himself in the Legal Services program hierarchy would see, in his own office, a supervisor, and in the downtown office, an overall program director and a handful of subject-matter specialists available for consultation. In 1980, the novice neighborhood staff lawyer saw, in the neighborhood office, a supervisor and perhaps a senior lawyer who had been relieved of intake responsibilities; and in the downtown office or in specialized offices elsewhere, he saw a director, two deputy directors, five subject-matter "team" leaders (health, welfare, employment, consumer, housing) with their staffs, and several "projects" (elderly, handicapped, food, juveniles, prisoners, women's, immigration, migrants), each with a supervisor and staff.

Numerical expansion brought qualitative change to the social organization of LAF. The proliferation of teams and projects made the staff much more specialized than it was in the early seventies, with a consequent increase in the demand for administrative integration to coordinate the formally divided sections. Each team and project had its own specialized staff, but each also was capable of drawing staff and cases from the neighborhood offices. On formal and informal levels, there was a great increase in resources allocated to the direction, integration, and administration of staff work.

Reflecting this trend, the position of the neighborhood office supervisor was fundamentally transformed. In 1970, neighborhood supervisors were primarily expected to be professional leaders. Litigation experience was the dominant criterion used in hiring them. The offices most highly regarded by the downtown leadership, Uptown and East Garfield, were led by supervisors who took aggressive initiatives in client representation. In 1980, the neighborhood supervisor was expected to play much more of an administrative role. With a legal staff of about 10 (including Reggies and Vistas), he or she had two to three times as large a staff to administer as in 1970, an expansion which entailed a geometric increase in potential personality conflicts. The program of proliferating team and project units with specialized litigation responsibilities resulted in additional, external sources of professional leadership for neighborhood staff lawyers. Neighborhood supervisors assumed the burden of administering fluctuations in the availability of staff for intake responsibilities stemming from irregular working alliances established on particular reform cases between staff lawyers and team or project leaders.

LAF's leaders exported routine administrative work to the field offices and imported professional talent and policy-making responsibility downtown. Administrative matters such as office space allocation and furniture acquisition, which in 1970 under the leadership of United Charities Legal Aid were central concerns of the downtown leader of the neighborhood offices, became the joint responsibility of neighborhood supervisors and a nonlawyer administrative officer located downtown. The deputy directors and the special litigation leaders, most of whom were located downtown, had as their main concern final responsibility for the program's voluminous federal court class-action and state appellate litigation. "Significant" reform litigation clearly became the organization's highest priority, well above community group representation and individual client service, the values to which the neighborhood offices were originally dedicated.

As LAF proliferated downtown layers, it also built organizational buffers between neighborhood lawyers and the local social environment. No longer were neighborhood lawyers confronted by the unmediated client demands which recurrently reached crisis levels in the sixties, precipitating sudden turnovers and threatening administrative chaos. When Legal Services first established neighborhood offices in Chicago, staffs of two to four lawyers struggled to serve a stream of walk-in clients, with no more than literally transparent glass partitions marking their distance from overflowing waiting rooms and with virtually no expert assistance from downtown. In the mid 1970s, almost all of the neighborhood offices went on appointment systems to manage the inflow of clients. Lines of specialization were drawn. Commitments to spend time on pieces of major litigation were encouraged, further removing neighborhood lawyers from the front lines. Working alongside 8 to 10 colleagues instead of 2 to 3, the neighborhood lawyer found more readily at hand an everyday culture within which to redefine and resist the pressures of the local environment.

Organizational Development: Internal Conflict and External Anchors

Both in the changed relationship between LAF's downtown and neighborhood offices, and in the changes within the neighborhood offices, there were signs of an increasingly hierarchical, formal, centralized control. They suggest a classical pattern in organizational history: the empowerment of a rigid oligarchy after it has overcome a period of initial uncertainty about the collectivity's ability to survive. Internal flexibility and democracy have often been found to perish in the organizational aging process. Organizations originally distinctive for commitments to diverse, locally responsive grassroots operations are likely gradually to coordinate and subordinate field personnel into a centralized hierarchy.[5]

LAF's staff leaders in the seventies—its executive director and the two deputy directors—had reasons to try to turn their organization toward the classic pattern. They were intimately familiar with the anarchic sixties in Legal Services programs—the organizational weaknesses represented by high staff turnover and by the constant pressure from staff lawyers for independence from superordinate control. LAF did in fact engage in an elaborate program of organization building in the seventies that could be expected to cure these weaknesses.

Yet instead of terminating the weakness of internal authority in the sixties, the organization building of the seventies served only to dramatize its continuity. While the staff specializing in reform litigation became ever more experienced and sophisticated (in 1980, LAF had perhaps unparalleled in-house experience in its senior litigating staff),[6] the neighborhood-office staff below the supervisory level remained relatively inexperienced. The 1980 neighborhood staff had about the same median tenure as did the 1973 staff: two years.[7] From 1975 to 1980, an average of about one-quarter of the neighborhood staff left each year.[8] This is about the same rate as obtained in Legal Services nationally, a rate considered pathological throughout the institution (Legal Services Corporation 1977). As had been the case in neighborhood offices before, personality conflicts continued to become so intense at times as to precipitate wholesale office turnovers. In the Legal Services neighborhood offices of the late seventies, one could find discontinuities in the interrelation of staff careers similar to those observed in the sixties (see chapter 7).

An equally emphatic sign that the internal order in the seventies was not smoothly integrated from the center was the advent of staff strikes. Chicago barely missed a strike when a contract was signed with a new union in late

1979, after a strike vote had been taken. The Boston and the major New York City Legal Services programs went on strike in 1979—New York for the third time—and with a unionization movement sweeping LSPs nationally, more staff strikes were expected. The advent of unionization and employee strikes has no single meaning across institutions for the integrity of a strong authority system. Nonetheless, in the history of Legal Services, the strikes of the late seventies gave the public glimpses of anarchic, conflict-prone, individualistic tendencies that had been characteristic of Legal Services since its start. At virtually any time in the late seventies, one could scan the country and find at least one major Legal Services program embroiled in personality conflicts within neighborhood offices or in a staff revolt against the professional executive leadership.

When staff turmoil did not take the form of strikes, it generally escaped public notice. Within the Legal Services community, there was an understandable embarrassment about the phenomenon which evidently kept reports of internal turmoil out of the institution's trade journals.[9] Large LSPs in the Northeast led the pattern. In late 1979, staff organizations challenged the centralized program authority structure in Philadelphia as well as in Boston and New York. In Connecticut during the late seventies, a staff revolt led to the ouster of the director of the New Haven program, and dissension in the statewide Connecticut Legal Services program spurred the resignation of its director. On the West Coast, staff lawyers rebelled successfully against their leaders primarily in the smaller programs such as in Berkeley and Contra Costa County. In the Los Angeles area, tensions in internal hierarchies provoked turnover at the top of two "back-up" centers, the National Health Law Center and the Western Center on Law and Poverty.

The chaos stimulated by the early stages of the unionization movement may well have been a temporary effect. More clearly, the overall historical movement in the seventies was toward staff-lawyer autonomy from any form of centrally imposed, hierarchical authority. Centralization of power was often denounced as "elitism." Staff revolts were typically led by neighborhood lawyers against downtown leaders and their supervisory associates. Material benefits were at issue in New York, Boston, and Chicago; significantly, substantive program priorities were not. Even in Chicago, where the issue of program priorities might have been raised in an extreme form, the complaint was not that reform litigation was being subsidized to the detriment of neighborhood or individual service. Instead, the issues about the exercise of authority were over its form. The complaints were typically phrased as due-process objections against uncontrolled discretion and the arbitrary exercise of power—just the sort of due-process grievances Legal Services lawyers had often brought against their clients' adversaries. The Chicago staff organization wanted to abolish merit increases and to block the creation of a position of senior attorney, arguing that these benefits seemed inherently beyond the governance of prescribed, impersonal criteria. They also pressed for a policy giving attorneys rights of approval over evaluations. Staff revolts have thus expressed a deep distrust of arbitrary, central executive leadership without necessarily expressing any criticism of the leaders' professional quality or substantive institutional philosophy.

The customary internal explanation for staff dissension within Legal Services, an explanation provided both from above and below in the staff hierarchy, refers to personality factors and to self-selection in the staffing process. Lawyers come to Legal Services instead of to more prestigious and remunerative private firms because, in addition to political sympathies, they dislike working in hierarchical organizations. A few seek a collectively or communally run work environment; but far more generally, the explanation goes, Legal Services lawyers could not or would not work in any strong authority system. They are people who have always had trouble "accepting authority."

Taking a comparative perspective, personality variables seem to be overshadowed by structural organizational factors. Compared with many young lawyers in other public agencies, Legal Services lawyers do not appear unusually disposed to criticize the constellation of power in their organizations. As noted in chapter 4, research findings in Chicago and in a national sample ran against the common belief that Legal Services lawyers significantly differ in philosophy from the young bar as a whole. I have interviewed assistant U.S. attorneys in large offices on both coasts and have found them quick to demean their chiefs' pretensions to professional superiority and the personal and political values that distribute and shape the exercise of power in their offices (Katz 1980; see also Weaver 1977, p. 53). Yet there is virtually no experience of revolts by young staff in U.S. attorneys' offices. In large governmental and private law offices, junior staffs must occasionally share a deep disrespect for the internal hierarchy. I suggest that they are deterred from revolt less by conformist dispositions than by structural barriers.

Specifically, the current structure of LSPs contrasts with similarly large public and private law offices in the extent to which the internal authority system is anchored by its ties to external constituencies. Assistant U.S. attorneys do not mobilize critical views of superiors into revolts because it would be pointless; they cannot reach the political powers that appoint the U.S. attorney. Securities and Exchange Commission enforcement-staff lawyers limited their challenge to Director Stanley Sporkin to anonymous cooperation in the writing of critical news stories ("Why the SEC's Enforcer" 1976) because, as recent law graduates, they have no accumulated influence over the commission of established securities lawyers that appoints their chief. Young corporate lawyers have reasons to swallow their feelings of injustice against senior partners because they know who has the clients. Legal Services lawyers began to go into public revolt against their program leaders in the seventies, even though they apparently did not differ in personality from the staffs of the sixties, because, over the decade, the internal authority system was progressively cut off from the external forces that had anchored it in earlier years.

In Chicago, there were movements toward staff revolt against executive leadership almost from the start (see chapter 8); but as in many other programs during the sixties, the local political environment was a strong restraining influence. To the extent that the staff did mobilize, it was to push their leaders toward freedom from *external* policies and power. The struggle against Mayor Daley's control of Legal Services in Chicago had to take priority over a battle against the internal executive leadership.

Shortly after independence from the Democratic machine had been secured, some of Chicago's poverty lawyers began talking about unionization. A CLC lawyer actually set up an organizing meeting, but it was poorly attended. The staff at that time had another prior concern, achieving independence from United Charities Legal Aid. Again, it made little sense to unite in opposition to the program's executive leadership before challenging the external constituency that controlled the selection of that leadership.

The eight-year process of winning independence for Chicago Legal Services lawyers, which culminated with the establishment of the LAF in late 1973, was followed a few months later by the creation of the national Legal Services Corporation, which itself symbolized a national victory for LSPs in surviving the Nixon administration and obtaining independence from partisan political influence. As local program staffs began to realize their new capacity to influence the internal authority structure free from external political influence, they also watched a doubling and then a tripling of the congressional appropriation for Legal Services. Within three or four years, the earlier paranoia about bare survival had been dispelled, and staff revolts had mushroomed.

The national Legal Services leadership also contributed to internal battles over authority by abandoning its role of influencing substantive policy and top staffing. In the sixties, the Office of Legal Services was a significant force in shaping priorities and the distribution of power in the Chicago program. From the start, when Clinton Bamberger, then OEO Office of Legal Services director, pushed United Charities to develop its Appellate and Test Case Division, through the merger in the early seventies, when national and regional Legal Services officials gave substance to CLC's vaporous bargaining position, the national office had promoted a priority on reform litigation—a role it had been playing across the country (Johnson 1974, pp. 163–184). The role did not survive the sixties. The first president of the new Legal Services Corporation, Stanford Law Dean Thomas Ehrlich, fashioned a wholly nonideological administration which steered clear of philosophic disputes over priorities and intervention in turbulent local programs. He focused on increasing the congressional appropriation, carrying as his banner a quantitative, minimum-access resource goal: one Legal Services lawyer for each 10,000 poor people.

At the local level, the LAF experienced an overall reversal in the direction of influence between its staff and the organization's external constituencies. In the break from control by United Charities, the role of community representatives on the board had been crucial. But the decline of the sixties social movements eroded client or community representative power on the board. The Chicago Welfare Rights Organizations, which informally won a permanent seat on the LAF Board, stopped functioning in the early seventies as a service organization with a mass base. With the dismantling of OEO, the federal government stopped providing the subsidies that once drew aggressive members of poor communities to seek careers as generalist representatives of the poor. LAF Board meetings were no longer invaded by militant spokespeople for poor communities.

The lawyer-directors on the board also came more under staff influence. The power of the CBA over the early boards of Chicago LSPs was reduced to token representation, and of course the United Charities influence was eliminated entirely. Replacements were largely corporate law firm lawyers who served as concerned individuals, not as representatives of organized interests; others came from a handful of public-interest and human rights groups. To the extent the board was not predisposed to defer to the staff leadership, its fragmented character made it less likely than the boards of the sixties to mobilize an independent voice.

Finally, staff lawyers were no longer tied, as they once were, to independent, prior socializing forces. In the sixties, the staff brought in personal experiences in war resistance, southern civil rights protests, Catholic social activism, urban community organizing, and a number of other sixties forms of involvement that disappeared or faded in the seventies. Legal Services itself indirectly became the provider of a significant measure of prior socialization for its recruits. Law school clinics became the major recruiting agents; and over the seventies, clinics at almost all major law schools came to be staffed by ex–Legal Services lawyers. The expectations about proper organizational direction which new Legal Services lawyers brought with them thus came to be shaped within the Legal Services community itself.

In the seventies, Legal Services staffs became increasingly autonomous, free to set their own priorities, as well as autochthonous, capable of producing leaders from their own ranks. The second Legal Services Corporation president and successor to Ehrlich, Dan Bradley, came with a background as a Legal Services lawyer and administrator.[10] Sheldon Roodman, the second staff head of LAF, was promoted in 1976 from within Legal Services, as were his two deputy directors.

In short, over the decade in local programs a series of constraints from external constituencies were weakened, with the result that the internal authority system became less anchored, less restrained externally against disruptive pressures arising from within. The staff demands which emerged were certainly not new in kind—readers may recall the petition by Chicago neighborhood lawyers in 1970 for democratic decision making. The emergent factor appears to have been a structural opportunity to exert pressure from below.

Despite formal indicia of increased centralization and stabilization of authority, LSPs did not become smoothly integrated organizations. The trend was in the opposite direction, toward an organizational form in which neighborhood lawyers have equal citizen rights with superiors, are free from unpredictable sanction from above, and negotiate constantly over their practical work responsibilities—which team or special project to participate in, for how long, with what reduction in home-office case load. A familiar picture of the aging of a grass-roots organization shows a conservative hierarchy emerging as the central leadership, through commitments it makes to powerful external constituencies, and then restraining the adaptive flexibility of field units. LSPs have undergone the opposite evolution, pulling up ties to their original constituencies in the sixties, ties which initially anchored internal authority systems so that they were relatively little swayed by waves of staff discontent.

Institutional Development

The advance of U.S. government commitments toward equal justice has flowed, not steadily from the implications of a generally embraced political ideology or jurisprudence, but sporadically, out of contexts of societal crisis. In the case of civil legal assistance for the poor, the Legal Services Program was established as part of the Office of Economic Opportunity, which was part of a national Great Society program, which was central to the domestic conflicts of the sixties. The 1970s produced another example on the criminal law side: the surge of law enforcement against white-collar crime during the series of scandals known as Watergate. If expansions of public organizational commitments to equal justice seem generally to require a push from broader political forces in order to start off, the history of civil legal assistance to the poor suggests that such new organizational commitments soon acquire an internal impetus to persist after the originating context of crisis has faded.[11]

The Chicago program illustrates several ways in which the drive toward an institutional expansion of Legal Services's mission survived the sixties. First, Chicago's LAF expanded by tapping income streams off of emergent currents in popular moral concern. In the mid seventies, when national attention turned for a time to the problem of hunger on a national and international scale, LAF initiated the Food Law Project. Later, a sudden turn of mass-media attention to wife and child abuse enabled the organization to form a special project for battered women. As national sensitivity to the problems of the handicapped grew in the seventies, the LAF found funds to institute the Developmental Disabilities Project.

Another sign of continuing institutional strength—a persistent ability to expand collective resources—appeared in the subsequent activities of existing staff. As noted earlier, there was very little turnover in the reform litigation positions. Because replacements in slots for reform were often made from within Legal Services, the reform capacity suffered even less loss of experience. In the neighborhood offices, turnover continued in the seventies at a rate similar to that of the sixties. From 1975 through 1979, figuring an average of 40 positions in each of the five years, 37 percent of neighborhood staff lawyers turned over every two years.[12] But also like the staffs of 1966 through 1973, a high rate of those leaving continued to remain within the institution. Of the 67 lawyers who left LAF from any position from 1974 to mid 1980, less than 25 percent went into private practice.[13]

Almost 50 percent stayed "within the institution," using a conservative definition of the phrase, that is, going to other LSPs (one to direct the Vermont, another the Minnesota, Legal Services program), to public-interest firms, or to government agencies historically related to Legal Services in the general legal rights movement of the sixties. If the definition is expanded to include "teaching" and "government jobs," categories used in LAF's records, about 70 percent of those leaving remained within the institution. The turnover pattern indicates a continuation of organizational weakness in smooth succession and efficient exploitation of training but growing institutional strength through the increasing retention of personnel resources to benefit the clientele.

Recruitment patterns indicate that the organization also continued to develop its institutional capacity in staff career perspective. Chicago's Legal Services program continued to be demographically diverse. New recruits continued to feature social identities such as "male WASP" and backgrounds such as corporate law firm that were not represented on the 1950s Legal Aid staffs. Elite law schools which virtually never supplied lawyers to Legal Aid, such as the University of Chicago, Yale, and Harvard, were represented at a much higher level (about 35 percent[14]) in 1980 than they were in 1969 (about 15 percent). There was a corresponding drop in hiring from local proprietary and Catholic law schools, schools which had provided the bulk of Legal Aid's modern staffs. Apparently, lawyers were not coming to Legal Services in Chicago primarily with a view of the job as the best available to them for money and prestige. These staffing trends indicate an increase over the decade in the internal pressure to experience "professional growth" through involvement in significant reform litigation.

As noted previously, LAF in the seventies tripled the staff occupying specialized reform litigation positions. The form used to structure this expansion had an unanticipated consequence for institutionalizing the organization's commitment to reform. Instead of constructing a single, large litigation hierarchy containing 25 to 30 lawyers, the special litigation staff was expanded through the proliferation of parallel units, each with a supervisory lawyer and a staff of from one to six attorneys. When the drive for unionization developed, a group of some 20 neighborhood and downtown supervisory lawyers was separated out from the staff's bargaining unit. Staff lawyers in the special projects were lumped in the bargaining unit with neighborhood staff lawyers and thus arrayed against superiors with whom they had worked closely on reform litigation. Organizational structure therefore deterred a shaping of the unionization conflict of the seventies into the form common in LSPs in the sixties: a struggle between proponents of individual service and proponents of reform litigation.

In 1974, LAF emerged out of the struggle for dominance with Legal Aid bent on implementing a clear priority on reform litigation, an impetus maintained throughout the seventies. The organization's formal priorities placed forms of impact litigation unambiguously at the top of the list; individual service did not appear until the fourth priority. Several policies attempted to streamline the organization's individual-service case load into a flow of potential impact suits. LAF removed neighborhood staff lawyers from a large number of cases that previously had pitched them into battles between poor people. "Plaintiff-evictions" (representing the landlord in an eviction action), which had presented recurrent moral dilemmas to antipoverty lawyers in the sixties, were declined as a matter of formal policy. Domestic-relations matters other than uncontested divorces were often referred to the LAB. Specialized downtown operations stripped from the neighborhood offices masses of cases that had distracted staff from social-class issues in the sixties: uncontested divorces and personal-injury property-damage suits ("fender-benders") requiring defense.[15]

Finally, LAF's actual conduct of reform litigation developed dramatically in quantity and quality after the sixties. In the seventies, Chicago's Legal Service program became one of the most, perhaps the most, productive and sophisticated reform litigation units in Legal Services. I only note LAF cases here, but that the Chicago experience of progress in reform litigation was part of a national pattern can be verified by a comparative glance over the pages of early and recent issues of the *Clearinghouse Review,* a Legal Services–funded journal that has published summaries of significant poverty litigation since the late sixties.

In an annual "Docket," Chicago's LAF published summaries of federal litigation, appeals, and state court class actions in order to advertise itself within the general legal rights community. The 1978 year-end "Docket" ran 73 pages. In the 1972 "Work Program" jointly submitted to Legal Services headquarters by CLC and the United Charities Legal Services operation, 27 pages were used to describe law reform activity. More telling than this gross quantitative increase were the novel lines of qualitative growth in the organization's adversarial stature.

One sign of increased adversarial sophistication was a rise in the status of entities made defendants. Employment-discrimination actions (which were not mentioned at all in the 1972 review by Chicago's Legal Service leaders of their significant litigation) were brought in the late seventies on behalf of thousands of potential beneficiaries against the Rock Island Railroad (for discrimination against ex-offender CETA applicants), Allied Van Lines (for excluding blacks from Allied's main office), Rush-Presbyterian St. Luke's Medical Center (for discrimination against Latinos as applicants and in all phases on the job), and the Chicago Transit Authority (for discrimination against Latinos as applicants and on the job). Class-action suits began to reach beyond local retail sources of debtor grievances to giant financial backers. Although a number of notorious auto dealers remained opponents of poverty lawyers in debt-collection actions, consumer-credit suits also reached General Motors Acceptance Corporation and Ford Motor Credit. Demands for payment by local hospitals had always been everyday sources of new Legal Services cases, but a new line of attack was developed to challenge a strong contributing force in the background: refusals by Blue Cross to cover hospitalization costs on assertions that a "medically necessary" standard was not met.

The Illinois Department of Public Aid (IDPA), in its administrative roles in the cash-benefit, food stamp, and Medicaid programs, became a constant defendant of Chicago poverty law suits in the seventies. The range of institutional defendants expanded in various directions beyond this central target. A litigation unit which in the sixties focused on judicial and residential treatment of juveniles in the criminal law system turned in the seventies to the treatment of adult prisoners by the Illinois Department of Corrections. Legal Services prison suits began to challenge the adequacy of medical care and the placement of inmates in segregation. The immigration division of the U.S. Justice Department also became a new institutional target for reform by LAF. One case sought to increase immigration by tens of thousands by declaring illegal a policy begun in 1968 that unnecessarily used up part of the quota for immigration from the Western Hemisphere to admit Cuban refugees.[16] Another suit attempted to produce about 9000 visas for Mexicans by challenging the dates used by the Department of State in counting visas toward a statutory quota.[17] The exercise of power in Chicago's public schools, an area virtually untouched by Legal Services suits in the sixties, came under a series of attacks: against the imposition of fees on students; against the refusal of state scholarships to refugees; against the assignment of Latino and black children to classes for the mentally handicapped on the basis of IQ tests. Unions, attacked only weakly and rarely in individual cases of pension denial in the sixties, became defendants in Legal Services suits to compel effective representation and to structure fair elections for dissident challenges to union leadership.

In addition to expansions in types of institutional defendants, reform litigation reached previously sacrosanct domains of defendants' powers. A case against the secretary of HUD[18] indicates the atmosphere of innovative, aggressive lawyering that came to characterize Chicago's reform litigation. The attempt was not only to direct the administrative policies of HUD at the highest level but to impose restraints on the ability of this public social welfare agency to act in the legislative arena. In an earlier legal action that had ramifications across the country, Chicago Legal Services lawyers had won a judicial order compelling HUD to implement a program to rescue low-income homeowners from mortgage foreclosure. In mid 1980, HUD Secretary Moon Landrieu faced contempt charges for failing to implement the program administratively and then attempting to get Congress to repeal the mandating legislation.[19]

Other indications of expanded reform litigation capacity appeared on the plaintiff side. Class-action suits, brought in the sixties and early seventies on behalf of poor people throughout Illinois, were used in the seventies to represent poor people in region-wide and nationwide classes. Million-dollar monetary recoveries for class plaintiffs, an exceptional event in the sixties, were reported with regularity. LAF won a Supreme Court decision invalidating a lower level of public assistance payments to nonrelatives, as opposed to relatives, acting as caretakers in the foster care program. LAF reported that there would be about 1500 immediate beneficiaries in Illinois, receiving in the aggregate about $1 million in additional annual benefits. A dozen other states were also affected. The *Los Angeles Times* quoted a state public assistance official for an estimate that the cost would be $30 million a year in California (Mann 1979). LAF reported that it won a judicial order restoring about $2 million in back payments to eligible households in the food stamp program, benefits that had been lost when the IDPA changed its method of calculating them.[20] In the health area, LAF won, for a class of about 40,000 participants in the Illinois Medicaid program, a judgment that raised the income eligibility standard and increased annual benefits by an estimated $10 million a year.[21]

In another line of institutional development, LAF expanded its capacity to effect reform through litigation by acting as what might be termed a metaplaintiff. Starting in the mid 1970s, the organization brought a series of suits to activate the powers of other agencies to take legal action against adversaries of the poor. One suit attempted to speed the processing of employment-discrimination complaints at the Chicago-area office of the Equal Employment Opportunity Commission (EEOC).[22] The local EEOC allegedly was holding up complainants as long as four years before beginning to investigate their charges. The Fair Employment Practices Commission was sued to compel administrative action on more than 300 backlogged employment-discrimination complaints which had been placed on "indefinite suspension."[23] A petition pressured the Illinois Department of Insurance to enforce statutory maximums on rates for credit life and disability insurance.[24] In an effort to block an agency enforcement action against the poor, the state's attorney was sued for sending threatening letters to compel civil settlements of debt claims at the behest of alleged creditors.[25]

In addition to the increased size and status of defendants and plaintiffs, LAF increased its capacity for reform by entering forums of greater jurisdictional competence. Institutional defendants such as the Illinois Department of Unemployment Insurance, who were occasionally sued in state courts in the sixties, were instead pulled into federal court in the seventies. The organization developed an ongoing Supreme Court case load, and Supreme Court decisions in LAF cases began to appear in law school textbooks.[26] Administrative petitions, which can act as omnibus vehicles for the airing before a federal administrative agency (HEW or HUD, for example) of a complex of grievances against a subordinate state bureaucracy [e.g., IDPA or the Chicago (Public) Housing Authority], grew from tentative drafts in the early seventies into a viable alternative to narrowly focused federal cases against the state agency. An administrative complaint brought before HEW alleged 63 separate violations by Illinois of federal Medicaid law,[27] including failures: to help mentally disabled persons apply; to deduct child-care expenses in determining income for eligibility; to pay after recipients win administrative judgments granting retroactive benefits; and to place recipients on advisory committees.

The development of awards of attorneys fees in significant Legal Services cases stands as a dramatic symbol of the progress made in the late seventies toward institutionalizing a commitment to reform. LAF's lawyers began regularly to win sizeable orders from federal judges requiring defendants in successfully prosecuted reform suits to compensate LAF for its costs in salary expenditures. According to an estimate made by LAF's executive director, defendants in 1979 (primarily IDPA) were ordered to pay LAF about $200,000 in attorneys' fees.

The Professionalization of Reform

In short, Legal Services expanded its institutional competence in the seventies, enlarging its capacity to advance the rights of the poor and developing self-perpetuating forces to support the process of expansion itself. The collective commitment to reform in Legal Services not only survived the dissolution of the social movements of the sixties; in several ways, the commitment was significantly increased. That the Legal Services program, virtually alone among the original components of the OEO's War on Poverty, survived, even thrived in the seventies, was due largely to its unique ties to the legal profession.

Powerful segments of the bar provided political support for the reform emphasis at crucial junctures, often reversing traditionally conservative stands when approached strategically by Legal Services lawyers, as in the Chicago example in chapter 8: corporate law firm lawyers appointed by United Charities were moved to vote for the subordination of the UCC LAB under an administration headed by Legal Services lawyers who voiced unambiguous preferences for reform litigation over individual service.

Chapter 5 showed how, in the sixties, the general movement toward activism established the political conditions for the founding of the Legal Services Program and induced lawyers to enter Legal Services with expectations unprecedented in Legal Aid; but then the overall activist movement hindered as much as promoted reform action in Legal Services. Specifically in chapter 7, as well as generally throughout the book, I have argued that the impetus toward reform as carried by the individual attorney has always been independent of distinctive moral or political outlooks. For lawyers doing the work of representing the poor in civil matters, the persistence of a sense of progressively valuable experience, often termed "professional growth," depends on involvement in reform litigation.

Themes of professionalism have sustained the impetus toward reform, but in the process they may have obscured a transformation of its meaning. As poor people's lawyers faced the 1980s, they had reason to question the social function of their efforts to reform the structure of poverty.

Chapter 10

Legalizing Poverty

As the sixties declined, "reform" in Legal Services increasingly meant litigation. With the disappearance of OEO's "community action" policy, the representation of community groups lost a major stimulus. Organizations of the poor often made headlines briefly and then disbanded. As Handler (1978, pp. 161–162) has noted in the context of welfare rights, reform litigation by Legal Services lawyers actually achieved its greatest success after the dissolution of welfare recipients' organizations. At the same time, poverty lawyers with a mandate to represent community groups turned, seemingly ineluctably, toward the attractions of downtown offices and reform litigation. This process was unusually clear in Chicago, as seen in the collective career of CLC, the organization in which LAF's director and deputy directors had previously worked.

Reform in Legal Services came to mean the conventional, professionally structured activity of litigation. Not only did community organizing and the personal representation of controversial radicals fade; LSPs other than the specialized "back-up" centers rarely played a role even in lobbying.

In the late seventies, reform activity in Legal Services was treated officially as a professional, apolitical matter. Within the administration of Legal Services, antipoverty rhetoric passed from being an officially sanctioned routine (LSPs originally had to report annually to the OEO Office of Legal Services on the year's progress in reducing poverty) to being an embarrassment, to being but a dimming memory. Ever since its creation in 1974, the Legal Services Corporation has steered clear of indignant commentary on the social reality of poverty in the United States. The research projects funded by the corporation have emphasized standard professional and administrative concerns such as how to keep the federal courts open to Legal Services litigation and how to reduce staff turnover, not the development of a guiding social philosophy on the relation of the law to social-class justice for the poor.

One of the consequences of the professional narrowing of reform concerns is that there has been little written commentary on the sociopolitical implications of the process. A few attempts have been made to calculate the economic benefits of Legal Services reform litigation. Some commentators, using a formula that estimates the size of the class and multiplies by the anticipated average benefit, have tried to measure the wealth redistributed by class-action suits (Levy 1969, p. 254; Carlin 1971, pp. 140–141; Johnson 1974, pp. 187–234; Aaronson 1975, p. 124; Stumpf 1975, pp. 273–281; Weisbrod 1978). But victories won at one stage of a case may be lost at another, and triumphs in one suit may be canceled by the outcome of the next. Judicial orders are rarely "final" in the sense that such accounting operations must assume. Moreover, increases in benefits paid out of one section of a public welfare program may be made up fiscally by contractions elsewhere. Legal Services lawyers are not unaware of these ambiguities. The million-dollar victories reported by Chicago's LAF may suggest unreasonable self-satisfaction, but the public bravado masks private humility. In interviews conducted in early 1980, senior LAF lawyers gave estimates varying from 10 to 50 percent as the measure of the program's paper gains that survive countervailing readjustments by the government. In the context of the conservative political victories of the fall 1980 election, far more modest expectations, including that of counterproductive backlash, would be reasonable.

In assessing the impact of poverty litigation, there has been virtually no commentary on structural effects: the implications of reform litigation for the quality or form of poverty. Yet with respect to formal characteristics, there is a notable coherence to poverty reform litigation. Reform litigation in Legal Services became more efficient in the seventies. With increasing ease, lawyers in one program could write for the pleadings used by poverty lawyers in another jurisdiction and quickly file a major suit. Reform litigation in Legal Services became more consistent and systematic, as indicated by the increased commitments over the decade in Chicago's LAF. Reform litigation became more nationwide because of high turnover within programs coupled with a high level of retention within the institution; broader "classes" represented in suits; and advocacy in forums that encompass wider jurisdictions. In short, as the commitment to reform in Legal Services became professionalized, it became rationalized.

More important, the ends as well as the means of reform litigation developed in the same direction. The central thrust appears to be to transfer the distinctive, segregating treatment of the poor out of the irrational workings of the private sector and into the routines of public bureaucracies. Reform suits have attacked personal, emotional, inconsistent exercises of private economic power against the poor; and they have promoted a construction by government of a social category of the poor that is increasingly total, formally predictable, internally consistent, duly applied, and uniformly differentiated from the working and middle classes. I first examine the structural thrust of poverty reform litigation, then describe the role of professional administrator of poverty as constructed in the U.S. political context by poor people's lawyers. Finally, I outline the policy dilemma that has developed for poverty lawyers after the decline of the social movements of the sixties, a dilemma dramatized by the conservative political victories of 1980.

The Structural Thrust of Reform Litigation

To appreciate the reform role played by contemporary lawyers for the poor, it is useful to recall the situation almost a hundred years ago (see chapter 2). Legal assistance organizations were then sponsored privately, by contributions not primarily from lawyers but from the civic elite in general. The targets of reform were almost exclusively abuses in the private sector. Reform was concerned with classic problems of class injustice, such as the inability of employees to obtain earned wages and to receive compensation for injuries sustained on the job. Legal assistance lawyers worked aggressively, primarily on the plaintiff side, suing to collect debts owed to their clients. Reform was pursued through the eminently political, marginally professional activity of lobbying for legislation. Beneficiaries of the reforms championed by the nineteenth-century legal assistance organizations, reforms such as workmen's compensation boards and state labor commissions, were frequently spread throughout the urban working class in general.

By 1970, public funding of legal assistance lawyers had completely overshadowed the private funding of Legal Aid societies. Funded by the federal government, Legal Services's reform activities became increasingly national in scope in the seventies. The Legal Services Corporation provided training services and materials on a national scale, and its *Clearinghouse Review* disseminated descriptions of significant litigation among LSPS. A national market for Legal Services jobs flourished as the number of program lawyers grew from some 2000 early in the decade to about 5000 in 1979. Patterns of transfer and promotion between programs also flourished. The targets of reform litigation were predominantly public agencies. Reform litigation by lawyers for the poor had become overwhelmingly a matter of and about government policy.

The thrust of reform litigation on behalf of the poor may be characterized in two complementary parts, that in the private and public sectors. In the private sector, reform litigation attacks practices which segregate the poor or maintain the poor as a qualitatively separate class: practices that keep the poor out of, or marginal to, the working class and practices that exercise economic power over the poor in qualitatively distinctive ways. The thrust in this sector is to alter not so much the "what" as the "how" of the participation by the poor in market relations. The objection is to the creation by the private market of a separate, specially treated category of poor people. This category of litigation includes suits against employment discrimination and suits to enhance the ability of migrant and menial laborers to organize. It includes suits attacking methods to exact private profit that are rarely applied to the middle classes: wage garnishments, repossessions of personal property, summary evictions, and evictions for nonpayment of rent from apartments that fall substantially below housing-code standards.

Within Legal Services, and increasingly in the eyes of the general public, the distinctive methods used by the private sector to order its economic relations with the poor have become almost too unseemly to be condoned. Over the last 30 years, racial discrimination in employment has become indefensible across the effective political spectrum. Collection practices are too vicious to withstand public scrutiny in congressional hearing. Migrant farmworkers outside the protection of the National Labor Relations Board receive massive public sympathy. Evictions often appear too vindictively motivated to appear legitimate, however proper the landlord's formal notice. Ugly ethnic tensions are suggested in the popular picture of the white European merchant acting as creditor in the black or Latino ghetto. The private sector's special methods for structuring relations with the poor are too inconsistent, too emotional, too personal, too feudal—in sum, insufficiently rational to pass review in the modern moral conscience.

The thrust of litigation against such exploitation is not to eliminate poverty but to civilize it. Academic commentators have argued that the consequence of elaborating tenants' and debtors' rights is to make it increasingly uneconomic to extend private credit to the poor (Hazard 1969, Bolton and Holzer 1973). Although the argument has been made more on the basis of elegant theory than on researched fact, it seems compelling. Unless poverty lawyers are to make personal moral judgments about clients, they will be obliged to use technical defects in eviction procedures to keep defaulting tenants in well-kept buildings, with a consequent disincentive to maintenance. If technical defects in consumer-credit contracts routinely block the collection of deficiencies on the contract, either the cost of credit will increase or the amount offered will decrease. Some poverty lawyers take the admittedly paternalistic view that poor people too easily take on consumer debts. But whatever the lawyers' motivations, their thrust is to make the persistence of poverty less outrageous by eliminating collections and evictions charged with personal emotions, ethnic tensions, and racial prejudice.

While reform litigation in Legal Services has attacked qualitatively distinctive, differential treatments of the poor in the private sector, it has also promoted the distinctive treatment of the poor by the state. With perhaps unusual proficiency in Chicago, but on a general basis throughout the country, Legal Services lawyers in the seventies routinely recruited the poor into public programs run especially for the poor by suing government agencies to implement outreach or notification obligations in food stamp, Medicaid, public assistance, and public housing programs. Poverty lawyers sped the enrollment of the poor into class-segregated public programs by attacking administrative delays in processing applications. (After an LAF lawyer won Supreme Court decisions on the issue in the early seventies, his colleagues almost automatically thought of a delay suit whenever they came across a public-benefits program for the first time.) Lawyers for the poor continually pressed to expand the number of the poor actually covered by public-benefits programs by knocking down irrational, moralistic, noneconomic distinctions. LAF attacked differences in benefits based on such moral distinctions as those between: legitimate and illegitimate children, relative and nonrelative caretakers, welfare recipients in vocational school and in college, new and old residents of Illinois, and public mental hospital residents above and below age 21. Legal Services reform litigation also further promoted the rationality of the state's differential treatment of the poor by bringing due-process suits to make the application of poverty program categories procedurally acceptable and apparently fair.

To test the accuracy of this characterization of the thrust of poverty reform litigation, I asked a sociology graduate student and a law student to use the following typology to code the Legal Services cases described in two issues of the *Clearinghouse Review,* June 1974 and August 1979.[1] Two dimensions were used: is the target of the legal assistance lawyer a public or private party; is the projected effect segregated to poor people or does it promote similar treatment of the poor and the nonpoor? The categories were described (almost verbatim) as follows:

1. Target is *public*; projected *effect* is *segregated* to poor people.
The following defendants, programs, or issues justify a presumption that the projected beneficiaries are distinctively poor: AFDC, SSI, GA (general

assistance); Medicaid; food stamps; state mental hospitals–involuntary commitments; public utility cut-off; jail–juvenile delinquency–prisoners; public housing projects; parental custody—neglect, dependency (state social work agency presumably involved). *Not* social security, Medicare, unemployment compensation, FMHA. As to HUD, unless the context makes clear whether the program in question is distinctively for the poor, code the case under "5," inadequate information. The context may make clear that a case against one of the above agencies or programs substantially affects "working-class" people. Thus AFDC cases on employment-related expenses should be classed under "3," public-integrating. We can justify the above list while recognizing that a significant percentage of beneficiaries in some of the listed public programs are marginally "working class." (Thus, according to 1971 statistics, about 30 percent of AFDC mothers currently work or worked in the last year.)[2] In popular understanding, AFDC is a program distinctively for the poor; and in historical perspective, it is a program through which the state has organized poor people and segregated them in basic life contingencies from the working class, even though a sizeable minority may be employed temporarily in the "secondary" labor market. The coding assumes that AFDC, juvenile homes, state mental hospitals, etc., reflect a separation between "the poor" and the working or middle classes that is well established in the public mind.

2. *Target* is *private*; projected *effect* either would be shared by *poor and nonpoor* or would promote treatment of the poor in the manner in which the middle class is treated. "Private target" covers economic (landlord–tenant, consumer-credit) and domestic-relations cases. Other examples include: adoption—notice to natural mother; migrant work conditions and unionization movement; sex or race discrimination by private employers. Interpretation: Many eviction and consumer-credit issues have little relevance for nonpoor people; much of the legislation and case law in these areas is in fact class-specific to the poor. Although the litigation creates a segregated body of law, it promotes a similarity between poor and nonpoor in the quality of experience when participating in private market transactions.

3. *Target* is *public*; objective or *effect* is *integrating,* or shared with nonpoor. *3A*: Case aims to end segregated or differential treatment of poor by state: *Serrano* (equalizing expenditures across school districts); stop urban renewal; get public services for migrants; voting

rights for prisoners. Interpretation: such cases do not put the poor in the same schools, neighborhoods, etc., with the middle class; they do promote integrated or uniform administrative treatment. *3B*: In 3A, the beneficiaries are distinctively poor persons. In 3B, cases promote reforms beneficial to poor and nonpoor. Examples: employment rights of prison guards, nurses, housing-authority employees; police department height requirements; attacks on prohibition of drug advertising; unemployment compensation; social security; Medicare; FMHA; public utility rate cases (where a general rate increase is held up, or objective is consumer–commercial differential); educational rights of mentally retarded; students' rights; race, sex discrimination in state employment; aliens and public employment; AFDC-employment expenses; food stamps for college students.

4. *Target* is *private*; *effect* is to shape a distinctive treatment of the poor, or *segregating*. Not many examples here. Include: Medicaid patient, doctor can't bill directly or end service arbitrarily; nursing home can't evict Medicaid patient without hearing; Hill-Burton. Theoretically, these might be thrown into "1," on the theory that they show poverty litigation expanding the public sector, making previously "private" parties into public agencies or agents.

5. *Other*: *5A*: Inadequate information. *5B*: Concepts too ambiguous. *5C*: Concepts too narrow.

From the 1974 to the 1979 monthly issues of *Clearinghouse Review* that we examined, the number of reported cases almost doubled, from 85 to 155. All but 7 were deemed codable. The categories and subcategories showed the same distribution in both years. The first category—public target, segregated effect—had 55 percent of all coded cases. Another 15 percent were in the second category—private target, integrating effect. Significantly, within the 29 percent of cases in the third category—public target, integrating effect—there were three times as many in 3B as in 3A; only 7 percent attacked a differential treatment of the poor by the state; the other 22 percent promoted benefits that would be shared by poor and nonpoor alike. Cases brought on behalf of the poor with spillover benefits for the working or middle classes do not confirm the tested characterization of poverty reform litigation; but unlike the 7 percent which pressed for a uniform state treatment of poor and nonpoor, neither do they directly contradict it.

These figures suggest that, overall, poverty reform litigation on the one hand attacks exclusions of the poor from the private job market and distinctive methods for exercising economic power over the poor in consumer transactions; and on the other hand, it spurs public agencies which specialize in a clientele of poor people to activate recruitment, speed the processing of applications, and discard moralistic in favor of economic criteria for defining beneficiaries. The thrust seems to be to incorporate "poverty," as a distinctive set of behaviors, into the state, where it can be systematically examined and rationally governed by professionals.

The process of transforming the social organization of poverty was not an invention of legal assistance lawyers. As Grønbjerg, Street, and Suttles (1978) observe from their institutional study of social welfare policy in the United States:

> To be poor in present-day America has come to mean that one has been diagnosed as poor by bureaucracies and professionals. . . . American governmental activities have less reduced inequality than they have bureaucratized and professionalized it. Under these processes, the operations of the system of inequality become more sophisticated, definitions of poverty become more precise, policies for defining eligibility become more complicated, and programs of help receive greater expert attention. (pp. 133, 165)

Legal assistance lawyers have developed a unique role in this long-term historical process.

Professional Administrators of Poverty

LSPs have developed a special structural competence to contribute to the state's governance of the poor. Consider the role they have played within the overall public administration of poverty. Legal Services lawyers have provided administrative leadership, from out-of-house, to the network of public agencies that specialize in establishing the basic conditions of life for poor people.

The social organization of this role has evolved gradually, without any explicit plan. Partly because of partisan political influence, partly owing to civil service rigidity, public welfare programs are typically administered poorly on the standard of rationality. To date, the federal government has been unable politically to discipline welfare administration by running programs directly at the local level. Legal Services lawyers were freed from partisan political influence over an initial eight-year period, 1966–1974, in which local forces (city bar associations, old-line charity bureaucracies, state politicians) were frequently overpowered by national organizations (the ABA, Legal Services's Washington-based headquarters, and finally, Congress). During the seventies, when LSPs lost many of the ties to external influences which had anchored their internal hierarchies in the sixties, they became sufficiently free externally, and sufficiently anarchic internally, to offer widespread opportunities for personal involvement in ego-gratifying, "significant" litigation. Supported by monies from the federal government, capable of tapping rich sources of professional motivation, reform litigation by Legal Services lawyers became an indirect method of overcoming bureaucratic and political limitations on the rationality by which the state administers the poor.

The objectives of poverty reform litigation have been as diverse as have been the limitations in government on the professional administration of poverty. Legal Services's reform litigation has struck down administrative irrationalities within local public programs. A recent example of a vanquished irrationality was a Chicago Housing Authority (CHA) eligibility policy, characterized as "stupid" by the judge on the case, which assumed that the entire military income of an absent spouse would be available to a CHA tenant, except if the spouse "is under hostile fire."[3] Legal Services litigation has rationalized the state's welfare programs for the poor by enforcing state adherence to federal regulations and by compelling state departments to regulate county agencies, in effect integrating governmental hierarchies that could not impose administrative discipline from within. Poverty lawyers have also litigated to impose a measure of rationality on the relationships among the various public agencies to which the poor are segregated. In the early seventies, Chicago Legal Services lawyers brought suit to compel public housing and public assistance officials to end a situation in which public housing tenants incurred penalty charges if they failed to pay rent at the start of the month, while welfare recipients in public housing with names beginning after "Bah" in the alphabet were not sent their assistance checks until later in the month.[4]

What accounts for the creation of a role for Legal Services lawyers as out-of-house, professionalized social welfare administrators? What are the political dynamics that have created the market for the poverty lawyer's emergent reform role? Thus far, only fragments of an explanation have appeared in the literature. But interestingly enough, the available fragments cover a wide political spectrum, indicating relevant dynamics both in conservative and in liberal U.S. politics.

Aaronson (1975) has written a detailed study of welfare law administration and Legal Services litigation in California during Ronald Reagan's terms as governor. According to Aaronson, Governor Reagan backed his conservative public opposition to welfare expenditures with administrative policies that were repeatedly declared illegal in poverty law suits. Instead of treating judicial reversals as political liabilities, Reagan incorporated legal losses into his conservative rhetoric, launching a series of public attacks on Legal Services lawyers. Three aspects of this history are especially instructive: (1) Reagan's fiscal objectives apparently were not achieved; welfare costs rose during his administrations by $1 billion (Aaronson 1975, p. 287). (2) Moreover, the governor's insistence that cuts be made without a legally defensible basis actually cost the state substantially in expenses for repeatedly instituting and then reversing changes in the practices of the state's large welfare system [Aaronson (p. 230) reports the figure of $2.6 million for just one set of reversals]. (3) Despite the judicial reversals and dubious fiscal benefits, over time, Governor Reagan appeared to regard his welfare record with, if anything, an increased estimate of its political value. In Aaronson's analysis, the combination of a celebratory official animus against welfare expenditures and a series of successful Legal Services suits led to a fundamental transformation of the state's welfare bureaucracy. It lost its character as an agency that implemented social welfare goals inconsistently through a largely discretionary administration; and it became a department for benefit payments, an expanded bureaucracy narrowly concerned with dispensing funds to the poor in mechanical conformity to regulations.

About the same time, across the country and at the other end of the conventional U.S. political spectrum, liberal politicians in New York invited poverty lawyers to play a similar role. In the late sixties, Mayor John Lindsay considered it impolitic to adopt the style of Governor Reagan and make an outright attack on the substantive justification for public assistance. Instead, as fiscal pressures increased and welfare expenditures loomed ever larger in the city's budget, New York's liberal political establishment became sophisticated in reducing welfare expenditures quietly by altering the process for receiving and responding to applications for public assistance. According to Lipsky (1980), welfare administrators expected to achieve substantial cost reductions by increasing administrative inefficiency in specific ways and by the hassling of recipients in general. Lipsky describes a memo written by the city's budget bureau in 1969.

> The bureau recommended four administrative changes. . . . A new intake procedure was proposed that would require applicants to be actively seek-

> ing jobs . . . it was hoped [that this] "would have a deterrent effect on applications for welfare." . . . Closing seven outreach centers would save . . . the costs of . . . the centers, but more importantly, "larger savings are anticipated from secondary effects. . . . The most important of these is the opportunity *to build up and maintain the maximum legal backlog* between intake and eligibility increasing average backlog from two weeks to a full month." Among other secondary benefits of center closings, the author . . . expected that "the relative inconvenience to the client . . . may have some deterrent effect on [those] marginally eligible for welfare." Further, stronger management audits would provide better checks on welfare employees, who are portrayed in the document as more interested in enrolling clients than in controlling welfare costs. (p. 103)

By increasing the regulation of welfare workers' discretion and by increasing the uncertainty, inefficiency, and overall burdens of the system for recipients, New York City's government made rational administration a major variable in public assistance policy, thereby defining for Legal Services lawyers the issues for reform litigation.

In sum, the limited administrative capacities of both conservative and liberal domestic politics to govern effectively set up for poverty lawyers a role as external, professional rationalizers of state social welfare agencies. Conservatives attacked welfare expenditures with public rhetoric and with policies that often ended counterproductively in judicial reversals of administrative practices, all at greater cost to the state. Liberals attempted to decrease the street-level administrative efficiency of the welfare bureaucracy in order to reduce outlays with minimum publicity. In both political settings, lawyers for the poor were virtually invited to protect a threatened administrative rationality.

In mounting reform suits, Legal Services lawyers are not properly understood as autonomous, outside agents attempting to impose rationality on the administration of public welfare services over the opposition of a univerally hostile state. At times, state officials, aware that politically they cannot effect administrative justice for the poor, have explicitly but secretly issued invitations to Legal Services lawyers to take up the slack. Poverty lawyers have increasingly played overt political roles at the covert behest of sympathetic executives and legislators.

Typically, at least some people in the legislative or executive branch want poverty lawyers to oppose the state's administration of welfare expenditures, and at times they consciously help. Aaronson reports an instance in which sympathetic legislators worked with a poverty lawyer to rewrite a hostile bill so that it would be more abusive of the rights of recipients and thus easier to strike down through litigation (Aaronson 1975, pp. 206, 239). Legal Services lawyers in Chicago and elsewhere have reported to me that state welfare administrators, after apologizing that they cannot do what they recognize as legally required because of partisan political pressures, often encourage suits against specific policies so that they can obtain the cover of judicial compulsion. No doubt similar instances of covert legislative and executive assistance could be reported by civil rights and civil liberties lawyers who sue government units to implement regulations to desegregate schools, reform prisons, and humanize mental hospitals. The emergence of an out-of-house, professional administrator's role for poverty lawyers reflects a trend that has characterized the legal rights movement generally.[5]

Historical Formation of the Current Dilemma

When legal assistance organizations began operating in the late nineteenth century, being poor carried no legal status as such, except in the sense that some forms of poverty were illegal. In the 1890s, when successive depressions made "tramps" of thousands of men in search of work, "vagrancy"—a legal category applied in many jurisdictions to people from outside the given state, who "follow(ed) no labor," were "without visible means of support," and could not give a "reasonable account of their business"—was, numerically and politically, a significant crime.[6] To the extent it was legally recognized at all, poverty was a prosecutorial allegation used to lock up and to export indigents.

In 1980, legal assistance lawyers worked with a clientele whose poverty was legally sanctioned. Now the state, instead of invoking its criminal law powers to banish the public spectacle of poverty, officially recognized and routinely administered the material existence of large segments of the poor through publicly funded programs. Legal assistance lawyers played only a peripheral role in the transformation of poverty from a sporadically prosecuted crime to a bureaucratically maintained legal status, but the transformation profoundly altered the social meaning of their role.

The initial legal assistance lawyers were not serving "the poor" in the contemporary sense of the term. Primarily, they represented indigent working men and women on problems of class exploitation. In three stages, the clientele at legal assistance offices became a distinctive category of poor people, a group noticeably differentiated from the working or middle classes.

First, during the Progressive Era, several state remedial agencies were established with the legal competence to resolve employment-related disputes of the types that had dominated the original legal assistance case loads. In this process, legal assistance agencies played a constant, but in context minor, lobbying role. By 1930, in most states where Legal Aid societies operated, small claims courts, state labor commissions, and workmen's compensation agencies were hearing complaints by workmen against employers and creditors. The clientele left at legal assistance could then be seen as distinctively deficient psychologically and culturally and hence in need of essentially defensive legal advocacy and supportive social work.

In the second stage, the national social welfare programs created during the Depression years, in particular by the Social Security Act and the Wagner-Steagall public housing act, laid the basis for the state's organization of poor people into a culturally identifiable, institutionally segregated class. These programs did not represent a Machiavellian capitalist social-control plan to create and differentiate a class of the poor from the working class. Public housing was originally understood to be for a "submerged and potential middle class,"[7] a group culturally and morally from the middle classes but temporarily short on income because of the Depression. Similarly, the AFDC program, which in political rhetoric later came to symbolize "welfare recipients" uncommitted to the work ethic, was initially intended for dependents of the working class and was expected to "wither away" as coverage expanded in the payroll tax–financed, working class–based parts of the social security system (Steiner 1966, pp. 18–47). Public housing began to be an endemic poor people's institution as income levels rose during and after the Second World War, encouraging aspirants to the middle class to anticipate private home ownership; and also as government rechanneled housing subsidies to aid a massive move by veterans to private home ownership in the suburbs (Friedman 1968, pp. 116–117). The AFDC program became a major state institution for the poor at first quite slowly and then very rapidly. The number of AFDC families, which was only 360,000 in 1940, actually dropped by 25 percent between 1940 and 1945. The number rose by 132 percent between 1945 and 1950, increased only 17 percent in the fifties, and then exploded in the sixties, increasing by 107 percent, or 800,000 families, from December 1960 to February 1969 (Piven and Cloward 1971, pp. 116–117, 183). In their study of the phenomenon, Piven and Cloward attribute the rise in the sixties to an increased pressure on eligibility decision makers, and they credit Legal Services as making a significant contribution through suits to eliminate exclusionary criteria and, especially, arbitrary denials (pp. 306–320).

The advent of a third stage in the transformation of the social-legal organization of poverty was acknowledged by the antipoverty programs of the sixties. They proceeded from a recognition that poverty in the United States had already assumed an unprecedented form. Relative to the situation in the 1890s, "poverty" had become incorporated into the state as a statutory category represented by specialized ameliorative institutions. "Community action" programs were thus needed to stimulate indigenous pressures that might make government bureaucracies more sensitive to the needs of the poor; federally funded lawyers for the poor were to implement an antipoverty mandate which in part required attacks on the inadequacies of other public programs. The clientele at legal assistance offices was now understood to be poor in an institutionally sustained way. The role of the new "poverty lawyers" would be defined in large part by their response to the institutionalized, public administrative segregation of the poor.

An initial objective of poverty reform litigation, particularly litigation against state agencies with a distinctive clientele of poor people, was to break down the segregation of the poor. In the South, welfare rights litigation began as an extension of the civil rights movement. In the urban and typically liberal North, Legal Services litigation against public welfare programs was understood in some quarters as part of a larger strategy of structural change. In a 1965 article widely read in Legal Services circles, Cloward and Piven (1966) noted that only about half of those eligible were receiving welfare. They predicted that if welfare recipients demanded their rights—a process in which lawyers could play a significant role—liberal city administrations would fall into fiscal crisis; conservative state governments would not help; and national Democratic leaders would step in to enact a guaranteed annual income, thus ending poverty.

If, in the 1980s, proposals for radical changes that might end the state's administrative segregation of the poor seem absurdly impolitic, it is essential to recall that, during the 1970s, several such ideas were practical possibilities. For a while, President Nixon backed the Family Assistance Plan, which would have established a guaranteed annual income; and the concept of a negative income tax was in small part implemented in federal income tax returns in the form of the earned income credit. The idea that public-aid bureaucracies might be replaced by an IRS-administered system, an integrated system which would administer claims and distribute subsidies to members of all social classes, was not an idle academic thought. Similarly, in the early years of the Carter administration, there were reasonable prospects for national health legislation which, for the poor, might replace Medicaid with a system treating all participating patients, regardless of class, within a uniform process.

A small percentage of the reform litigation brought by Legal Services lawyers also contributed directly to the integration of state services to different social classes. The California Rural Legal Assistance program, through its services to the United Farm Workers union, aided the drive to bring migrant laborers within a state-level collective bargaining framework roughly analogous to the national labor-relations system from which agricultural labor was statutorily excluded. Also in California, a Legal Services suit, *Serrano* v. *Priest,*[8] secured a state supreme court judgment to equalize expenditures in school districts, the implication being not that classrooms would be integrated economically but that the public school system would deliver equal value in education to all income groups. In health services, income payments, educational opportunity, and to a lesser degree in other areas (e.g., school lunches), there were notable signs of movement away from the state's differential treatment of the poor. In this context, legal assistance lawyers could understand their litigation against inequitable coverage and low-quality administration as contributing to a growing dissatisfaction with state institutions that exclusively served a poverty clientele.

As politics in the late seventies became increasingly conservative, ideas for major institutional reforms which might have produced similar facilities and accounting procedures for the poor and the middle class (such as a federalized welfare system administered through the IRS and a national health plan) were deemed impractical. Independent of the general social movements of the sixties, the impetus persisted within Legal Services to use litigation to reform poverty. Professionalism, in the form of a drive to sustain involvement in work, was a sufficient motivational base. No publicly visible culture remained in Legal Services to celebrate an antipoverty role. Most reform litigators in Legal Services were grouped within their local programs along organizational lines that reflected the divisions among the state's bureaucracies for poor people: units to litigate issues of welfare, food, health, housing; the special needs of the handicapped; the special problems of the elderly poor, and so on. By the late seventies, Legal Services reform litigation had become thoroughly professional and, arguably, more of an adjunct than an enemy of the state's administration of poverty.

Foucault (1978) writes that, progressively since the democratic ("bourgeois") revolutions of the late eighteenth century, the state in capitalist societies has employed the philosophy of rational humanitarianism and the personnel of the modern professions to establish an exacting surveillance and a disciplinary administration over deviant elements of the working classes. Historically, the institutions first exhibiting the new methods for defining, segregating, and supervising a morally discredited lower class were the prison and the state mental hospital. The professional group of humanitarian rationalists who created intelligible frameworks for control were social and psychological scientists. Professions of help—to rehabilitate rather than punish the criminal, to cure rather than abhor the mentally ill—established the conditions for an unprecedented extension of state control in class-segregated institutions. The tactics of the new discipline were indefinite sentences and involuntary commitments; intimate psychological investigations and elaborate typologies for differentiating antisocial tendencies; and a routinized tracking of everyday life.

There is a chilling plausibility to an analogous perspective both on the twentieth-century trend in the social organization of poverty in the United States and on the role of sophisticated poor people's lawyers in conservative political epochs. In 1981 reactionary national policies tried to sharpen the state's administrative segregation of the poor, for example by cutting subsidies for school lunches for the middle class; by cutting college students off food stamps; and, through a reduction in the amount of child-care expenses figured into welfare eligibility, by cutting working poor women off the rolls. Liberal humanitarianism appears less likely to help indigents by pressing for class-integrated administrative formats than by continuing to dramatize the need for a greater differentiation of the poor. Consider the special educational needs of the child whose first language is not English. Consider the special nutritional needs of the unborn. Consider the special energy costs borne by the elderly poor in the Frost Belt. Consider also the special legal needs of indigent abused wives. Conservative politicians may be expected further to discredit the moral status of the state-defined poor by alleging massive fraud and by demanding more administrative surveillance and investigation of claimants, all the while removing burdensome regulations from the business classes.

If legal assistance lawyers manage to retain federal funding, they may well encounter severe restrictions on their capacity to litigate significant cases, especially those cases that seek to integrate or jointly benefit the poor and other social classes. Conservative opposition to Legal Services has been especially sensitive to poverty reform litigation which battles differential treatment of the poor by the state or which promises to benefit groups of poor and nonpoor alike. Thus Agnew provoked publicity about "radicals" in Legal Services by sympathizing with the frustrations of the mayor of Camden, New Jersey, when his plans for urban renewal, colloquially known as "black removal," were being stopped by a Legal Services lawsuit. California's Governor Reagan and U.S. Senator George Brown, responsive to the interests of growers in keeping migrant labor out of the union ranks, tried to terminate funding for California Rural Legal Assistance. In Congress, conservative Democratic opposition to Legal Services has come disproportionately from representatives of rural areas threatened by the migrant labor union movement. A succession of legislative proposals to restrict the role of Legal Services lawyers has aimed at prointegration suits (representation of migrant labor, school desegregation litigation) and at suits with spillover benefits beyond the poor in the areas of Selective Service, environmental protection, gay rights, and students' rights.[9] In the presidential campaign debates of 1980, Reagan attacked a public policy favoring equal treatment of residents of private and state mental hospitals. The policy was then being articulated in the Supreme Court by Chicago's LAF. At stake was a monthly payment to indigents in public mental hospitals of about $25 "pocket money," a payment that similarly situated residents in private mental hospitals were receiving. Candidate Reagan commented:

> I think it's disgraceful that the disability insurance fund in Social Security finds checks going every month to tens of thousands of people who are locked up in our institutions for crime or for mental illness and they are receiving disability checks from Social Security every month, while a state institution provides for all of their needs and their care. ("Debate Transcript" 1980)[10]

Throughout this book I have traced the changing perspective on equal justice for the poor as it has been enacted by legal assistance lawyers. For readers expecting a conclusive characterization or a confident prediction, the ending will be a disappointment. As I write these lines, President Reagan's proposal for zero funding for the Legal Services Corporation is working its way through a surprisingly conservative Congress: the House is beginning to consider a Senate proposal to continue funding at $100 million—more than a two-thirds cut from the current level; and the news has just been reported that the president was shot. I will have to leave the fate of the reform impulse in legal assistance as an open question. The drive to reform poverty had the internal motivation to survive the decline of the sixties; indeed, it substantially matured and became more powerful in the seventies. It is obvious that aggressive poverty lawyering has not been "institutionalized," however, in the sense of being secure in federal funding regardless of changes in the national political climate. But against a historical background of indifference and hostility to federally funded Legal Aid, in the 15 years from 1965 to 1980 the Legal Services program did develop in the elite of the bar and in the news media a reliable, virtually unqualified, politically potent set of allies. Structurally, poverty reform litigation seems fundamentally vulnerable to the political tenor of its times. In the early 1980s, the cause of legal assistance to the poor faces an ominous conservative coalition in Washington and the suspicion that, if it is sustained at all, the techniques of reform litigation which began as methods for fighting poverty may become, willy nilly, a means of legalizing the state's administrative segregation of poverty.

Appendix

A Theory of Qualitative Methodology: The Social System of Analytic Fieldwork

There are perhaps four questions about evidence which readers of this book are most likely to raise. They may be characterized as four *R*s that haunt participant observers in sociology.

1. *Representativeness*. I studied the legal assistance programs in Chicago through historical documents, organizational files, and 18 months of fieldwork in 1972 and 1973. Since 1973, I have had numerous interviews with lawyers who have worked in LSPs in Chicago, Connecticut, and California, but my report primarily covers experiences and events in Chicago in the early seventies. The study may have some value as a historical document of local interest, but I offer it as a general institutional analysis of the careers of legal assistance lawyers and their organizations. Can such generalization be justified?

2. *Reactivity*. In Chicago, I observed and talked with staff lawyers sometimes for minutes, sometimes for hours; in court, their offices, their homes; without anything approximating a fixed questionnaire. Perhaps the differences I report in the data simply reflect differences in my behavior. I might be asked, "How do you know it looks the way you describe it when you're not there looking?"

3. *Reliability*. I typed up about 2000 pages of field and interview notes, presented only a fraction in the final report, and have not specified the criteria I used to select those data I published. A sympathetic but concerned reader might well observe and ask, "There is an infinite amount of background context that you could have included or excluded from your original field notes and the final text. The meaning of the behavior described would change with a change in the description of its context. How can you say your descriptions are the right ones?" A less kind reader might put it, "How do we know you didn't overlook disconfirming data, or even make it all up?"

4. *Replicability*. I began the study at a time when I learned that the legal assistance organizations in Chicago were about to merge. My initial interests were twofold. "Merger" seemed an attractively elusive phenomenon, one on which there seemed little useful sociological literature. The other interest was in the analysis of personal and collective careers and their relations. This interest grew out of my fascination

with Georg Simmel's writings, and from my training in symbolic interaction, with its perspective on the processes in which people shape individual and collective identities.

I began by interviewing organizational leaders, asking about their personal careers and their expectations for the merger. Then I began sitting in on lawyer–client interviews. When meetings began at the merged organization, I attended. I recorded my observations and interviews, sometimes contemporaneously, sometimes within an hour or two, often that night, occasionally weeks or even months later. The "career interviews" were loosely structured, to say the least. I would typically begin with questions about how the lawyer came to the job, move to initial experiences, then encourage a recollection of stages and changes in internal career, and finish by asking about expectations for the future. I changed the focus of my observations and interview questions in innumerable, unrecorded moves.

In light of such broadly formulated interests and inconstant methods, one might well ask, "If we wanted to test your analysis by repeating your research, how would we know what to do?"

Qualitative field studies appear especially vulnerable to criticism because they do not proceed from fixed designs. They do not use formats for sampling which could produce statistics on the representativeness of data. They abjure coding books which might enhance reliability by spelling out in advance the criteria for analyzing data. They fail to give detailed instructions for interviews—the questions to ask, their order, when to give cues and when to probe—which might give the reader faith that differences in subjects' responses were not due to variations in the researcher's behavior. Because of their emphasis on informal and flexible methods, qualitative field studies seem to make replication impossible.

Unfortunately, qualitative researchers have customarily conceded fundamental methodological weaknesses when faced with the four *R*s.[1] Not displaying significant statistics, they acknowledge the "merely exploratory" status of their "case" studies. Citing the importance of "getting close to the data," participant-observation fieldworkers concede risks of reactivity (Scott 1965, p. 266). Symbolic interactionists discard coding books, and along with them the goal of verification, as a necessary cost of developing "grounded" theory (Glaser and Strauss 1967). As for replicability, some qualitative methodologists recommend reporting a natural history of the study but ultimately attribute success to "having the gift" (Lofland 1976, p. 318).

Something important is missing from methodological thinking.[2] On the one hand, as both Becker (1970, pp. 6–7) and Glaser and Strauss (1967, p. 12) have noted, the sociological community, despite its neglect of the rationale for qualitative methods, frequently rewards qualitative empirical research. On the other hand, forceful questions have been raised as to whether formal research designs ever could be implemented according to their prescriptions. In fact, the argument increasingly goes, research designs never do anticipate fully the social relations that emerge in the research process. However random the sample, research subjects are never chosen through logical deduction from the theory purportedly tested (Camilleri 1962). Inevitably there are unscheduled influences on the understanding by respondents of the questions or stimuli (Cicourel 1964). Unexplicated bases for interpretation are ubiquitous (Garfinkel 1960), and they undermine the effort to establish that one has performed a replicable study.

These considerations raise two sets of related questions. Are not the methodologies of social surveys and experiments premised on a substantive sociological claim that supposedly pre-fixed features of the research, such as plans for probability sampling and coding rules, can actually determine and accurately predict the social relations established by the researcher with subjects, readers, and subsequent researchers? What is the methodological value of the formal research design if it does not in fact govern research? This essay takes up the converse set of questions. If qualitative field research can produce what the scientific community is willing to regard as valuable results, must there not be methodologically valuable empirical implications of the qualitative field researcher's behavior? Perhaps we should look for the methodological strength of qualitative fieldwork not by comparing it with an image of research from fixed designs but by examining the social relations which may be built up with research subjects, readers, and subsequent researchers by the fieldworker's conduct, from initial entry into the field to the final write-up.

This essay outlines a sociological theory for evaluating qualitative field research. It takes three substantial rhetorical risks. The first is to offer a general theory of a distinctive social system that can be constructed by field research, rather than to illustrate and qualify elaborately one subset of hypotheses. Some may prefer a more "grounded" approach, but my immediate objective is to undermine a habitual critical perspective, and for this the emphasis is best kept on the possibility of a comprehensive alternative methodological stance. The second risk is to ignore diversity in methods and focus on one qualitative research strategy, analytic induction. Once the subject of intense debate, analytic induction has not been much discussed since it was given a forceful critique by Ralph Turner almost 30 years ago. But the method has lived vigorously if subterraneously, surfacing occasionally in the footnotes of symbolic-interaction field research reports.

The dependent variable—the social relations shaped in the research process—is drawn quite broadly to suggest an emergent social system; the independent variable—the characterization of qualitative fieldwork—is defined quite narrowly, as analytic induction, a method for which there are precious few pure examples. The third risky decision is to formulate the distinctive strengths of qualitative field research in the standard terminology of methodological discussion, as in the discussions of the four *R*s. To some readers, the argument in places may appear simply to be giving a different meaning to established standards so that field research will look good where it has looked bad in contrast to surveys and experiments, and vice versa. In a sense, that is precisely the contribution the essay attempts to make to the literature of field methods, from which it admittedly borrows and rebottles much. As indicated by the opening paragraphs, my motivating concern has been a practical dilemma, the need for a rhetoric with which to respond more directly to standard methodological questions than claims of "discovery rather than verification" and "pretesting" allow. The need is to outline an alternative perspective for interpreting such issues as representativeness, reactivity, reliability, and replicability and also simultaneously to indicate that the customary readings are at best arbitrary.

Analytic Induction Revisited

The fundamentals of analytic induction can be stated simply. The researcher is committed to form a perfect relation between data and explanation. When encountering a negative case—evidence contradicting the current explanation—the researcher must transform it into a confirming case by revising the definition of either the explaining or the explained phenomenon. The researcher is enjoined to seek negative cases and the resulting opportunity to modify the explanation. There is no methodological value in piling up data of a sort already determined to be consistent with the theory. Quantification therefore plays no logical role.[3]

I used analytic induction throughout my research on the careers of legal assistance lawyers. At an early stage of my study, I worked with a two-year cutting point. Legal Services lawyers had often referred to "two years" as a meaningful benchmark when commenting on their careers. After separating a number of lawyers into groups with tenures at exit time of more and less than two years, I began looking for features common and unique to the former. Not finding any, I eventually moved from obviously false hypotheses to the final version of the theory in the following way. I drew up a list of lawyers who had stayed more than two years and who had certain biographical features in common, and another list of lawyers who lacked the specified biographical features and who had stayed less than two years. Then I considered "exceptions," lawyers who fit neither list. I made a series of changes in the definition of the explanandum (initially, staying two years) and the explanans (initially, activism before joining Legal Services) to remove the exceptions and place all the lawyers on one of the mutually exclusive lists. I was manipulating the meaning of the concepts which distinguished the lists in order to restore the perfect correlation with which I had started. In the process, the definition of the explanandum was changed from staying two years, to desiring to stay two years, to desiring to stay in a frustrating place, to involvement in a frustrating place, to involvement in an insignificant status; and the definition of the explanans was changed from features of preorganizational biography to methods of transcending pressures to assume routine work, including the use of legal strategies for reform and participation in a collective culture of significance.

After working this way with sketches of biographies, I developed the concepts further in a two-step process of coding field materials. In this part of the research operation, the codes represented the concepts of the explanation, and problems in making coding decisions represented problems in the explanation. First, I altered the codes to fit one-sentence summaries previously made from typed interview and field notes. Then, in writing the text, I adjusted the analysis when the quotes extracted directly from the original notes were not what the summaries had led me to expect. When a quotation showed both the presence and absence of involvement in a lawyer's experience at the same time, the concept of involvement had to be further refined; when a section of an interview showed the presence of involvement and the absence of the condition stipulated as explanatory, the explanation had to be revised. Theoretical development continued from early in the research throughout the writing.

One can characterize analytic induction as a distinctively qualitative methodology. One can also distinguish it clearly from methods requiring pre-fixed designs. True, the overriding commitment to seek negative cases is a pre-fixed feature. But the injunction to alter the contents of the theory during data collection gives the research process a distinctive openness. In practice, one does not begin with a hypothesis and then encounter exceptions one by one. Instead, one begins with multiple hypotheses and is confronted with a mass of hostile evidence. Analytic induction permits the researcher to flounder interminably in the choices of: which hypothesis to select out and stick with, then which datum in the disconfirming mass to select as an "exception" while consciously ignoring temporarily the discouragement of the rest, and then whether to alter the explanans or the explanandum.

Symbolic interactionists have sensed but not fully spelled out their affinity with analytic induction. (Indeed, many of the arguments that follow have been suggested by these sociologists but not integrated into a self-conscious methodological stance.)[4] The affinity is natural. Analytic induction is well suited to the practical flexibility demanded in qualitative field research. The ethnographer who uses analytic induction need not step out of the field for analytic repair each time a negative case is encountered. The guiding purpose will often be simply to collect a rich array of closely related data; the explicit process of formulating an explanation may be put off until fieldwork ends. The qualitative researcher serves the logic of analytic induction in the meantime, because the pursuit of data that are similar but qualitatively different effects a search for substantively relevant negative cases.

Field researchers generally have not embraced analytic induction as a doctrine. This reluctance appears related to problems historically but not necessarily associated with the method. As originally proposed, analytic induction claimed a superiority over "enumerative induction" by promising perfect correlations and "universal" explanations rather than probabilistic findings. But then very few if any perfect explanations appeared. Yet this embarrassment misconceives the methodology. Analytic induction ought to be evaluated in the same way in which field researchers practically gauge the value of their work. The test is not whether a final state of perfect explanation has been achieved but the *distance* that has been traveled over negative cases and through consequent qualifications from an initial state of knowledge. Analytic induction's quest for perfect explanation, or "universals," should be understood as a strategy for research rather than as the ultimate measure of the method. Analytic induction is a method for conducting social research, not a perspective from which to evaluate findings. The argument I develop in later sections is that we can evaluate social research by examining the social relations built up in the research process; within this perspective, the use in field studies of the core principle in analytic induction—the search for negative cases—appears to have great advantages.

In addition to their claim of "universal" explanation, early proponents of analytic induction[5] unnecessarily raised hackles by arguing its superiority over "statistical enumeration" for developing "genuinely causal laws." Against this background, Turner's critique—essentially that the concepts of explaining and explained phenomena in studies using analytic induction shade into each other and suggest tautology—was especially forceful. Analytic induction appeared to produce good definitions at best, not causal explanations.

The case for analytic induction can be made stronger with a number of revisions. If we view social life as a continuous symbolic process, we expect our concepts to have vague boundaries. If analytic induction follows the contours of experience, it will have ambiguous conceptual fringes. Its independent and dependent variables will inevitably shade into each other, suggesting tautology. But this weakness is only remarkable if exceptional claims are made for the method. Analytic induction and enumerative induction (in other words, survey statistics) differ in the form, not the fact, of uncertain results. For the statistical researcher, practical uncertainty is represented by statements of probabilistic relations; for the analyst of social process, by ambiguities when trying to code borderline cases into one or the other of the "explaining" or "explained" categories. In application to given cases, predictions on the basis of probabilistic explanations will sometimes be wrong, and predictions on the basis of explanations of social process will sometimes be so indeterminate as to be useless. (Turner did not claim that all explanations by analytic induction would be circular, nor that all its predictions would be indeterminate. See this chapter, note 8.)

Field researchers also have reason to be uncomfortable with analytic induction's preoccupation with theory. Disregarding time and space boundaries, analytic induction appears to slight the specific for the general. It seems to call for a narrow, utilitarian interest in the specific site solely for what it can contribute to theory. But many highly regarded case studies are overtly more respectful of specific historical periods and places than of the glories of scientific theory. Here too the tradition for discussing analytic induction has misled it into disfavor. Sociologists can use analytic induction to study particular historical dramas, ethnic communities, or principled institutions without compromising a belief that the ultimate value of social science thinking is in its application to the concrete, not in its form as theory abstracted from history. But whether the goal is to develop theory or to grasp concrete experience, the way of qualitative field research is to seek a series of negative cases as a means of qualifying a comprehensive analysis.

A final difficulty for using the tradition of analytic induction is its apparent emphasis on an epistemology of "induction." What field researchers actually do when they use analytic induction would be described more properly by philosophers of science as "retroduction" than as induction: a "double fitting" or alternate shaping of both observation and explanation, rather than an *ex post facto* discovery of explanatory ideas (Hanson 1958, pp. 85 ff.; Baldamus 1972).[6] To signal both my departure from several aspects of the tradition of analytic induction and my debt to the tradition's essential guide to research practice—the injunction to search exclusively for negative cases—I drop the reference to "induction" in favor of the rubric *analytic research.*

Analytic field studies will not produce "proof," that is, artifacts of evidence which speak in a standard language or specialized fashion about representativeness, reliability, and so forth. The exclusive commitment to search for negative cases implies that there ought to be a different conceptual point for each reported phenomenon. Each datum reported should make its own substantive and not solely evidentiary contribution to the analysis. But analytic fieldwork does create an elaborate framework which can be used by researchers to assess how well they are doing and by readers to make evaluations. That framework is a social system, of which I sketch the following aspects.

Applied consistently in field research, the search for negative cases will: force the researcher to focus on social process as experienced from within; induce research subjects to act toward the researcher as a meaningful member of the native world; enfranchise readers as colleagues competent to make an independent analysis of the relation between data and explanation; and shape a role which subsequent researchers can readily take up for testing substantive findings. I suggest that this is a social system distinctively constructed by analytic fieldwork, in contrast with quantitative social research from fixed designs, and that this social system can be invoked to spell out answers to a wide variety of methodological questions frequently asked of qualitative field studies. This system of social research relations promotes generalizability, reduces the problem of reactivity, establishes constraints toward reliability, and enhances replicability.

Representativeness

The strategy of analytic research is to expand constantly the domain to which an explanation validly can be generalized. The sequential process in which theory is altered upon discovery of a negative case, in turn changing the meaning of a "negative case," allows each new datum to function as a rival hypothesis. This method invests research energy with maximum efficiency to improve the generalizability of theory.

Analytic research rests the external validity of a study on its internal variety. The more differences discovered within the data, the greater the number of possible negative cases, and thus the more broadly valid the resulting theory. From a perspective on the sociology of social research, the analytic method, if it is followed, actually promotes the discovery of internal variety and thus its logic for establishing external validity.

In practice, the analytic method shapes a particular researcher perspective on research subjects. It leads researchers inexorably to examine social process as subjects experience it from within. Once researchers have been led to examine the emergence in subjects' experience of the phenomena to be explained, they find that their basis for generalization—qualitative variation—has expanded vastly. Thus, use of the method has systematic empirical results which are methodologically beneficial for approaching the value of representativeness.

Blumer (1969, p. 82) indirectly asserts that a search for explanations that avoid contradiction must lead to an examination of social process. In his symbolic interactionism, he views behavior as built up through a process in which a person identifies features of his situational context and biographical background, interprets some as relevant, and shapes a line of action in response. Blumer challenges the reader to "find or think of a single instance" inconsistent with this perspective. If social action is the result of a problematic symbolic process, then explanations that relate background factors directly to behavioral outcomes should soon stumble on contradictions. It follows that researchers who commit themselves to revise analysis in order to avoid negative cases will develop theories of social process.

This has in fact happened in every known instance in which analytic induction has been used expressly to discipline social research.[7] At the start, the researcher's conceptual units have often been static background factors and discrete acts. As the study has developed, the units have become processes with vague boundaries. Lindesmith (1968) discovered that he could not explain the first act of taking opiates, only addiction, a sustained use. Rejecting explanations by personality type, he offered a motive developed in the process of use, a "craving." In my study, an early concern was to explain turnover among poverty lawyers. This was a focus on an *act* of leaving an organization. I ended with an explanation of "involvement," a perspective on continuing a line of activity as intrinsically compelling.[8]

Analytic research forces researchers to turn explanatory concepts in naturalistic directions so that they capture the processual nature of social life as experienced from within. The result of this transformation in the researcher's outlook is to expand immeasurably the evidentiary powers of a given period of social life and of research on a given number of people. At the start, the analytic researcher often works with demographic categories and conceptualizations of acts that will rarely change for each member during the course of the study: sex, ethnicity, personality type, neighborhood location, socioeconomic status, intergenerational mobility. On such dimensions, each subject typically will be counted once. Analytic researchers then go on to develop concepts identifying "moments" and forms of experience which repeatedly emerge and disappear in individual biographies: the emergence and decline of cravings, variations in the expression of political perspective (Moskos 1967), the cyclical experience of becoming involved and uninvolved in work. At different times, each subject may appear at different points on each dimension. Rich diachronic contrasts become available for tests.

If this hypothesis of the effects the use of the analytic method has on the researcher's perspective is true, it implies a principle to guide qualitative research. Given the strategy of exploiting internal variety in order to warrant generalizability, the ideal site is one that both is in a period of historical change and has the most differentiated members. These do not appear to have been the principles typically guiding the selection of sites for qualitative research.

Critics might respond that the fact that a site is distinctive in the heterogeneity of its members and in the drama of its historical change makes it unrepresentative. The researcher's naturalistic focus on symbolic social process suggests a strategy to work on this problem. Take the charge that unique features of the research site—extreme differentiation of members, large scale of organization, rapid change in collective character—bias all the data collected. The qualitative researcher can examine the range and fluctuations of members' situated experiences and may discover tests for the rival hypotheses. If the objection is that a smaller, more homogeneous and static context would alter members' behavior, the researcher may locate exceptional members who, for a time at least, were situated in a homogeneous subunit isolated from the influences of a general historical trend.

To use this logic, one must assume that there are not complete discontinuities on the dimension at issue between the case studied and the place or time invoked in the rival hypothesis.[9] For example: I tried to explain involvement and alienation from work among poverty lawyers by studying organizations in Chicago in the early 1970s. I would like to determine whether my theory requires qualification when applied to lawyers working in rural California poverty law offices, but I have no direct data. Is it reasonable to reject the hypothesis that the theory cannot be extended to the rural California site by examining the exceptional experiences of a lawyer who worked in Chicago's Mexican-American neighborhood legal assistance office and cultivated vineyards in abandoned West Side lots in preparation for a move to a poverty law job in his native Northern California? I would also like to test the validity of my theory for lawyers currently assisting the poor. One might object that political commitment and its collective mobilization was unusually strong and pervasive among poverty lawyers during my fieldwork, in the early seventies, and that there is a general malaise now. But is the contrast so complete that a close examination of the experiences of the earlier group *could not* have encountered instances of the currently dominant perspective? By definition, no researcher can prove continuity between what he has and what he has not studied, but the analytic method points a way for thinking the problem through.

This logic for generalization of course requires the researcher to make substantive sociological assumptions, but there is no special weakness here. To collect data from a sampling design that statistically will support claims of representativeness, decisions will have to be made to exclude some variables, times, and places.[10] In one respect, the analytic researcher actually relies less on sociological assumptions untested in the research. Because of the methodological status given the single negative case, he or she need not recognize an encounter with a precursor of historical change as such in order to reconcile theory with it. The sampling researcher, on the other hand, can purposively select for rare events thought to be harbingers, but he or she will first have to *have* that thought and bet on it.

Quantitative and qualitative strategies toward generalizability strike different bargains with the existential limitations of social research. In attempts to establish statistical significance, the more the researcher sees data as heterogeneous (the greater the number of variables examined in a given number of data), the less likely it is that levels of significance will be reached. The goal of specifying the explanation by testing it against rival hypotheses through partial correlation or elaboration analysis may be pursued only at the cost of weakening the argument that the patterns examined are significantly representative of a larger population (cf. Camilleri 1962). Statistical evidence of representativeness depends on restricting a depiction of qualitative richness in the experience of the people studied. A similar practical trade-off confronts inductive research, but it makes the opposite choice. By searching for data that differ in kind from instances previously recorded, analytic research creates a picture of the scene researched that is strategically biased toward much greater variation than random sampling would reveal. Brilliant qualitative studies such as Goffman's *Asylums* (1961) overrepresent the richness of everyday life in the place actually observed in order better to represent social life outside of the research site.

Reactivity

By using the analytic method, qualitative field researchers join in methodological strategy with historians, literary critics, and other humanistic scholars who derive lessons of general significance by mining internal variation in a given case. Used in the field, in direct contact with subjects, analytic research does confront special methodological problems. I have asserted as an empirical proposition (or perhaps more accurately, reasserted after Blumer) that when sociologists committed to hunt for negative cases examine theories that explain discrete acts by background psychological or social characteristics, they will inevitably transform their theoretical perspective into a focus on social process as experienced from within. When this research perspective is used in direct contact with subjects, it becomes a form of participant observation. Participant observation appears to exacerbate the problem of reactivity—subjects' responses to a study's methods that confound substantive findings. Among approaches to participant observation, the analytic method might appear the worst.

Styles of participant observation differ depending on the way the researcher participates in the lives of the social group's members, how much as participant, how much as observer (Gold 1958). Common to all varieties is an effort to induce members to participate in defining the study through the absence of a rigid research design. Within interviews, in selecting scenes to observe, and in deciding when to ask informants about group reactions to collective events, the participant observer attempts to ask questions about, and to be present during, the phenomena that make a difference to members. Flexibility and fluctuation in research behavior is required. A participant observer committed to search exclusively for negative cases might constantly change the content of questions or the angle of observation; and as a result, any difference in the behavior of research subjects could be attributed to a change in the researcher's behavior.

Spokesmen for participant observation have taken a defensive position on the issue, noting dangers for "objectivity" (Scott 1965, p. 266) and for "contaminating" the scene examined (McCall 1969). Reasonably courageous sociologists might well be frightened off by such metaphoric warnings. To use participant observation appears to risk not only destruction of the scientific self but the pollution of society!

But interaction between variations in research methods and variations in members' behavior does not necessarily produce a methodological problem. It does when the resulting behavior is irrelevant to the researcher's objectives, or when the researcher fails to interpret correctly how he is perceived by members. Yet it is precisely on these grounds that analytic field research shows distinctive methodological strength. In contrast to research that attempts to fix the researcher's behavior with a design for gathering data, the analytic field method makes valuable substantive data out of the responses of members to the researcher's methods. Moreover, this qualitative approach distinctively creates opportunities for testing the meaning to members of the researcher's presence.

It is my thesis that, in order to recognize the strength of qualitative field methods on the standard of reactivity, we must develop a sociology of social research. A key virtue of the analytic field researcher's lack of preset methods is that it deters the presentation of a "scientific" self. If the researcher influences members, it will not necessarily be as a "researcher." Members have reason not to take as a "researcher" the sociologist whose methods take shape in response to native concerns.

In relations with researchers, members will take what is to them significant action by identifying researchers as significant others. To consider participant observers significant, a member must cast them into identities rich with indigenous meaning. In field studies of communities or organizations, researchers may be grilled as informants, sworn in as confidants, and debated as representatives of the views of various groups and leaders. In these relations, members reveal their concerns, not about the world of social science research as understood by the researcher, but about everyday aspects of their own social lives. If by their presence analytic field researchers change the scenes in which they participate, the data they take out are still about those communities and organizations.

By *not* insisting on a uniform meaning for the research role, the analytic field researcher minimizes the problem of creating irrelevant, "artificial" data. Conversely, the use of fixed methods to combat reactivity paradoxically exacerbates the problem. By attempting to control the research setting rigidly, so that differences in members' behavior cannot be attributed to variations in research methods, experimental and survey researchers define artificial "research" settings and induce members to become hypersensitive to accidental and unplanned variations in researcher behavior (Becker 1970, p. 44).

Just as on the standard of representativeness, so also on issues of reactivity: not only does the analytic method avoid weaknesses that traditionally have been attributed to fieldwork; it creates resources of evidence where traditional methodology only sees problems. Analytic field methods not only minimize the risk that members will act "artificially" as research subjects; it lets them shape an identity for the researcher that itself provides valuable substantive data. Two distinct sources of data are made available. One source has been recognized in a classic social science tradition that seeks to understand members' social lives by examining the researcher's subjective experiences in trying to shed an alien "research" role. Anthropologists have long taken their emergent problems in learning how to act as natives for substantive data on the implicit rules of a society.[11]

The other source of data, one more neglected by field researchers, is member efforts to define a role for the researcher.[12] Consider the question of access. It is usually discussed as a problem faced only at the start of a study, before substantive data gathering can begin. In fact, the negotiation of access is ongoing, continuing, from situation to situation and from the beginning to the end of each interview, in the researcher's efforts to establish and maintain rapport. Indeed, once the process of developing rapport is over and researchers with fixed questionnaires are ready to begin serious interviewing, qualitative researchers are often ready to leave. By this point they have realized which questions make no sense to an interviewee and have found substitutes that do. An appreciation of such qualitative distinctions is more important for the analytic researcher than learning which way the questions are answered this time.

Rich data are available in members' efforts to place a field researcher in a role and at a distance useful for native purposes. A process through which members attempt to keep the researcher further out is revealing of the nature of the scene studied. So are ploys by members to draw the researcher further in. On the former: For virtually the entire course of an 18-month field study, Wieder (1974) failed to build rapport with the residents of a halfway house for parolee-addicts. By examining his frustrations in "learning the code," and by investigating similarities in the alien roles residents shaped for him and for the staff, Wieder detailed the techniques used by residents for achieving segregation. The very fact that the residents persisted in reacting to the researcher as nothing more than an irrelevant researcher provided relevant data on the dominant culture in the institution. On the latter: Gusfield (1955) turned into data the sometimes frustrating reactions of WCTU leaders to his efforts at maintaining a formal interview role. Cast by them not as an indifferent, neutral, scientific "researcher" but as an informed member of the public, he was berated and subjected to proselytizing efforts. The concerns of members about the boundary between outsiders and insiders and their ability to define it are significant features of all social systems.

Of course proffered interpretation of the meaning of members' behavior toward researchers may be wrong. But member behavior that has been shaped in response to the researcher's methods is not necessarily more problematic as substantive data than behavior shaped in any other interaction. Field researchers have missed this point. Common topics in the literature on participant observation concern whether members are lying, being superficial, or showing racial deference to the researcher. There is no fundamental difference between these problems of interpretation and those about whether members are lying, being superficial, or showing racial deference to each other.

Just as analytic field methods have distinctive strengths for decreasing the likelihood that reactive behaviors will be artificial or substantively irrelevant, so they have distinctive strengths for detecting artifacts of researcher behavior. The possibility that the researcher may be giving cues without being aware of the fact is treated like any other ambiguity in the interpretation of members' behavior. An interpretation is made consistent with previous evidence and revised if contradicted by subsequent evidence. The very absence of systematic regularity in the researcher's behavior promotes the creation of a wide range of research situations available for such tests. Specific methods may systematically be made unsystematic, and the abandonment of method may be pursued as an unattainable goal throughout the research. Analytic field research should be considered not *a*methodological but strategically *anti*methodical (cf. Phillips 1973).

Reliability

Reliability is an appropriate methodological concern in all empirical research. Just as we should always inquire into the representativeness of data and the reactivity of methods, so we should always question whether the researcher has been constrained to be rigorous when working data into an analytic scheme. Has the researcher overlooked disconfirming data or used concepts inconsistently? Are the concepts so ambiguous that different observers would not apply them similarly?

Quantitative sociologists have developed complex measures of reliability, many of which have been described in the annual American Sociological Association publications of *Sociological Methodology*. One old and relatively simple quantitative strategy for providing evidence of reliability suffices to indicate the apparently unreliable nature of qualitative field methods. If rules for coding are specified before data are gathered, the researcher can produce specialized, statistical evidence on the extent of agreement among "judges" who independently apply the scheme to the same data. This strategy is inconsistent with qualitative research. By definition, so long as a researcher's encounters with data are governed by preset coding rules, they cannot be exploited to develop qualifications in substantive analytic categories.

But qualitative research is not necessarily "impressionistic." The search for negative cases leads the qualitative researcher to a holistic analysis that binds propositions and data into an intricate network.[13] Seen within the social relations that analytic observers develop with members and readers, the network constrains the researcher toward consistency in selecting and interpreting data. Such a network holds together my thesis on the careers of lawyers for the poor.

I have argued that the social environment presented to legal assistance lawyers—clients, adverse parties, courts—characteristically defines the problems of the poor as insignificant. In turn, poor people's lawyers typically experience expectations that their work should be routine. To maintain intense involvement in client representation, the lawyers must struggle to treat problems as significant by doing a specific kind of work: reform. Because the environment calls for routine, their maintenance of involvement depends on reform.

An elaborate network of analysis and data underlies this summary statement. There are two main themes in the analysis, a warp and a woof, each of which has multiple strands. Thus "the environment" includes the expectations presented by clients and by the adversaries and court settings brought in their wake. The "reform" activities of the lawyers include not only litigation objectives but the creation of an everyday intraoffice culture that resists and transforms "routine" messages received from outside.

Each of these propositional strands is itself a combination of evidentiary threads. I support the assertion of a judicial expectation for routine treatment by direct evidence. For example, I quote a poverty lawyer's account of an instance in which a state court judge responded to his argument of a far-reaching constitutional issue literally by throwing the pleadings out of court. I treat some data as neutral on the proposition, for example reports of courteous judicial hearings of routine motions. I offer many types of indirectly supporting evidence, for example, explanations by legal aid lawyers that a court's failure to comprehend routine arguments represents judicial senility or alcoholism or prejudice against the poor. *A fortiori,* judges experienced as having such incompetencies would appear to be unresponsive audiences for complex arguments. Similarly, varied evidence bears on the characterization of the expectations of clients and opposing counsel.

To convert disconfirming into confirming data, it was necessary to qualify concepts and generate explanatory propositions. On the generation of explanation: If the environment defines the lawyers' work as routine, then one should find that the lawyers' development of reform strategies is a necessary condition for their involvement in work. Further, if some lawyers who are litigating reform issues describe themselves as disengaged and demoralized, then another necessary condition must be added to the explanation. This second condition was found to be participating in a peer-sustained culture that expresses a reform perspective. On qualifying concepts: If lawyers who are not litigating for reform nevertheless recount extended periods of immersion in work, the theory must be refined by elaborating the meaning of "being in the institution's environment." I found that these lawyers were occupied with internal leadership projects of institution building such as training other lawyers, not with directly representing clients in an adversarial setting. The result: A complex analytic framework supports any proposition, although the framework is illustrated by what may seem superficially to be casually selected "anecdotes."

However unconvincing the reader may judge this institutional analysis of routine and reform, the point here is to indicate the many ways in which it could be embarrassed. There is no insurance that analytic researchers will make rigorous interpretations, but readers can easily guard against being misled. As a result, as a practical matter, the researcher faces strong constraints toward reliability. On the mundane level of mechanics, self-deception and biased selectivity in recording data will involve substantial difficulties.

Considering the social relations created in the research process, there are several methodologically salutary features of participant observing. Analytic field study builds relations with members such that the researcher will often be unable to grasp immediately whether what he is recording is supporting or contradicting his current analysis. I assume I share the following experiences with other qualitative fieldworkers. In the field, I often wonder whether I should be elated or depressed for my theory in response to the course an interview or observation is taking. Group scenes usually contain much that is obvious to members but challenging for me to comprehend. In interviews I must restrain analytic commentary in order to remain respectfully attentive and in order to provoke respondents to keep responding. I have no forms on which observations can be checked off and no set formulas for probes. A fieldworker inclined to ignore disconfirming data and record only confirming data often could not easily make the discrimination.

Once the qualitative researcher is out of the field and constructing a text, the social relationship of writer to reader presents elaborate constraints against inconsistent and unexplicated interpretations. If the qualitative data-gathering and text-construction process seems inarticulate, even mysterious, it helps to recognize that, irrespective of how unruly the analytic researcher's practices, the reader has rules available to detect error in the text. Blumer's classic critique of *The Polish Peasant* (1939) demonstrated the multiple objections that a discerning reader could make to qualitative research reports. Charges of a lack of fit between data and analysis may come from many sources: from multiple interpretations by the reader of the data presented, from the apparent irrelevance of the member's meaning to the analyst's point, from the connection between the analysis and the data being made through interpretive commentary rather than through the data itself, and from inconsistent implications of data presented in different parts of the text.

The weblike character of the text means that each datum will ramify in implications throughout. To insulate a careless analysis from critical readers, the researcher would have to engage in a laborious process. Each quote or episode would have to be edited carefully so that it might avoid contradiction elsewhere in the analytic framework. For example, if I had characterized the legal assistance lawyer's professional environment loosely as disreputable or demeaning (one of my earliest hypotheses), then I would have had to purge, from all quotes, any indication that a local judge or opposing counsel may have acted respectfully. To protect the initial, casual analysis, an extensive chopping-up of quotes would have been essential, and further, a meticulous effort would have been necessary to avoid the appearance of chopped data.

Authors of qualitative field research reports cannot escape a dialectical evidentiary bind. The analysis must be made dense to make the data representative, to claim, in other words, that the study is generally useful. If the network of field materials and propositions is very limited, it would be easy to indulge inclinations not to report inconsistent data. Of course this could be done, but after a point the deceit would become self-defeating. Who would care? The study then could not pretend to be very useful or significant.

Given the possibilities of misfit, a biased selection of data that would convince a careful reader is not easily achieved. Given the emergent character of the analysis, if a confirming quote is hard to find or invent, the alternative readily available is to alter the analysis so that the data at hand will suffice. The everyday stuff of writing qualitative analysis consists of an ongoing series of retroductive shifts: trying to convince oneself that a quote or episode can be interpreted to fit the analysis until frustration is sufficient to make stepping back and modifying the analysis seem the easier course.

Analytic field research establishes a distinctive social relation between researcher and reader. The reader of a survey or experiment is asked to find reliability less on the face of the text than in the consistency with which a pre-fixed design has been operationalized. True, there will always be means of inspecting the text critically for signs of internal inconsistency. Sample size and the marginals reported for the relationship between any two variables will constrain the interpretation of statistical associations among other variables. But *by design,* judgments about the reliability of quantitative data are made independent of judgments on the strength of relationships between variables.

That reliability and representativeness are more interdependent in analytic qualitative research than in surveys and experiments can be seen in differential practical constraints in the research process. Consider the researcher's selection of relationships among data for inclusion in the report. It has been noted that the logic of significance statistics is vitiated when a report of significance at the 5 percent level belies 19 unreported statistics not reaching that level (Selvin 1957, pp. 525–526). The text will not necessarily indicate an indulgence of this bias in reporting. Consider also the researcher's dilemma in remedying suspect data. There are different constraints on qualitative and quantitative researchers for recognizing mistakes made in coding. The analytic researcher may simply return to the site to pick up a more reliable example of the phenomenon. But for data that are to be treated as part of a probability sample, "cleaning" by discarding suspect items would undercut the logic of the significance statistics.

In the traditional view, qualitative fieldworkers seem relatively free of practical constraints on recording and interpreting data wishfully and carelessly. Analytic research must be kept small scale in its human organization. Arrangements to deploy numerous researchers and coordinate their activities would compromise the method by requiring a prespecification of the data that they are to look for. Thus, little if any mutual consent must be achieved to invent qualitative field notes. Qualitative research produces bulky field notes recorded with abbreviations meaningful only to the researcher. The interpretation of field notes often depends on a knowledge of context supplied by prior field notes or known but not recorded by the researcher. Field notes cannot as readily be transferred to other sociologists in original state as can responses to fixed-choice questionnaires because they cannot as easily be masked to preserve confidentiality without altering their meaning. The analytic strategy, which never separates data gathering from inspection of "results," may tease the qualitative researcher to disregard disconfirming data selectively, perhaps through an unconsciously biased inability to understand "inarticulate" responses. In contrast, the collection of quantitative data from a preset design may block the researcher's awareness of what findings would be disconfirming until data collection is complete and the computer has finished its run. The rules which preset the meaning of data to be gathered through surveys are used in large-scale research as a framework for an organizational hierarchy which gets the work done. An elaborate conspiracy might be necessary to manufacture findings. Moreover, the frequent practice in survey research of hiring specialized data gatherers who lack responsibility for analysis would appear to insure motivational neutrality.

On the other hand, this arrangement carries the risk of building alienation and indifference into a study at its most basic level (Roth 1966). In contrast, the close relationship between field researcher and subjects should make it more likely that the researcher will take the people studied as significant others. This audience can provide powerful constraints on reliability. To dismiss their objections to interpretations, the researcher might have to renounce an emotionally significant segment of his or her life. It would also seem to be easier to alter the number in a category than to invent quotations that sound like 75 different research subjects. Working with hypotheses, one could specify statistics on significance and correlations which would be confirming. One could instruct a machine to figure elegant equations backward and manufacture the data necessary to make the math succeed. Just as it would be easier to change the number entered in a category than to invent a quote, it would be easier to figure out what that number should be.

My purpose is not to impugn the integrity of statistical researchers but to outline an empirical theory for evaluating reliability in analytic field studies. I have used the issue of manufacturing data as a way of shortcutting a more lengthy argument that would cover in detail allegations of morally lesser methodological sins. If there are constraints inherent in analytic field research which automatically place the dishonorable researcher between the Scylla of apparent unreliability and the Charybdis of apparent insignificance, *a fortiori* the merely careless analytic researcher should be found in the same straits. To develop in detail a theory of the constraints against fraud in qualitative and quantitative social research, one might examine real cases of serious allegations.[14] But for the present, if the methodological strength of research depends on the social system it actually fashions, qualitative field researchers need not be deferential in evidentiary debate.

Replicability

To the extent that researchers pre-fix their decisions for gathering data, they can easily present readers with a format for testing findings by repeating the study. Questionnaires and sampling procedures defining the boundaries of the relevant population may be included in an appendix; the coding book and written instructions for administering the survey instrument may be copied and mailed to subsequent researchers. Apparently inviting replication, psychology experiments traditionally have been reported in articles that neatly separate the description of methods and findings. The format takes the posture: You don't believe it? Go see yourself.

Analytic field research changes procedures for gathering data in order to encounter negative cases, then changes the analysis, and so on, in an interactive relation of method and substance. Innumerable *ad hoc* judgments are made in the field, decisions on when to visit the research site and when to move from observing one situation to another, decisions on when and how to probe in interviews. They could be reported, if detected, only through retrospective reconstruction. Because standards of substantive relevance change rapidly within the research process, much of the data considered will not be reported or even recorded. The difficulties of specifying the research procedures used and of accounting for all the data considered add up to an inability to define what a replication would be.

Despite these facts, the analytic field research strategy promotes relations with other researchers that facilitate the subsequent testing of substantive findings. Elaborate prespecifications of research procedures both define what must be done to repeat a study and impede subsequent tests of its findings. Such studies call for rigorous attention to standard procedures for gathering data both by initial and replicating researchers. In contrast, the claim in analytic research that no negative case can be found invites the testing of findings without repeating the original research. A subsequent researcher can simply pick up where the study left off, looking for a single contradiction.

If the costs of subsequently testing qualitative field research findings are relatively low, so the rewards are relatively high. It has been notoriously difficult to publish failures to reject null hypotheses (Sterling 1959, Tullock 1959). Publishing criteria are biased toward disconfirming and innovative results. An attempt to replicate a study with a fixed design and determinate findings runs the risk of becoming nothing more than an unpublishable confirmation. The risk is a significant deterrent. In contrast, subsequent tests of qualitative field studies will never be merely attempts at disconfirmation. If only because the original research fails to specify what an exact repetition would be, a subsequent researcher should be confident of documenting new types of phenomena, valuable for other theoretical purposes, in his search for disconfirming cases.

Analytic field research also more democratically empowers readers to become subsequent testers. Research that proceeds from a fixed design produces probabilistic propositions. (When variables are selected at the start, unless the researcher's initial understanding is perfect, the correlations will not be.) As a member of a percentaged category, an individual in the sample or an individual reader cannot contest the findings authoritatively by citing personal experience. In contrast, the claim made in analytic research that propositions stand without exception enfranchises research subjects and readers, giving each the logical right to falsify and require modification of the theory.

If the question is considered closely, it is clear that we assess qualitative research reports by whether they not only invite but induce subsequent tests. Qualitative research reports properly may be regarded as good to the extent that readers test them in application to new data in the very process of reading. Underlying the reader's experience in "recognizing" as valid or rejecting as "artificial" an analytic formulation in a qualitative text is an implicit application to phenomena within the reader's experience, to new data existing beyond the reach of the original research.

To appreciate the reality of such testing, compare the implications of two allegations, that when writing *Asylums* Goffman invented his portrait of the mental institution, and that Hollingshead and Redlich invented the survey responses and the computations presented in *Social Class and Mental Illness* (1958). Assume it is 1961, and follow-up studies have not yet been attempted. Readers of both works would, I submit, respond differently. There is a sense in which a reader would judge that the former charge could not be true. If Goffman was never a participant-observer in St. Elizabeth's Hospital, as he said he was, he must have been in some other mental hospital; or he must have talked to people who were; or read accounts by people who were. Ignorant of his methodology, one takes his results as evidence that he did something right. One can judge the value of his text immediately with as wide a variety of methods as he *might* have used. For the quantified survey study, the allegation of dishonestly reported methods and fabricated findings is much more crucial. One can readily imagine how the allegation could be true; if one wants to test it, one faces a sizeable task; and if one believes the allegation, the work is worthless. To evaluate such claims requires an accurate and detailed account of how the findings were produced from a pre-fixed design.

In a fundamental way, the allegation of fictive data is less meaningful when applied to qualitative field studies. In fact, many of the best interweave observational and interview data with excerpts from novels written by earlier participant observers. An example is the use of Melville's *White Jacket*[15] in Goffman's *Asylums*. Another legitimate use of fictive data is illustrated in a book by Rosett and Cressey (1976). Drawing on wide but unspecified prior research and participant-observation experience, they invent a criminal case, a cast of players, and a multistage decisional process—a whole social organizational setting and drama—in order to demonstrate the collective construction of guilty pleas. They offer their work not for the "theoretical" purposes traditionally invoked to justify ideal types, but as a way of making an empirical argument.

When such authors blur the line between fiction and data in their texts, they are obeying tendencies natural to their methodology. Phenomenologically, the distinction between "created" and "recalled" data becomes ambiguous in qualitative field research. Observations can be recorded at any time, contemporaneously or long after they are made. No rules govern the timing. Researchers can credit as data their own experiences in interaction with members.[16] Given this methodologically sanctioned freedom, the researcher may often be unable to assert confidently whether his image of a research scene is recalled or "made up."

But given the relation between author and subsequent researcher, this is a very constraining freedom. Qualitative researchers obtain no license from their affinity to the novelist. After all, the analogy between the novel and the participant observer's qualitative text is not complete. The requirement for an explicit analysis that is more general than the case under study, plus the discipline of the negative case, breed a compelling concern that one is not manufacturing data. On what else other than the accuracy of his analysis in the scene researched can the author rely to avoid a subsequent researcher's discovery of disconfirming data and the consequent charge that the analysis offered exists only in its author's mind? For the analytic researcher, methodological constraints are experienced as existential matters, not as matters of methodical convention.[17]

Researchers' Social Relations and the Evaluation of Analytic Fieldwork

By recommending a sociological perspective on methodology, I mean to call attention to implications for evaluating research findings that may be discovered by examining the system of social relations created in the research process. I have proposed hypotheses on the social relations created by analytic field research with reference to four familiar standards of evaluation. First, representativeness. By searching exclusively for negative cases, a researcher gives distinctive shape to his or her perspective on the people studied. To avoid contradiction by negative cases, analysis inevitably turns to the examination of social process as experienced from within. Continued study of a given segment of social life turns up increasingly refined discriminations between states of phenomena as they emerge in and vanish from experience. In qualitative variation, where sampling designs find limitations on their ability to assert the statistical representativeness of relations, the analytic sociologist seizes on resources for warranting the generalizability of his analysis.

Researchers who gather data from fixed designs acknowledge that statistics on significance measure only the uncertainties of extrapolating from the data examined to the specific population sampled, not the prospects for extrapolating to later times and other places. Since any use of the findings of a study will necessarily be in application to a different population, a showing of statistical representativeness is necessarily an incomplete achievement. Analytic research cannot measure the uncertainty with which the scene it describes reflects any larger population, but its single-minded pursuit of qualifications in order to enhance the prospects of accurate application to other times and places raises the question whether this failing should be troublesome.

In its present state, the methodological literature assumes that reactivity in participant observation is a contaminating problem. But if we examine how research procedures shape the meaning of the study to members, we may conclude that field research without a formal design makes interaction between researcher and member into a substantive data resource. In a sense, analytic field research dissolves the problem of reactivity, whereas formally rigorous methods actually create it by enhancing the appearance of "research" and by limiting variation in the meaning of the research process to members.

Qualitative researchers typically concede an inability to verify the reliability of their interpretations of data. Yet even sociologists who labor to show high levels of statistical agreement among indicators acknowledge a logical gap between indicators and what is indicated (Blalock 1968). True, field researchers make themselves vulnerable in special ways to questions of objective interpretation by elaborating a network of idiosyncratic observations and informally fabricated explanations. But does this imply methodological weakness? From a sociological perspective on the relation between researcher and reader, the analytic method confers on readers unique powers to make their own judgments on reliability from independent encounters with data. Is that not preferable? Unlike statistical measures of the relations between several items in an index, or of agreement scores on a given item administered at different times, the analytic qualitative approach does not separate the evaluation of reliability, or consistency in interpretation, from the evaluation of validity, or the mesh between the researcher's concepts and the meanings expressed by subjects.[18] Is that not preferable?

Qualitative researchers often admit to an inability to describe what would have to be done to repeat a study. They also have questioned whether a study is ever so disciplined by pre-fixed designs that, by adopting a published account of social research, anyone could ever really repeat it. The strength of analytic field research for replicability lies in the relationship it creates between original and subsequent researchers. When used in participant observation, the analytic method induces the researcher to credit as data his or her own experience as a member, minimizing the barriers to subsequent researchers for continuing the verification process. If qualitative field research offers no insurance that the researcher did not make up findings, it also raises the question of whether social research need be conducted in such a way that fabricated data can become a meaningful problem.

The analytic approach to fieldwork maintains an interaction between method and substance, breaking down their separation. Analytic field studies will not produce "proof," or artifacts which stand apart from substantive findings and can measure, or otherwise speak in a standard language about, representativeness, reliability, and so forth. The process and perspective for evaluation must be different. Acting within a system of social relations constructed in the research process, readers can make evaluations and researchers can assess how well they are doing.

Applied consistently in field research, the search for negative cases will force the researcher to focus on social process as experienced from within; induce research subjects to act toward the researcher as a meaningful member of the native world; enfranchise readers as colleagues competent to make independent assessments of the trustworthiness and general significance of the analysis; and facilitate subsequent tests of the findings by readers. This social system, which contains dimensions that have been barely outlined in this preliminary essay, can be invoked to spell out answers to numerous methodological questions frequently asked of qualitative field studies. For each qualitative field report, readers can assess how richly the researcher has perceived internal variation in the data; how radically the researcher varied his approaches to subjects; the density into which data and analysis have been interwoven; and the practical ease of testing the theoretical claims on new data.

Notes

Introduction

1. Although formally a jurisprudential essay, Fuller's (1969*a*) famous fable of the failed attempts by King Rex to construct a legal system makes a phenomenological claim. Such features as a general, public, and consistent reasoning are inherent in "law" as a distinctive, lived perspective on the workings of power.

2. For example: "From the dawn of Anglo-Saxon legal history, this idea has been manifest. The earliest laws continually directed that justice be done alike to rich and poor. The equal right to law was asserted in the Charter of Liberties of Henry II. The idea received its classic embodiment and statement in the fortieth paragraph of Magna Carta, where was inscribed '*nulli vendemus, nulli negabimus, aut differemus, rectum aut justiciam.*' As a purely historical fact this did not signify, or inaugurate, an era of absolute freedom of justice, but it was a first step in that direction. Its supreme importance, however, lies in the tradition which gradually attached to it, and which glorified the ideal—an ideal which steadily persisted in men's minds throughout five centuries, and which was brought by the colonists to the New World" (Smith 1919, p. 3).

3. Thus one of the most significant recent works in legal philosophy ends with the existentialist's cry: "But our days pass, and still we do not know you fully. Why then do you remain silent? Speak, God" (Unger 1975, p. 295).

4. A theme that contributes to *The Fall* (Camus 1956).

5. Such surveys have occasionally been attempted (Sykes 1969, Curran 1977), but they have not been institutionalized to allocate resources.

6. The forces that determine the perception of unequal access to the legal system are often barely visible. For a provocative discussion of one subtle point—how the structure and procedural rules of court systems implicitly "ration" justice, despite the celebrated ideological prohibition—see Hazard 1965.

7. This commitment would seem to be implicit, or at least immanent, in the establishment of the public prosecutor's office. But it must be acknowledged that historical research has not described the actual purpose behind the U.S. decision to deviate from the English tradition of private prosecution. Indeed, legal historians have rarely even speculated on why eighteenth-century U.S. jurisdictions, when still colonies of Britain, began to place the function of prosecution in a public office, seemingly following a Continental model (Van Alystyne 1952). But cf. Langbein

1973, p. 318: "The obvious drawback to any system of gratuitous citizen prosecution is that it is unreliable. There will be cases where there are no aggrieved citizens who survive to prosecute, and others where the aggrieved citizens will decline to prosecute, or be inept at it. Because the public interest in law enforcement cannot allow such gaps, the English had to admit an official element into their system of citizen prosecution." In other words, the office of the public prosecutor probably originated from a concern with "law and order," not with equality. Supporting this theory, the historical background for the change was a criminal trial in which, typically, neither side was represented by counsel (see Langbein 1978, p. 282). The symbolic commitment of the public prosecutor's office to equal justice in the initiation of criminal suits has developed quite gradually, without formal notice, seemingly as a response to the power of expertise that became available to the wealthy with the expansion of the private legal profession in the twentieth century.

8. But see Abel 1979.

9. In developing this theme, I have been provoked by the writing of Foucault (1978) on the historical role of professionals in assisting the state toward an increasingly comprehensive, meticulously applied, highly differentiated system of rules for controlling the lower classes.

Chapter 1

1. Also listed were types of "services rendered" on 34,718 "completed cases." They showed over 23,000 completed either with "consultation only" or with "consultation and referral"; 6320 after "representation without court action"; and 4647 after "representation with court action." The first two categories indicate dispositions after a single client interview, but to read within these categories for the amount and kind of preparation invested is to open a methodologist's Pandora's box. For example, included in the last and presumably most involved category are over 1700 uncontested plaintiff divorces.

2. "Heavy case loads" has been found to be an inadequate explanation of routine treatment in lower criminal courts. In Connecticut, jurisdictions with relatively low case loads and those with large volumes both employ summary processing (Freeley 1979).

3. In recent years, legal assistance lawyers have been disproportionately young relative to the bar as a whole (see chapter 4). They often sound like young physicians in hospitals (Miller 1970), energetically discriminating against "routine" cases and in favor of novel ones.

4. "People work," a term applied by Erving Goffman to minor officials supervising institutionalized populations, has introduced a field of study of "social institutions . . . whose primary goal is the shaping, reshaping, removing, overhauling, retooling, reassembling, and recording the physical, psychological, social, legal, or moral aspects of human objects" (Kitsuse 1970, p. 163).

5. On the elusive nature and moral implications of imputations of personal competence, or "essences," see Katz 1975. That the professions distinctively, though not exclusively, invite their members to pursue the discovery of essential truths about the self is implied in much of the work on charisma by Shils (1975).

6. For an earlier statement of this situation, see Katz 1978.

7. This is a clear, if diplomatically unstated, implication in Horsky 1952, pp. 59–117.

8. A Legal Services lawyer in Chicago's Uptown office wrote a pseudonymous account of his frustrated attempts to bring even minimal sophistication to the defense of evictions prosecuted by lay landlords (Davies 1971).

9. On the economic organization of lawyers' large-volume collection practices, see Grant 1967. On the distinctive pressures toward unethical conduct in practices which concentrate on handling, in lower municipal courts, personal-trouble cases—matrimonial, personal-injury, and collections—see Carlin 1962, pp. 162–200; 1966, p. 166. Leff (1970) has written on the economic rationality underlying the working personality of consumer-credit collection agents: "It pays to exaggerate how much "the law" favors you, how much you can do to the other party (via the law or without its help), how intransigent you always are (that is, how much spite is worth to you . . .). It pays to lie—at least in the short run. . . . If one views modern collection practice as another species of mass transaction, it becomes quite clear that the same economic constraints lead to most of its imperfections: it is too expensive . . . to be handled individually on the basis of the peculiar needs of particular parties in particular instances" (pp. 41, 38).

10. Despite recurrent calls in legal assistance circles for "community education" programs that would bring clients in for more anticipatory or preventive assistance, there is a rational basis for the poor person's crisis-centered search for help. A *personal ability* to plan for the long range is not solely a matter of personal preferene or personality organization but a *collective product* that depends on the willingness of others to take one's plans into consideration.

11. A client's refusal to leave the office, like a client's willingness to leave after receiving little or no service, often proceeds directly from the expectation that his problems will not be given much attention by others. Both privately retained and legal assistance lawyers may rebel against "menial" work expected by their clients. In either setting, the lawyer may consider a client able to handle an accounting or reporting task on his own. But legal assistance lawyers have unique problems for negotiating a role they consider suited to their competence. Citing their rights to "free" service and afraid that without the service they would be ignored, clients may insist on a right to be less competent than the lawyer cares to define them.

> *This was the most extreme mess of a lawyer–client interview that I have witnessed. For at least 25 minutes, L. and Cl. fight over whether L. or Cl. would go to eviction court and show the judge receipts which, L. claims, make out a solid defense. Cl. argues that she wouldn't be paid the same respect by the judge*

> *as would L. L. privately insults Cl. by thinking her unstable (as his comments later show), all the while explaining in a therapeutically calm voice,* "I refuse to insult you by handling this case. You're fully capable of doing this yourself." *Cl. retorts angrily,* "This is Legal Aid; I'm a poor person, so I'm your boss; and if I want you to insult me, you'll insult me."

12. Tasks pejoratively labeled "social work" in legal assistance offices have their parallels in private practices. But with paying clients, where personal services requiring no professional competence can be perceived as helping maintain long-term relations, such services seem not to be thought quite so demeaning.

> From the first day I was at Legal Aid, I wanted to give the same service that I had at the firm, the same quality. I was amazed when I read in the [Legal Aid] manual: if clients come in for a divorce, ask them if they've got their marriage certificate; and if they don't, tell them to get one and come back. Well, that's right; often people, especially the Legal Aid clients, won't really know if they're legally married or not, so you should check that. But I felt, hell, at the firm we'd never treat a client that way. We'd write to court for the document. That's when, right at the first, I began to perceive the differences, that you couldn't do that and also do volume work.

13. Here again I prefer a structural to a culture-of-poverty explanation. Actually I have no choice: I gathered no data on whether poor people are personally disorganized and untrustworthy outside of their behavior at legal assistance offices. Within the office itself, all that can be observed are the terms and qualities of the relations. It is, however, interesting to note that legal assistance lawyers themselves often prefer the culture-of-poverty explanation. The culture-of-poverty thesis is questioned in Leacock 1971. O'Gorman (1963) draws a distinction between legal practices with transitory and with permanent clientele. He describes the private matrimonial lawyers he studied as in the former category and presents their typical views of clients: emotionally upset, ignorant of the law, and irrationally demanding of help on personal rather than legal problems (pp. 62–64, 81–109).

Chapter 2

1. The Protective Agency's legislative program was exclusively and extremely punitive, contemplating at one point the "sterilization of habitual criminals, imbeciles, idiots and rapists in institutions" (Chicago Legal Aid Society 1908, p. 12). When it became part of the Legal Aid Society, the agency's emphasis on incapacitation began to lose force; civil rather than criminal laws became the preferred remedies. The society's president scathingly criticized its Women's Committee, successor to the agency, for the role it took in prosecutions, which was to induce children to relive sexual assaults in accounts elicited under pressure at trial. He noted that the evidence in such cases consisted solely of a contradiction between testimony from the child and the defendant and that "our own experience and the experience of those

who are better able to judge than we are teaches us that there will undoubtedly be an acquittal" (Chicago Legal Aid Society 1910, pp. 9–10).

2. The bureau's original milieu was recalled by a participant, Rudolph Matz, in Chicago Legal Aid Society 1914, p. 13.

3. I took Martindale-Hubbell ratings for 1914, specifically the top av rating, as an indicator of a "prominent" reputation in the legal community. Two ex-staff lawyers of the five I checked (a complete list was unavailable) had received an av rating, as had several of the early board members.

4. The general pattern of institutional transformation in social work, from settlement house reformer to professional caseworker, is described in Lubove 1965.

5. In 1903, a drop in employer–employee cases was attributed to the rise of unions in the building trades (Chicago Bureau of Justice 1903, p. 11). In 1936, Smith and Bradway (p. 52) attributed historical trends in Legal Aid's work to the rise of an analogous role by state labor and industrial-accident commissions.

6. Typescript of oral report made to the Legal Aid Society by Maud Parcells Boyes, Superintendent [Chicago Historical Society n.d. (1919?), p. 2].

7. In the national association of Legal Aid Societies in the early 1920s, a major "problem was the relationship between legal aid work and social work. Legal aid work nearly split on the question as to whether its service was purely legal or purely social" (Bradway 1926, p. 164).

8. The procedural version of justice was not seen as sufficient justification, however. The case for Legal Aid was often couched in terms of benefits for social control and improving the citizenry. Johnson (1974, p. 13) threw himself into the spirit of the Legal Aid philosophy in order to describe it; commenting on Reginald Heber Smith's praise in 1951 for Legal Aid as an anticommunist device, he maintained: "Each man, rich or poor, deserves his day in court; that is what this country is all about; and besides, if we do not insure that access, the masses will revolt and tear down our system of government. Entirely missing is an evident stake in the outcome of the poor man's day in court and its implications for his other social and economic problems."

9. In the same vein, Hunter wrote: "The Bureau's office is a law office, and its counsel are bound by the Code of Ethics of the American Bar Association. Not only is the office free to refuse to take unworthy claims, but it cannot afford to do so [*sic*] because of its unique position in the community. It is most important that the Bureau, by its good reports, earns and keeps the good will and respect of judges, officials, lawyers, and of the community in general. While the Bureau recognizes that every man is entitled to be protected in his legal rights, and while it does not purport to make itself the judge of its applicants, it does refuse, and refuses without equivocation, to have any part in matters which are morally wrong, or which run contrary to the spirit of enlightened justice" [Chicago Historical Society n.d. (1920s?), p. 11].

10. Historically, the New York Legal Aid Society has been almost unique among Legal Aids nationally both in not receiving funds from a Community Chest and in

receiving a major portion of its funds from a bar association. For the financially precarious national pattern before the formation of Community Chests, see Smith 1919, pp. 193–196; for the situation in 1933, Smith and Bradway 1936, p. 147. For 1947, Brownell (1951, p. 237) reported that nationally about 60 percent of the financial support came from Community Chests, about 8.5 percent from "bar associations and lawyers." Legal Aids were not creations of lawyers, and it was not until 1922 that a formal "arrangement" for contributions was made between the Legal Aid Bureau of United Charities of Chicago and the Chicago Bar Association. The deal, which required the bar association to raise one-half of the bureau's funds (Gariepy 1926, p. 36), was not carried out. According to annual reports issued by the United Charities, the Legal Aid Bureau received in 1965 about $475,000: $100,000 from law firms, lawyers, and the Chicago Bar Association; $250,000 from the Community Fund; and $91,000 from United Charities funds. In 1972, for the joint Legal Aid and Legal Services programs, $2.5 million was received: $165,000 from law firms, lawyers, and the bar association; $380,000 from the Community Fund; $270,000 from United Charities funds, and $1.6 million from federal funds.

11. I have no basis for asserting that the growth of social distance was cause rather than effect of the abandonment of reform. The point—continued in later chapters on Legal Services—is simply that the relationship has been systematic over the evolution of the institution. The pattern is evidently applicable beyond civil legal assistance to the poor (see Rabin 1976, pp. 218–219).

12. Within the legal community, the dominant theme in appeals for support and in commendations from Legal Aid supporters was how justice was compromised because access to the judicial system depended on the ability to pay a lawyer. It was often stated with poignant examples and couched as a violation of ideals ranging from the Magna Carta to the Bill of Rights. Samples of such statements, typically made by and to lawyers at annual meetings, can be found in the published proceedings of the national Legal Aid conventions starting in 1912 and in the national organization's periodical, *Legal Aid Brief Case,* starting in 1942. In Chicago, the high point in attracting symbolic support was apparently achieved in 1915, when Woodrow Wilson, Theodore Roosevelt, and William Howard Taft were enlisted as honorary vice-presidents of the Legal Aid Society.

13. In Chicago: Hale 1949; Lortie 1959; Carlin 1962, pp. 17–25. In Detroit: Ladinsky 1963, pp. 47–54, on discrimination, pp. 52–53. In New York: Smigel 1964 on discrimination, pp. 44–46; Carlin 1966, pp. 22–37.

14. I searched for listings in regional and national *Who's Who* of the 18 members of the Legal Aid Committee in 1955. I found entries on 15 members, only 4 of whom were exceptions from the pattern: one woman, who held a succession of offices in the local and national Girl Scouts, leading to the national presidency; a Notre Dame B.A.–Harvard law educated vice-president of the First National Bank and the Catholic Charities; a Harvard B.A.–Harvard law educated, Republican, senior-senior partner of the city's oldest large Jewish-founded law firm; and a "social

and civil welfare worker," the only graduate in the group from a non-"national" law school and the only one indicating participation in the Urban League, the NAACP, or any form of civil rights work.

15. In 1962, the Legal Aid staff director summarized for the Legal Aid Committee the difficulty of finding "suitable people" for Legal Aid positions and suggested a "reemployment plan with our supporting firms" whereby a "bright young man" might be induced to come to Legal Aid for a year or more. The idea was generally discounted, but two members said they would "be interested in a man with proper qualifications who may desire to spend a year" at a Legal Aid office before "attaching himself" to a "large firm" (United Charities of Chicago 1962).

16. Epstein (1970, pp. 160–161), drawing on her New York research on women lawyers, terms Legal Aid: "a haven for women lawyers, although many who begin practice there leave it for other work. This semi-welfare agency typically handles a high proportion of family cases: desertion, abandonment, and juvenile problems. (Some officials have estimated these as high as 40 percent.) Not only have men avoided legal aid work because of the low salary it pays, but family law cases are believed to be paralegal—more social work than legal work. . . . Thus, legal aid work has not typically been the first choice of aggressive and ambitious male lawyers and in consequence has been relatively open to women lawyers."

17. The 1950 census (U.S. Dept. of Commerce 1950) reported 10,006 employed lawyers and judges in Chicago, of which 239 were "non-white," of which 13 were female (at pp. 276, 279, 281). The 1960 census reported for the comparable categories 10,699, 225, and 8 (U.S. Dept. of Commerce 1960).

Hale (1949) studied black lawyers in Chicago in the late 1940s, using a large though unsystematically selected sample of 112. He found that, whereas many black clients went to white lawyers, 71 of the black lawyers had exclusively black clients and only 9 had a clientele over 10 percent white. Among the staff, but not at the board level, Legal Aid broke down the pattern of segregating lawyers from each other by race and the pattern of segregating clients from lawyers by race. It provided black and white clients for black and white lawyers who were governed by white corporate lawyers who had a white clientele in their practices.

The Legal Aid Bureau also promoted the integration of clients and lawyers in the lower levels of private practice. Hale termed the bureau an "unwitting partner" to the channeling of black clients to white lawyers through its referral policies. According to Legal Aid Bureau records, 27 percent of its 13,500 "cases received" in 1947 were "Negro," and 22.5 percent of the Negro clients were deemed ineligible and referred to a panel designated by the Chicago Bar Association (Hale 1949, p. 137). There were no black lawyers on the panel, and blacks were refused admission to the bar association until some time after the Second World War. The ambiguity concerning the precise date at which the color bar was lifted is described in Goldman 1972, p. 356.

18. For examples of culture shock among young associates of New York blue-chip

law firms who volunteer to work in Legal Aid offices, see Hoffman 1973, pp. 198–199. In one of his short stories, Auchincloss (1963, p. 22) indicates the personal competence thought compatible with Legal Aid work by senior partners in prestigious firms: Legal Aid work is one of the few alternatives remaining in the desolate and semialcoholic life of a senior partner who is forced to resign from the firm after a stunning defeat in a battle over ethics.

19. Chicago Historical Society n.d. (1919?), p. 1. Ethnicity was identified and recorded in a careful, highly differentiated manner. This elaborate social accounting reflected the practical need to allocate interpreters to client interviews.

20. According to a national study, in 1967, in cities of over 600,000 population, blacks, as opposed to "whites" and "other" (Chicano, Native American, etc.), constituted by far the single largest group of legal assistance clients, or 45.3 percent (Handler, Hollingsworth, and Erlanger 1978, p. 63).

Chapter 3

1. With unique specificity and provocative examples, albeit with characteristically mystifying brevity, Simmel (1971, p. 257) compared relations between the identities of members and their groups. He suggested a pattern in the nature of a dialectic that, with some reading between the lines, works in application to legal assistance lawyers and organizations. Viewing Legal Aid societies as "distinctive," or differentiated, from other efforts in the legal profession from 1920 to 1960; and viewing Legal Services programs as relatively undifferentiated from the rest of the broad legal rights movement of the sixties and seventies, I can agree with Simmel that, in this institutional setting, "the elements of a distinctive social circle are undifferentiated, and the elements of a circle that is not distinctive are differentiated." The next three chapters illustrate *how* such a dialectical relationship might obtain, an issue Simmel never directly addressed.

2. The perspective on the Chicago Legal Aid Bureau of one of its aristocratic lawyers of the fifties is available in Roberg 1957. I would like to thank Silvie Bizzio for assistance in translation.

3. See text in chapter 4, soon after the heading "Staff Ties to Social Movements."

4. Everyday methods of resolving existential uncertainties have been a major concern of ethnomethodology (see Garfinkel 1967).

5. U.S. v. Barr, 295 F. Supp. 889 (S.D.N.Y., 1969). Cf. U.S. v. Wiseman, 445 F.2d 792 (2d Cir., 1971), *cert. den.* 404 U.S. 967 (1971).

Chapter 4

1. As others have pointed out, these figures are necessarily rough owing to the flux of personnel and the administrative informality of the program in its early years.

See Handler, Hollingsworth, and Erlanger 1978, p. 33, n. 8. (Hereafter the Handler-Hollingsworth-Erlanger book is referred to as the Wisconsin study.)

2. For the reasons given in note 1, this is a loose estimate, based on staff reports at CLC and on personnel records and the annual report of the United Charities Legal Aid Bureau for 1970.

3. See generally Johnson 1974, pp. 82–86. Poverty lawyers and representatives of the poverty community in San Francisco allied successfully to win a Legal Services grant in a competition against an alliance between the existing Legal Aid Society and the local bar association (Wright 1967).

4. One could say there has been an inverse relation in the history of legal assistance organizations between historical and contemporaneous distinctiveness. In sociology, the concept of organizational distinctiveness was introduced by Selznick (1957), who examined how organizations come to be prized for their unique qualities —their distinctive identity within their contemporaneous context—through developing long traditions. There are compelling reasons to suspect a systematic trade-off between the ability of an organization to depart radically from its predecessors and its ability to be the unique embodiment of communal values.

A dialectical relation between the contemporaneous and historical distinctiveness of a collectivity's identity has been argued in diverse fields. See Perrow 1972 and Niebuhr's (1957) classic study of the careers of Reformation churches. Shils (1958) has studied the infusion of "charisma" into institutions, a process he describes in ways (and in language) that parallel Selznick's discussion. Shils finds anomie in charisma: activities seen as creative are in one sense understood as distinctive, in another as amorphous or vaguely bounded. Fuller (1969*b*), drawing explicitly on Simmel, finds an intrinsic trade-off between the principles of legality and commitment as bonds in human associations. The governance of social relations by rules imparts a distinctiveness to the group's nature in the sense of articulated clarity. At the same time, legality outlaws *ex post facto* norms and thus impairs the formation of shared dedication to inarticulate strivings, which promote distinctiveness in the sense of creative purpose and collective progress. Yet Selznick appears to have no interest in breaking distinctiveness into two dimensions.

5. Sociologists have long been fascinated with the careers of social-movement organizations. Almost invariably their analysis has failed to question the extent to which external influences were responsible for an organization's initial activism. This has often led to a spurious imputation of "inherent bureaucratic tendencies," or some such internal organizational cause, to explain conservative transformations that might as well be attributed to the decline of an initially supporting, initially encompassing social movement. Theoretical commentary has warned against assuming a "pathos" of bureaucratization (Gouldner 1955), but case studies continue to find elements of bureaucratization and "professionalism" inexorably promoting a shift from goals of social reform and structural change to individual service and adjust-

ment. See, for example, Helfgot 1974 on the social work leadership of Mobilization for Youth. Zald and Ash (1966) purport to avoid an assumption of pathos when offering a general framework for analyzing "growth, decay and change" of social-movement organizations. Their references to the effects on a social-movement organization of a decline in the broader movement consist, however, only of the following. They predict a direct relationship (see their Proposition 1): as the movement fades, the organization's ability to survive and grow will decline. And they offer a single qualification (see Proposition 2): pressure toward a conservative transformation will be less in organizations with "exclusive" memberships (i.e., where moral commitments are required) that aim at changing individuals than it will be in organizations with inclusive memberships that start to achieve structural social change. The application of those abstract formulations to Legal Services is not obvious (was it originally an exclusive, social-reform organization?). In any case, Zald and Ash do not examine closely the ways in which organizations may initially receive support from broader social-reform movements, much less consider how given supports, once removed, may be replaced by functional substitutes.

6. For decades, the LAB's main office was at 123 W. Madison St. One LAB staff lawyer was assigned to a student clinic at Northwestern Law School, also located downtown; starting in the late 1950s, another staff lawyer directed the Mandel Clinic at the University of Chicago Law School, on the South Side.

7. In 1972, the addresses of Chicago's neighborhood Legal Services offices (and their colloquial names) were: 2931 W. Madison St. (East Garfield); 1413 W. 18th St. (Eighteenth St.); 6508 S. Halsted St. (Englewood); 422 E. 47th St. (Grand Boulevard); 911 S. Kedzie Ave. (Lawndale); 2029 W. North Ave. (Northwest); 4564 N. Broadway (Uptown); 1105 E. 63rd St. (Woodlawn).

8. In 1970, CLC had its main office at 116 S. Michigan Ave., and it had four neighborhood offices, existing in various degrees (1) in Lawndale, at 3324 W. Roosevelt Rd.; (2) related to TWO, The Woodlawn Organization, in Woodlawn, at 1133 E. 63rd St.; (3) related to Charles Geary's organization in Uptown, at 4700 N. Kenmore Ave.; and (4) related briefly to KOCO, the Kenwood-Oakland Community Organization, at 1358 E. 47th St.

9. For example, the legal director of Mobilization for Youth gave a critical review to the New York Legal Aid Society (Rothwax 1969, p. 139).

10. The most elaborate use of the military metaphor was in a widely read article by Cahn and Cahn 1964. The national OEO Office of Legal Services required local projects to produce annual "work programs" featuring enumerated priorities and critical self-evaluations.

11. On the relation between internal structural change and rapid development in the 1960s of the NAACP Legal Defense Fund and the ACLU staff litigation unit, see Rabin 1976.

12. Law academics were only one among many types of professional reformers shaping the experiments (Johnson 1974, p. 29).

13. Information was compiled from United Charities personnel files, which during the period of research included only those CLC lawyers on staff in 1972. "Legal Services" included Reggies, but not Vista lawyers, and excluded about 10 CLC lawyers who had left that organization before 1972. The determination of the coverage of "major national law schools" and "nationally prestigious colleges" is inevitably artificial, since the referent in both cases is the views of an ill-defined and uncoordinated audience. I drew the list of law schools narrowly to include those schools I hear most frequently credited with "national" status (in student and professorial recruitment, in access of students to labor markets, and in law journal audiences): Harvard, Columbia, Yale, Chicago, Pennsylvania, Berkeley, Michigan, and Stanford. In selecting "nationally prestigious" colleges (undergraduate degrees), the purpose of showing a difference between Legal Aid and Legal Services did not require judgments on small colleges of specialized repute, and a short list consisting of the Ivy League schools, plus Chicago, Berkeley, and Stanford, sufficed.

14. I am using "social movement" as Blumer (1957, pp. 129–130) defined "collective behavior": "a sense of transcending power" which arises "when one identifies himself with a large group or participates wittingly in a large group enterprise"; social relations that "tend . . . to be indirect, segmental, and orientated toward broad categories of peoples"; a process of "mobilizing for action" that relies on bridging links between social units "which in themselves have a different positional and functional nature"; and "large group activity that comes into being and develops along lines that are not laid out by pre-established social definitions. Such activity and the organization of people which it presupposes are formed or forged to meet undefined or unstructured situations."

15. For the features of and organizational requirements for sustaining, a genuinely "radical" outlook, an outlook which was only marginally present in Legal Services, see Bittner 1963.

16. In the sixties, an everyday drama of political symbolism on public streets afforded constant opportunities to join "the Movement" with a slight gesture. This drama emerged so informally and has disappeared so totally that its membership is impossible to recount. I recall a moment when I was driving on the Outer Drive in 1971, a year in which my hair was "long," when a boy of about 7 in the car ahead appeared to check discreetly whether his parents in the front seat were watching, then furtively flashed me a V sign. What I see on the streets of Los Angeles today is a sizeable percentage of self-absorbed drivers singing and dancing in their seats.

17. A lawyer who had worked at the Woodlawn Neighborhood Legal Services office reported:

> I first turned on in my last year of law school, and there was a separate group who were turning on, and not very into being lawyers. It was like I just found myself in law school, then in Vista to beat the draft, and then into Legal aid because it was the most removed thing from working in an office. [Answering my earlier question] I wasn't considering other legal jobs; I was con-

sidering giving up the whole lawyer thing and teaching English. Legal aid was the only way I could have stayed in law then.

18. Erlanger's (1978, p. 260) statistics on lawyers graduating from law school after 1964 show that Catholics were overrepresented in Legal Services as contrasted with the bar, and the difference (45–21 percent) was substantially greater than the overrepresentation of Jews (31–19 percent).

19. A study based on interviews in 1968 with Catholic graduate students in Chicago-area universities indicated that those who had left the church and those still "in" differed more clearly on issues of personal choice (sex, intellectual freedom) than social responsibility (Kotre 1971). For an extensive, subtle description of changes in the political and moral self-conceptions of Catholics in the sixties, especially among the well-educated, see Wills 1972.

20. The most comprehensive review of these controversies is in Blumenthal and Soler 1971.

21. This charge worried the Wisconsin researchers.

22. Strong opposition came from bar associations at the local level (Pye and Garraty 1966, Stumpf, Schroerluke, and Dill 1971).

23. The day after she was elected president of a tenants' organization, Joyce Thorpe was ordered by the Durham City Housing Authority to vacate her apartment, and she was refused an explanation. The Supreme Court enforced a HUD Circular, dated 7 February 1967, directing that federally assisted, local housing authorities give reasons and an opportunity to reply before evicting tenants. Thorpe v. Housing Authority of City of Durham, 393 U.S. 268 (1969).

24. See, e.g., R. S. Boston Co. v. Chapman, 131 Ill. App.2d 385, 266 N.E.2d 767 (1970), which gave judicial recognition to defenses against collection actions based on a merchant's failure to fulfill requirements of the Illinois Retail Installment Sales Act (S.H.A. ch. 121 1/2, pp. 501–533, 1967) for the listing of the buyer's name in the *body* of the contract. It was not sufficient that Chapman had signed on a printed line designated "Buyer" at the *bottom* of the contract.

Suits brought by Chicago legal assistance lawyers have created virtually the entire case law on many sections of the Retail Installment Sales Act, the Motor Vehicle Retail Installment Sales Act, the Consumer Fraud Act, and other Illinois consumer protection statutes originally enacted or procedurally strengthened in the 1960s and early 1970s.

25. Although the Supreme Court made no mention of the fact, the complaint as popularly understood in Alabama and among the lawyers was one of racial oppression. The context and makings of the case are recounted in Garbus 1971. The Court signaled its readiness to cut down a host of other restrictions by depicting the state as so cruel as to be morally untrustworthy. In his majority opinion, Chief Justice Warren gratuitously noted that, after the regulation was enacted, Mrs. Smith and her four children were dependent on "a salary of between $16 and $20 per week which

[their mother] earns working from 3:30 A.M. to 12 noon as a cook and waitress." 392 U.S. 309, at 315 (1968).

26. Jack Spring, Inc. v. Little, 50 Ill.2d 351 (1972).

27. Johnson v. Robinson, 296 F. Supp. 1165 (N.D. Ill., 1967) aff'd. 394 U.S. 847 (1968).

28. Shapiro v. Thompson, 394 U.S. 618 (1968).

29. Doe v. Scott, 321 F. Supp. 1385 (N.D. Ill., 1971).

30. Brown v. Board of Education, 71C-694 (N.D. Ill., 1971).

31. Contact Buyers League v. F & F Investments, 300 F. Supp. 210 (N.D. Ill., 1969); appealed under the name Baker v. F & F Investments, 420 F.2d 1191 (7th Cir. 1970). Defending was Robert S. Cushman, a long-time, highly influential member of the United Charities Legal Aid Committee. The development of the league's legal strategy is described in Fitzgerald 1975.

32. The first decision was Gautreaux v. The Chicago Housing Authority, 265 F. Supp. 582 (N.D. Ill., 1967).

33. The first step was Rodriguez v. Swank, 318 F. Supp. 289 (N.D. Ill., 1970), aff'd. 403 U.S. 901 (1971).

34. Chicago Welfare-Rights Organization et al. v. Richard B. Ogilvie et al., 71C-2618 (N.D. Ill., Nov. 1, 1971).

35. Compare Piven and Cloward 1971, pp. 183, 187: "During the 1950's the AFDC rolls rose by only 110,000 families or 17 per cent. But from December 1960 to February 1969, some 800,000 families were added to the rolls, an increase of 107 percent in just eight years and two months. . . . *the rolls went up all at once*—by 31 percent in the first few years of the decade, but by 58 percent in the next few years. . . . fully 71 percent of the huge welfare increase during the 1960's took place in the few years *after* 1964."

36. On the concept of "latent" identities, see Gouldner 1957, Becker and Geer 1960.

37. A popular history of Chicago's independent political movement is given in Mathewson 1974.

38. I took the list of officers and board members from a February 1972 publication of the council, "Report on Disciplinary Procedures for Professional Misconduct" (on the inadequacies of the CBA mechanism).

39. The Democratic organization in Chicago appeared to be so wedded to its public image as impregnably strong that it felt vulnerable to the weakest material challenge. Suttles (1978) has analyzed how Chicago officials elevated to the status of politically subversive forces three street gangs of unruly ghetto youth, the Blackstone Rangers, Young Lords, and Young Patriots. He notes that there were scores of other youth gangs in the city at the time and that these three were distinguished by their location in wards that led liberal opposition to the machine.

40. Complaint Before the Secretary, Department of Housing and Urban Develop-

ment (Requesting that the Secretary withhold approval and funds from Respondent's proposed Modernization Program until and unless . . .), Chicago Housing Tenants Organization v. The Chicago Housing Authority, 1970.

41. The phrase is from an analysis of political implications of the legal rights movement (Scheingold 1974).

Chapter 5

1. Grønbjerg, Street, and Suttles 1978, p. 163: "Much activity during the poverty program [*sic*] consisted of the marketing of old wine (e.g., the idea of motivating the poor through self-help) in new bottles (e.g., 'maximum feasible community participation')."

2. Opposition to LSPs by the organized bar was stimulated by economic self-interest at the local level (Stumpf, Schroerluke, and Dill 1971).

3. See the references to the Chicago Legal Services program in Blumenthal and Soler 1971, pp. 249–250; Balbus 1973, p. 38.

4. One of the ejected Reggies told an interviewer:

> There were two or three lawyers in Legal Services, and two or three law students who got turned on to criminal political cases. We had started to know Fred Hampton [a Black Panther party leader in Chicago who was killed by the police during an alleged shootout at a Panther apartment in 1969], and some of these people, and they had a very great influence on us.
>
> In Legal Services Daley controlled the money and he didn't want any criminal or civil rights cases done, or suing police officers or anything like that. So each month we'd continue doing these cases, and each month the lawyers would be reprimanded, fired, and then rehired. At the beginning of the summer of 1969 we just had to get away from Legal Aid because we just couldn't function and keep up any personal sense of existence. So we all started thinking about going somewhere else. (James, M. 1973, pp. 130–131).

5. This process was traced in one city by Carlin 1971, pp. 64–74.

6. For a recent argument against the strategic value of organizing the poor apart from alliances with labor unions, see Roach and Roach 1978 (analyzing the career of the National Welfare Rights Organization).

7. Piven and Cloward (1978) responded to the criticism (just cited) of Roach and Roach by reemphasizing the powerful, if historically erratic, political value of militant protest and civil disobedience.

8. SDS organizers had reached the same conclusion seven years earlier (Gitlin and Hollander 1970).

9. The case was Goliday v. Robinson, 305 F. Supp. 1224 (N.D. Ill., 1969) (Public aid department must provide notice and opportunity to be heard before reducing benefits). The opinion on the capability of welfare rights organizations is given in Piven and Cloward 1979, pp. 299–300. A study of welfare rights organiza-

tions reported that Chicago's recipient groups were unusually factionalized and strife ridden and that in January 1971 they had enrolled only 2.6 percent of adult welfare recipients (Martin 1972, pp. 149–150).

10. Piven and Cloward 1979, p. 272, n. 11 (characterizing litigation organized by Edward Sparer).

11. Cf. Oberschall's (1977) account of the decline of activist agencies of the sixties: "On balance, it must be concluded that internal weaknesses due to deficiencies in organization structure and to a lack of shared political culture were important factors in movement decline" (p. 269).

Chapter 6

1. On young doctors, see Miller 1970.

2. There have been many studies of "involvement," especially by "management scientists," for example, McKelvey and Sekaran 1977. Virtually all use a static, cross-sectional design. They compare different degrees of what they posit as indicators of involvement—for example, measures of "job satisfaction"—under different conditions of work. Their correlational statistics do not help to explain variations over time in the experience of given individuals while they work in a given environment. To explain these phenomena, it is necessary to consider subjects not solely as objects affected by environmental factors but as actors, as people interpreting, then doing something to, their external conditions.

3. Certain difficulties for social research follow from the nature of the experience of involvement. When people are involved in their work, they want to talk about *it*, not about extraneous issues in the sociology of work and personal careers. In interviews, I would repeatedly tune out as respondents began to discuss the details of legal doctrines. To have developed an explanation of how it is that poverty lawyers find legal questions interesting, I would have had to examine the implicit social structure underneath their professional distinctions (e.g., what differences in folk anthropological theories on the determinants of district court sensitivities to appellate courts might explain esthetic differences among poverty lawyers over writing styles in briefs?). That would have been a worthy line of investigation, one that has not yet been taken up in the sociology of law. But following that line would have meant departing from a focus on the world of legal assistance, for poverty lawyers do not appear to use institutionally *distinctive* standards for experiencing questions of legal theory and strategy as more or less exciting.

4. Compare the concept of involvement developed by Becker (1970, p. 302) in his effort to explain consistency in human conduct, a generic sociological problem: "Persons sometimes create a new and at least temporarily stable self by becoming deeply engrossed in a particular activity or group of people, becoming involved in the sense that they no longer take into account the responses of a large number of

people with whom they actually interact." Becker's (emphatically tentative) explanation of involvement refers to mechanisms which enable people to ignore, discount, or insulate themselves from discouraging expectations. As examples he mentions both the physical isolation of religious sects and peer-group education among drug users. For lawyers in Legal Services, involvement similarly depends on sustaining a culture with which they reject and transcend expectations that they act routinely. I have more to say about the need to reject discouragement, but I am first concerned with the experience of involvement.

Paradoxical in Becker's explanation of involvement is his neglect of the actor's relation with the object of involvement itself. As experienced, involvement is a perspective in which one's activity or affiliation seems intrinsically compelling, not a matter of indifference which one maintains simply because disparaging pressures are walled off by social structure. A method of buffering oneself from discouragement may be a necessary condition of involvement, but it does not provide a sufficient explanation.

5. My source is Legal Assistance Foundation personnel files.

6. It is not clear that this view is valid. Consider two occupations. One overpays its members in ego-gratification: 90 percent believe they are in the top 10 percent with respect to desirable working conditions. The other underpays: 90 percent believe they are in the bottom 10 percent. I suspect that their work environments tend lawyers in the direction of the former mass delusion. One of the contributing factors might be the institution of confidentiality. (You alone are entrusted with responsibilities of such magnitude! The world should only know!) Another might be the widespread potential for evanescent publicity. (You always clip the news blurbs on your cases, but you do not remember the momentarily celebrated triumphs of others.) Another contributing factor might be the phenomenological vagueness inherent in much collective law work. When many lawyers combine many kinds of effort to produce a work product with a zero-sum outcome (the case wins or loses), it is easy for personal perceptions of personal contribution to add to more than 100 percent. Each of 20 lawyers, from the lowest library researcher to the first drafter to the last drafter to the appellate arguer, may believe that his or her contribution was decisive in producing the victory.

7. But why does the first leave? Because it purports to be a "sufficient" explanation, the theory of involvement requires an answer to this question. First, as the next paragraph notes, it is not always the case that both partners in a culture-sharing dyad are "involved"; often only one litigates reform cases. Second, exits often developed unexpectedly for "involved" lawyers. A community group might suddenly fall apart or succeed in obtaining a grant so large as to make it ineligible for Legal Services. Another turning point out of involvement may occur during long vacations in foreign countries that are taken after extended periods of involvement. For a few neighborhood lawyers, such vacations became a convenient time to reflect on the significance of work and its place in a long-range career.

8. Sociologists have rarely attempted to explain the role of collectivities in the causation of individual behavior in this way. The mechanism of causation is usually said to be: (1) a "push" by the collectivity on the individual (whether by crude threat or subtle inducement); (2) the functional efficiency of participating in the group for achieving individual ends (either through group support for individual problem solving or because the group presents the most proximate, cheapest avenue to a previously desired individual end); or (3) the opportunity presented by the group for "sociability," providing satisfactions unrelated to the actor's practical goals. All of these mechanisms assume that the causal relationship between individual and group is one of means and ends. That assumption leaves no conceptual room for an understanding of the simultaneous creation and mutual causal dependence of collective and individual identity. An alternative view is that society and the person are brought into existence at the same time, through the same activity: people depending on each other to make sensible the project of creating a self.

9. For reform litigators, the neighborhood-office environment, with its constant expectation of routine treatment, fits Goffman's (1971, pp. 340–341) analysis of an "insane place," one in which there is a sharp and continuous conflict between "person" and "self." "The treatment that an individual gives others and receives from them expresses or assumes a definition of him, as does the immediate social scene in which a treatment occurs. . . . The ultimate referent here is a tacit coding discoverable by competently reading conduct, and not conceptions or images that persons actually have in their minds. . . . Persons and self are portraits of the same individual, the first encoded in the actions of others, the second in the actions of the subject himself." Goffman here explicitly draws on the distinction between "role commitment" and "role validation" sketched by Erikson (1957).

10. The peer culture of significance goes far beyond shielding the lawyers from frustration. It dramatizes the heroics of doggedly attempting to do good works in an "impossible" situation and the *Über-mut* of showing provocative disdain for considerations of job security. Berger (1962, p. 31 in Smigel) describes the precise inverse of this form of involvement in professional and executive work which pretends to no moral content ("the manufacture of hoola hoops [*sic*] or mink coats for dogs or refrigerators that never need defrosting"). He notes that, in such milieux, "it has become fashionable, almost de rigeur, to be cynical about one's work . . . the sophistication and the subtlety of one's cynicism can be highly rewarding, thus creating a situation in which one can be quite alienated from work but quite satisfied with one's job."

11. The dilemma of the modern civil rights lawyer has its precedent in the abolitionist's world, in a time before the popularity of existentialism when, one may presume, no one took it as funny. "Slaveholders were sometimes willing to negotiate a sale of the runaway so that freedom might be maintained. Such a sale was often more advantageous to the owner than retention of a potentially rebellious Negro . . . but many abolitionists condemned the purchase of a runaway as a concession on the

basic issue that there may rightly be property in man. The most famous struggle over this principle occurred with regard to the question of whether the great Frederick Douglass, the nation's most famous fugitive, might rightly negotiate a self-purchase so as not to face the threat of eventual recapture. Douglass split with Garrison and Phillips on this matter and ultimately purchased himself" (Cover 1975, p. 213).

Chapter 7

1. The earliest and still the most provocative general statement on the relation between the character of a group and the careers of its members is Simmel 1898.

2. The study of personal change in organizations and the study of organizational character have traditionally been conducted separately. The resulting research gap has been recognized by Wheeler 1966, pp. 99–100. "Career" studies are usually temporal but ahistorical. They examine the intraorganizational careers of managers, teachers, patients, and prisoners, but not the careers of their firms, schools, hospitals, and prisons. Representative studies are collected in Glaser 1968. Studies of organizational character focus on institutional history. They usually examine the relevance for this history of the nature of membership, but not the meaning of the organization's character in ongoing biographies developed by members. See, for examples, Selznick 1949 (a government agency), Sills 1957 (a voluntary association), and Clark 1970 (colleges).

A sociological objective of my study is to comprehend the interrelations of personal careers and collective identities that have existed in legal assistance work. In previous chapters, I have traced the role of collective characteristics—Legal Aid's day-in-court philosophy and Legal Services's origins in the social movements of the sixties—in the development of staff lawyers' careers. I now turn to the other, more elusive direction of the interrelationship: how the personal careers developed by staff lawyers influence the collective character of legal assistance work.

3. The body of research on the effects of succession on organizations is large and rapidly growing. A recent example is Allen, Panian, and Lotz 1979. A frequently cited modern statement of the sociological issue is Grusky 1960. When succession occurs at organizational levels lower than management, it is known and studied as "turnover." For a review of the voluminous literature on turnover, see Price 1977.

4. A well-known study of decline is Messinger 1955. A theoretical approach is available in Hirschman 1970.

5. A struggle against redundancy characterizes work on a massive level in many of the most "modern" sectors of the human services and personal services industries (Braverman 1974).

6. A rich source of data on this issue is available in the nasty series of cases that has tried to define the extent to which an employee's thoughts or ideas on the job can be retained exclusively by the organization when he leaves. The case is easy to decide in favor of the individual when the issue is defined as the integrity of

individual personality threatened by a potentially all-embracing corporate entity. But the higher the member in the organization, the more arguable that he should be deemed to have operated at all times for the exclusive interest of the organization's intended beneficiaries. The conflict then appears to exist not between the member and the organization but between the member and stockholders, consumers, clients, and other constituencies external to the organization. For a description of some recurrent problem situations, see Johnston and Dudley 1964.

7. The present comparison of the career perspectives of Legal Aid and Legal Services lawyers is related to, but does not quite fit, familiar distinctions in the sociological literature. Thus the descriptions of organizational conflicts in LSPs may seem to confirm a long line of findings about tensions between professionals and bureaucracy, but in a comparative analysis of two groups of lawyers, reference to that literature is not illuminating. At first glance, the two groups of lawyers also seem to fit the contrast drawn by Gouldner (1957) between "locals" and "cosmpolitians." But as introduced by Gouldner, the terms are mutually exclusive; one cannot be both local and cosmopolitan. It is specifically the simultaneous presence of local and cosmopolitan themes in the careers of legal assistance lawyers that illuminates their influence on the character of legal assistance work generally. Thus Legal Aid lawyers appear to be "locals" in comparison with litigators in Legal Services who keep their eyes on Supreme Court decisions; yet the lawyers who used Legal Aid as a stepping-stone to private practice demonstrated a detachment from the local organization and a preoccupation with developing a career outside, both of which were generally unmatched in Legal Services. The Legal Services lawyer's "involvement," on the other hand, while achieved through a "cosmopolitan" focus on "significant" cases, requires a distinctive immersion in the organization's work and justifies a disregard for career opportunities elsewhere. *Local–cosmopolitan* becomes ambiguous when it is applied closely to the experience of members in prestigious firms, scholars at leading universities, and citizens of major cities—places which may attract fast local loyalties precisely by being centers of cosmopolitanism. [It is pertinent to recall that the research sites out of which the distinction was originally developed were relatively parochial: small college in Gouldner's case, small community in Merton's (1968).] In his original article, Gouldner (p. 291) appears intent on discouraging such a dialectical use of his terms.

Whatever its problems, Gouldner's use of the local–cosmopolitan distinction is an advance over Merton's. Merton questions the value of trying to trace his use of the distinction to its "source" in predecessors (see p. 458, n. 13a). But he does refer to Simmel's articles as seminal, a reference which inadvertently makes his point: Merton's dichotomy reflects none of the tensions characterizing Simmel's *dualistic* understanding of society. Simmel does not compare separate social facts as opposites. Instead he typically shows that each fact has *two inversely related sides*; and he compares each set of opposites with the other as its mirror image. A recent review of the diffusion of Simmel's thought concludes by noting "the difficulty experienced by American sociologists in dealing with nonunivocal assertions: the ambiguities, dualistic conceptions, and dialectical aspects of Simmel's thinking have often been screened out by those trained in American modes of thought, which stress univocality and one-dimensional metrics. . . . Of all the basic ideas informing Simmel's social thought, that which has received the least attention in American sociology is . . . the conception of the fundamentally dualistic character of social life" (Levine et al. 1976, pp. 1128, 829).

8. This suspicion is the basis of a common cynicism about the movement of lawyers from government to private-sector jobs. A counterbalancing point is less often recognized. Government law jobs, particularly in civil and criminal law enforcement offices, do not facilitate mobility equally for all insiders. Those who have made their mark on their agency's targets by extending sanctions to unprecedented lengths have been better rewarded than those who cautiously have protected the interests of the regulated while on the public payroll. This is an unstated implication of a study of lawyers who were young when they aggressively took on regulatory roles in New Deal agencies and who later—and in part thereby—became prominent "Washington lawyers" (see Auerbach and Bardach 1973). A strong drive for personal professional mobility can be detected behind much of the entrepreneurial use of federal prosecution offices against white-collar crime in recent years (see Katz 1980).

9. See field note beginning "We were supposed," p. 111.

10. Conflicts over case control in the San Francisco Legal Services Program are discussed in Brill 1973.

11. A distinction between turnover as a statistical phenomenon and as a social problem is made in McNeil and Thompson 1971, p. 625.

12. The LAB staff from 1955 to 1965 ($n = 55$) was compared with the staff that entered Legal Services–funded positions between 1965 and July 1973 ($n = 131$), using personnel files held by United Charities of Chicago in 1973. The group of Legal Services lawyers was cut off with those who had entered by July 1973 so that the careers of those entering near the cut-off date could be followed long enough to place them definitively in relation to the median for the whole aggregation. Comparing the pre- and post-1970 entrants, the median remained at about two years but, looking at the extremes, the Chicago Legal Services program drew fewer short-term and more long-term members in the latter period. Of those entering from 1965 through 1969, more than one-third stayed 12 months or less, and only one-fourth stayed more than three years; of those entering later, about one in five stayed only 12 months or less, whereas about one-third stayed more than three years. For statistics on turnover in recent years, see chapter 9, notes 6 and 7.

13. See Homans's classic reanalysis of the Relay Assembly Test and the Bank Wiring Observation Rooms in the Hawthorne experiments, reprinted in Etzioni 1969. See also the dramatic decline in the success of the Vera project after law students

working on temporary jobs were replaced by career probation officers (Schaffer 1970).

14. Senior Legal Aid lawyers, those with tenures in the LAB of from 20 to 40 years, reported that virtually all rotating lawyers left for small firms or office-sharing, solo practices in the Loop. Of the 102 staff lawyers who left the United Charities Legal Services program in the period from its start up to 1974, I obtained information on the first subsequent job of 88, mainly through reports of contemporaries in the program. Of these 88, 27 went to other LSPs, to Legal Services administrative jobs, or to like jobs. If one adds the 5 who went into "radical-law" private practices and the 7 who began law teaching in clinical legal aid settings, 39 of 102, or at least 38 percent, did not bolt the institution on leaving the Chicago Legal Services program. About half a dozen each went off to the counterculture, to large or "fancy" firms, to medium-size firms, to government agencies not typically associated with public-interest work, and to miscellaneous pursuits; 22 went to solo or small practices, many of them economically marginal. (I suspect that a large percentage of the "unknown" departed falls in the last category.) The assertion, often made with cynical undertones, that Legal Services lawyers become disillusioned, drop their "naïve idealism," and turn to traditional legal careers appears from these figures to be untrue in at least half the cases: the 39 noted above, plus the 6 who left for the counterculture, plus about a dozen who were on staff in 1974 and had been in Legal Services for at least three years (57 of 114).

15. Johnson 1974, p. 370, n. 237, shows the growing budgetary strength of Legal Services within OEO in the fiscal years 1966 to 1972.

16. The Chicago experience was a middle case on the national continuum of relations between Legal Aid and Legal Services programs. Where Legal Aid societies had been much smaller, as in San Francisco, they placed less constraint on the development of a reformist Legal Services program in the area. For an account of the success in San Francisco of young activist lawyers and representatives of the poor in competition with the local Legal Aid society and bar association for the OEO grant, see Wright 1967. The potential for LSPs to take on an emphatic social-change mission arose most quickly where there had been no representation of Legal Aid, most notably in the form of California Rural Legal Assistance. New York City had the nation's oldest and best established Legal Aid society. It had close ties both to a prestigious local bar association and to the local court system. The New York Legal Aid Society successfully sued to stop a centralized LSP run independently by new poverty lawyers and representatives of the poor. Partly as a result, the New York City area developed a fragmented, relatively undistinguished initial set of loosely connected, small neighborhood Legal Services offices. Fragments on the experience in New York can be found in Frankel 1965 and in Weissman 1969, pp. 31–36, 137–143. The former is a critical piece by the type of constituent Legal Aid traditionally could rely on for support—a "liberal" law professor, later federal judge—

who was condemning efforts by the Legal Aid Society to block the development of OEO LSPs and retain monopolistic control. The latter presents the critical perspective on the New York Legal Aid Society of MFY's legal unit, a federally funded program that was an early leader in poverty law reform.

Chapter 8

1. In guidelines issued in 1966, OEO's Office of Legal Services formalized a requirement that LSPs give representation to the poor "on the board or policy-making committee." The formation of this policy is described in Johnson 1974, pp. 108–112.

2. United Charities of Chicago 1969 displays the development of the controversy.

3. For a review of the controversies and for investigative reporting on their strategic composition, see Blumenthal and Soler 1971; on support for California Rural Legal Assistance from conservative lawyers, Johnson 1974, p. 328, n. 44.

4. Economic Opportunity Act, 42 U.S.C. § 2791(b)(2) (1970).

5. A good illustration of positions taken and arguments offered by Legal Services and Legal Aid staff is available in Bellow 1969 and Getzels 1969.

Chapter 9

1. In a compilation entitled "Clippings," the Legal Services Corporation summarizes and reprints national and local news stories on Legal Services programs and lawyers. During the 1980 congressional appropriation process, the corporation observed: "Editorials in newspapers throughout the nation are supporting extension of the Legal Services Corporation, without further restrictions in the Act. From the East, North, South and West, newspapers are urging that the missions of poor people be given equal access to this country's system of justice" (Legal Services Corporation 1980, p. 8).

2. "The legal services program was finally scuttled by the Nixon administration" (Auerbach 1976, p. 298). Scheingold (1974, pp. 193–194): "Regardless of how the current legislative controversy ends, the handwriting is on the wall . . . the political utility of the program will be severely curtailed and eventually the services, or at least the dedication, of the most committed young lawyers will certainly be lost."

3. An early commentary on the Legal Services Program of OEO had predicted that, if staff lawyers were not freed from routine, the Legal Services Program would become a federally funded, national network of Legal Aid societies (Lowenstein and Waggoner 1967, p. 824).

4. They never quite disappeared, but they had been reduced largely to peripheral political forces until the election returns of 1980 came in. See U.S. Congress 1980. It should also be noted that amendments attempting to restrict lobbying and staff-attorney autonomy in reform litigation were included in the original act [42 U.S.C. § 2701 (1974); PL 93-355] and that attempts to restrict permissible cases were written

into the 1977 authorization act (PL 95-222, containing language hostile to, but not prohibitive of, abortion and school desegregation litigation). In the 1980 session, amendments were offered to transfer court awards of attorneys' fees from Legal Services programs to the federal Treasury; to cut down on or prohibit proabortion litigation, legislative advocacy, and the representation of homosexuals and aliens; and to shift a significant part of federal funding from Legal Services staff programs to a system for paying private attorneys to represent the poor. The last measure was endorsed by the ABA's House of Delegates in August 1980.

5. The classic statement is Michels 1949. Cf. Selznick 1949.

6. In August 1980, only 3 of the 13 LAF lawyers who had primary responsibility for major litigation (2 deputy directors, 5 team leaders, and 6 project supervisors) had less than seven years of experience in Chicago Legal Services programs (per LAF personnel files).

7. In August 1980, the median tenure of the neighborhood office staff (47 lawyers) was less than two years. Of the 47, 30 had been in LAF less than two years and four months. The upper half of the current distribution appears to contain much more internal experience, however, than did the more senior half of the staff in the early seventies. To a degree, rapid office expansion in the late seventies may account for the low 1980 median.

8. The one-quarter figure is a rough one based on the actual number of lawyers leaving each year and on an estimate of the number of neighborhood staff positions in existence each year, but the estimate appears accurate. For the 1976 and 1977 entering cohorts, over 37 percent (12 of 32) did not stay in LAF for three years.

9. There has been an occasional, thinly veiled public indication of the phenomenon. In late 1979, when the director of the Office of Field Services of the Legal Services Corporation offered his "management philosophy" to the Legal Services community, he advised that "we . . . must acknowledge that impermanence, dissension, uncertainty, and ambiguity can become virtues, leading toward new approaches in management techniques" (Lyons 1979, p. 2).

10. Shortly after Bradley's appointment, a commentator from Project Advisory Group (1979, p. 2), a national organization of Legal Services lawyers, noted a "vast improvement in communication between field and Corporation executives." See also Bellow 1980, p. 343:

> A complex accommodation . . . seems to have been worked out between the Corporation's staff and organized interests within the program, more particularly the Project Advisory Group (made up of representatives from the progams) and the National Client's Council (made up of representatives of clients from local programs—these will be called internal lobbying groups: ILG's). The elements of this accommodation with the Corporation look something like this:
>
> –The Corporation is generally supported by the ILG's in its efforts to get more funds for legal services.
>
> –The Corporation is also assisted by the ILG's in controlling (or attempting to

control) efforts of individual programs to get special privileges for themselves from the Corporation or to deal directly with Congress.

–In return, representatives of the ILG's have ready access to Corporation staff and regularly participate in the formation of Corporation policy.

–New funds are allocated in accordance with pre-established formulas so that competition among programs can be kept to a minimum.

–Policies follow relatively established and predictable lines. New initiatives require extensive (and sometimes endless) debate and participation throughout the "legal services community."

–ILG's as individual consultants and organizations receive Corporation funds to meet and otherwise carry out their activities.

–There is little Corporation scrutiny of the actual performance of programs.

–The ILG's are left to put such pressure on their "peer" programs as they deem appropriate.

11. For a similar argument on the persistence of the movement against white-collar crime, see Katz 1980.

12. This is a rough estimate. The size of the neighborhood offices expanded rapidly during this period; and the distinctions among neighborhood staff lawyers, lawyers in other units, staff supervisors, and Smith fellows are somewhat arbitrary.

13. My source was lists of exiting lawyers kept by LAF's executive directors, who made notations under "new job."

14. Or 31 of 91. For a list of the law schools classed as "elite" in this calculation, see chapter 4 note 13.

15. Case-load priorities and policies are described in LAF's fall 1979 grant application to the Legal Services Corporation.

16. Silva v. Bell, 605 F.2d 978 (7th Cir., 1979). All descriptions of LAF cases are paraphrased from reports periodically issued by LAF and distributed widely within Legal Services and the interested professional community. The reports are available from LAF or through the *Clearinghouse Review*. This chapter draws on Legal Assistance Foundation 1979, 1979/80, 1980.

17. Contreras de Avila v. Bell, 78 C-1166 (N.D. Ill., 1978).

18. Ferrell v. Hills, decided *sub nom* Brown v. Lynn, 385 F. Supp. 986 (N.D. Ill., 1974); aff'd. on rehearing 392 F. Supp. 559 (N.D. Ill., 1975).

19. The case proceeded under the name *Ferrell* v. *Hills*. A contempt order was never formally filed. Negotiations concluded the matter after a proposed order was drawn up by the plaintiffs.

20. Banks v. Trainor, 525 F.2d 837 (7th Cir., 1975).

21. Winter v. Trainor, 490 F. Supp. 788 (N.D. Ill., 1980).

22. Steward v. EEOC, 611 F.2d 679 (7th Cir., 1979).

23. Litigation growing out of the controversy produced a published opinion on an indirectly related issue. Board of Governors v. Illinois FEPC, 78 Ill.2d 143 (Ill. Supreme Court, 1979).

24. Miles v. American Bankers Life (petition to Ill. Dept. of Insurance, 1974).

25. Jackson v. Carey, No. 78L-2545 (Circuit Court of Cook County, 1978).

26. Among the more important LAF cases decided by the Supreme Court since 1973 are: Edelman v. Jordan, 415 U.S 651 (1974): Eleventh Amendment, retroactivity: federal judicial order of retroactive state welfare benefits held unconstitutional; Quern v. Hernandez, 440 U.S. 951 (1979), summarily affirming Hernandez v. Finley, 471 F.Supp. 516 (1978): abstention: federal court can intervene in state court attachment proceeding based on an unconstitutional state statute; Trimble v. Gordon, 430 U.S. 762 (1977): family law, sex and bastardy discrimination: Equal Protection Clause of Fourteenth Amendment invalidates a state probate law allowing illegitimate children to inherit by intestate succession only from *mothers*; Miller v. Youakim, 440 U.S. 125 (1979): social security, foster care: AFDC-foster care program covers children who reside with relatives.

27. Illinois Welfare Rights Organization Medicaid Conformity Petition (to U.S. Department of Health, Education, and Welfare, 1977).

Chapter 10

1. These two issues were chosen by chance. The separation of the two by several years was useful not only to check historical trends but to minimize duplicate coverage. We wanted to code cases, not motions or particular stages in litigation; a given case is often described in several different issues as its judicial fate changes.

2. Levitan, Rein, and Marwick 1972, p. 60, data from 1971 and from 1961.

3. James v. Chicago Housing Authority, No. 78C-4994 (N.D. Ill., 1978).

4. Mays v. Swank, No. 71C-21 (N.D. Ill., 1971).

5. Commentary has focused on a consequence of this trend, the development of a judicial role in the administration of public agencies (see Fiss 1979). Another consequence of the trend has been the hiring of ex–Legal Services lawyers by government agencies that had been their adversaries. Perhaps the most concentrated instance has been in California (see Drager 1979: "The early days of the Brown Administration began a trend toward appointees with backgrounds in legal services").

6. For a vivid historical account, see Harring 1977; the quoted phrases come from Foote (1956), who found vestiges of the institution in 1950s Philadelphia, in application to agricultural migrant labor.

7. The phrase is from Friedman 1968, pp. 20–21.

8. 5 Cal.3d 584, 487 P.2d 1241, 96 Cal. Rptr. 601 (1971).

9. There are of course exceptions, such as a proposal to ban representation of food stamp matters (see chapter 9, note 4).

10. Shortly after the debate, the Supreme Court decided the issue in the direction favored by President Reagan. Schweiker v. Wilson, _____ U.S. _____, 67 L.Ed. 2d 186 (1981).

Appendix

1. Qualitative researchers have often called for a reorientation of methodological thinking, but they have not transcended the conventional approaches. Becker and others (1961, pp. 33–45) have proposed a *post hoc* application, to informally gathered data, of methods used to guide the collection of data in more formalized research. For example, their remedy for reactivity is to count up all field notes bearing on a given proposition and to assign greater weight to observations of behavior in group settings than to reports of one-to-one encounters between researcher and research subject. They also recommend a *post hoc* quantification procedure to create evidence on representativeness. These steps lead to the acceptance of a proposition about a group if the total number of observations and the ratio of positive-to-negative observations exceed arbitrary standards.

These are, at best, second-best solutions. When enumerated data are offered as the product of surveys and experiments, they purport to describe the precise number of instances underlying the substantive analysis, and they treat each datum as having a discernible weight on the analysis. The observational researcher who has directly entered, diffusely experienced, and variously recorded a natural setting cannot support this claim. Some field notes are, after all, based on observations covering seconds, others on a day's experience.

McCall (1969) tries a sympathetic extension of Becker's approach and reaches what he appears reluctantly to appreciate as a *reductio ad absurdum*: "In summary judgment, then, the techniques advocated in this paper are crude, fallible, tedious, and yield somewhat ambiguous results" (p. 140).

2. Despite the rhetoric of discovery and exploration, we are asked to attend to qualitative studies not merely on the claim that they develop attractive ideas but on an assertion that something "out there" has been discovered—on an empirical assertion that the theory is in fact grounded. For a vigorous critique of the distinction between discovery and verification, see Feyerabend 1975, pp. 165–169.

3. Because of the irrelevance of quantification to the logic of analytic induction and because of the search for qualitative variation implicit in the hunt for negative cases, the following discussion frequently contrasts "qualitative" and "quantitative" research. In fact many, perhaps all, researchers use a combination of quantitative and qualitative methods. The possibilities for mutually beneficial combinations have been argued by Zelditch 1962, Reiss 1968, Sieber 1973, and Myers 1977, among others. The claim usually is that quantitative methods offer evidence or proof; qualitative methods, validity or insight. Whatever the merits of these conciliatory positions, they have failed to explain how qualitative methods can be rigorous in their own right.

4. Since Turner's (1953) review of the handful of studies then recognized as examples of analytic induction, there has been virtually no explicit discussion of the method. An exception is the extensive treatment in Lindesmith 1968 and by Manning

1978. See also Moskos 1967, pp. 104–105. The convergence of analytic induction and symbolic interactionism was clearly signaled in Becker 1953. It is indirectly indicated in Blumer's (1947) introduction to Lindesmith's first edition and in Becker et al. 1961, pp. 17–32; Bruyn 1966; Blumer 1969, pp. 1–60; and Lofland 1976.

5. In particular, Znaniecki 1968.

6. I treat the shaping of data by analysis in each of the remaining sections of the chapter (e.g., in "Reactivity," a focus on analyzing social process creates substantive data in members' reactions to the researcher), but especially in the section on reliability (reinterpreting data to fit existing analysis).

7. Cressey's (1953) use of analytic induction to explain embezzlement is an exception that proves the rule. Although narrower than the legal definition, the embezzlement to be explained by the theory was treated as a discrete act. Cressey was obliged to specify the occurrence of something precisely connected with the criminal act. Turner (1953, p. 606) seized on this point of vulnerability in his critique, noting that the explanatory conditions—having a nonsharable financial problem, recognizing embezzlement as a solution, and rationalizing it—would seem always to have existed for some time before the embezzlement occurred. Significantly, Turner explicitly softens his argument in turning to Lindesmith's theory, noting only problems ("in some cases") at the boundaries of explanans and explanandum.

8. See also Becker 1953. Understandably but paradoxically, most studies using analytic induction have begun as attempts to explain social problems: Lindesmith, opiate addiction; Cressey, embezzlement; and I began with an attempt to explain "staying more than two years," or the problem of turnover about which legal assistance leaders had so frequently complained. In pursuit of a perfect explanation, the researcher must initially rely on an outsider's view of what is homogeneous when choosing a phenomenon for study, and "deviance" by definition has already been singled out as such. Yet a consistent contribution of such research is to establish the inaccuracy of the outsider's perspective by redefining the phenomenon in terms of homogeneity from the *inside*. A major difference between the view of social problems held by outsiders and insiders is that outsiders pick out discrete acts for sanction or regret whereas insiders experience a process with vague boundaries.

9. A general evaluation of the capacity of analytic induction to warrant generalizations thus hinges on theoretical contentions about discontinuities across societies and over history. For some provocative questioning of several once-accepted discontinuities, see Riesman 1976.

10. A commonplace—yet commonly ignored. Robinson (1951, p. 818) seriously obscured the case for analytic induction with the following argument for "the necessity for representative sampling. Practitioners of analytic induction would then no longer have to cling with anxiety . . . [to propositions] but could openly state the confidence limits for the proportion of exceptions which might occur in the future."

11. For a recent statement, see Wallace 1962.

12. An exception is Gussow 1964. Psychiatrists exploit these phenomena as "transference."

13. Holistic studies are usually thought of as case studies that try to comprehend an entire organizational or community social system. I am indebted to Diesing (1971) for his empirical research on the methodology of such studies. I believe that analytic induction takes on a holistic character even when it seeks to explain a particular line of action and that therefore the following methodological comments are applicable to analytic induction in general. Of his attempt to explain opiate addiction, Lindesmith (1947, p. 15) wrote: "The actual process of the study may best be described as an analysis of a series of crucial cases which led to successive revisions of the guiding theory and to a broader and broader perception of the implications of that theory. Isolated bits of information and apparent paradoxes one after the other seemed to form integral parts of a consistent whole."

14. In an informal note, Mel Pollner suggests to me that the inquiry might start with a comparison of the controversies around the work of anthropologist Carlos Castaneda (Strachan 1979) and psychologist Cyril Burt (Hearnshaw 1979).

15. "This book is classed as a novel, but . . . it is chiefly documentary and descriptive; most of it is clearly fact rather than fiction, and it would not be rewarding to try and decide which is which, because they are combined in one grand revelation of truth" (Plomer 1956, p. v).

16. See Glaser and Strauss 1967, p. 252, for a defense of one such instance, Fred Davis's article "The Cabdriver and His Fare," which was based on personal experience but written long after Davis left cab driving and without benefit of contemporaneous field notes.

17. Compare the distinction drawn by W. James (1970) between truth as "reflection" and a "pragmatic" theory of truth.

18. Efforts to enhance reliability measures through administering multiple items that are to be combined in an index, and through panel studies which pose the same questions to the same people at different times, may be not only logically independent of the value of validity but empirically hostile to it. Schnaiberg and Armer (1972) conducted a rare empirical study into the sociology of panel approaches to measures of reliability. Repeated administrations produced stability coefficients that were unreasonably high. Their findings suggest that, the greater the number of items measuring the same concept, and the greater the number of panel waves, the more likely it is that subjects will want to be done with the experience, leading to the artificial appearance of consistency ("providing responses in such a way as to minimize the costs of going through the thought processes generally required [*sic*] e.g., using a variety of tactics such as acquiescence, deference, random responses, and so on") (p. 12). The study also suggested a pattern of biased attrition from panels of respondents likely to be inconsistent: those for whom the measured dimension has least salience.

References

Aaronson, Mark. 1975. "Legal Advocacy and Welfare Reform: Continuity and Change in Public Relief." Ph.D. dissertation, University of California, Berkeley.

Abel, Richard L. 1979. "Socializing the Legal Profession: Can Redistributing Lawyers' Services Achieve Social Justice?" *Law and Policy Quarterly* 1:5–51.

Agnew, Spiro T. 1972. "What's Wrong with the Legal Services Program." *American Bar Association Journal* 58:930–933.

Albert, Lee. 1968. "Choosing the Test Case in Welfare Litigation." *Clearinghouse Review* 1:4–6, 28.

Allen, Michael Patrick; Panian, Sharon K.; and Lotz, Roy E. 1979. "Managerial Succession and Organizational Performance." *Administrative Science Quarterly* 24:168–180.

Alschuler, Albert W. 1968. "The Prosecutor's Role in Plea Bargaining." *University of Chicago Law Review* 36:50–112.

Auchincloss, Louis. 1963. *Powers of Attorney*. Boston: Houghton Mifflin.

Auerbach, Jerold S. 1976. *Unequal Justice: Lawyers and Social Change in Modern America*. New York: Oxford University Press.

Auerbach, Jerold S., and Bardach, Eugene. 1973. "'Born to an Era of Insecurity': Career Patterns of Law Review Editors, 1918–1941." *American Journal of Legal History* 17:3–26.

Balbus, Isaac D. 1973. *The Dialectics of Legal Repression: Black Rebels before the American Criminal Courts*. New York: Russell Sage.

Baldamus, W. 1972. "The Role of Discoveries in Social Science." In *The Rules of the Game: Cross-Disciplinary Essays on Models in Scholarly Thought*, ed. Teodor Shanin, pp. 276–302. London: Tavistock.

Becker, Howard S. 1953. "Becoming a Marihuana User." *American Journal of Sociology* 59:235–242.

———. 1970. *Sociological Work: Method and Substance*. Chicago: Aldine.

Becker, Howard S., and Geer, Blanche. 1960. "Latent Culture: A Research Note." *Administrative Science Quarterly* 5:304–313.

Becker, Howard S.; Geer, Blanche; Hughes, Everett C.; and Strauss, Anselm L. 1961. *Boys in White: Student Culture in Medical School*. Chicago: University of Chicago Press.

Bellow, Gary. 1969. "Reflections on Case-load Limitations." *Legal Aid Brief Case* (NLADA) 27:195–202.

———. 1977. "The Legal Aid Puzzle: Turning Solutions into Problems." *Working Papers for a New Society* 5 (Spring):52–60.

———. 1980. "Legal Aid in the United States." *Clearinghouse Review* 14:337–345.

Bennett, Michael, and Reynoso, Cruz. 1972. "California Rural Legal Assistance (CRLA): Survival of a Poverty Law Practice." *Chicano Law Review* 1:1–79.

Berger, Bennett M. 1962. "The Sociology of Leisure: Some Suggestions." *Industrial Relations* 1(February):31–45, repr. in *Work and Leisure*, ed. E. Smigel, pp. 21–40. New Haven, Conn.: College & University Press, 1963.

Bittner, Egon. 1963. "Radicalism and the Organization of Radical Movements." *American Sociological Review* 28:928–940.

Blalock, Hubert M., Jr. 1968. "The Measurement Problem: A Gap between the Language of Theory and Research." In *Methodology in Social Research*, ed. Hubert M. Blalock, Jr., and Ann B. Blalock, pp. 5–27. New York: McGraw-Hill.

Blumenthal, Richard, and Soler, Mark I. 1971. "The Legal Services Corporation: Curtailing Political Interference." *Yale Law Journal* 81:231–286.

Blumer, Herbert. 1939. *An Appraisal of Thomas and Znaniecki's "The Polish Peasant in Europe and America."* New York: Social Science Research Council.

———. 1947. Introduction to *Opiate Addiction*, by Alfred R. Lindesmith. Bloomington, Ind.: Principia.

———. 1957. "Collective Behavior." In *Review of Sociology*, ed. Joseph B. Gittler, pp. 127–158. New York: Wiley.

———. 1969. *Symbolic Interactionism: Perspective and Method*. Englewood Cliffs, N.J.: Prentice-Hall.

Bolton, John R., and Holzer, Stephen T. 1973. "Legal Services and Landlord-Tenant Litigation: A Critical Analysis." *Yale Law Journal* 82:1495–1511.

The Book of Chicagoans 1905. S.v. "Tobey, Frank Bassett." Marquis.

Bradway, John S. 1926. "The National Association of Legal Aid Organizations." *Annuals* 124:163–166.

Braverman, Harry. 1974. *Labor and Monopoly Capital: The Degradation of Work in the Twentieth Century*. New York: Monthly Review.

Brennan, William J., Jr. 1968. "The Responsibilities of the Legal Profession." *American Bar Association Journal* 54:121–126.

Brill, Harry. 1973. "The Uses and Abuses of Legal Assistance." *Public Interest* 31(Spring):38–55.

Brownell, Emery A. 1951. *Legal Aid in the United States*. Rochester, N.Y.: Lawyers Co-operative Publishing.

———. 1961. *Legal Aid in the United States, Supplement*. Rochester, N.Y.: Lawyers Co-operative Publishing.

Bruyn, Severyn T. 1966. *The Human Perspective in Sociology: The Methodology of Participant Observation*. Englewood Cliffs, N.J.: Prentice-Hall.

Cahn, Edgar S., and Cahn, Jean C. 1964. "The War on Poverty: A Civilian Perspective." *Yale Law Journal* 73:1317–1352.

Camilleri, Santo F. 1962. "Theory, Probability, and Induction in Social Research." *American Sociological Review* 27:170–178.

Camus, Albert. 1956. *The Fall*. Trans. Justin O'Brien. New York: Knopf.

Caplan, Gerald M. 1970. "Career Inhibiting Factors: Problems of the Public Prosecutor and Defender." In *The Politics of Local Justice*, ed. James R. Klonoski and Robert I. Mendelsohn, pp. 206–210. Boston: Little, Brown.

Carlin, Jerome E. 1962. *Lawyers on Their Own: A Study of Individual Practitioners in Chicago*. New Brunswick, N.J.: Rutgers University Press.

———. 1966. *Lawyers' Ethics: A Survey of the New York City Bar*. New York: Russell Sage.

———. 1971. "Store Front Lawyers in San Francisco." In *Culture and Civility in San Francisco*, ed. Howard S. Becker, pp. 125–151. New Brunswick, N.J.: Transaction.

Carlin, Jerome E., and Howard, Jan. 1965. "Legal Representation and Class Justice." *UCLA Law Review* 12:381–437.

Chicago Bureau of Justice. 1903. *Annual Report*, 16.

Chicago Historical Society. 1919. Agreement between Northwestern University and the United Charities of Chicago, 1 September.

———. 1938. "Legal Aid Bureau of the United Charities of Chicago." Paper delivered by A. D. McDougal, Jr., at a meeting of the Legal Aid Society of Milwaukee, 6 May.

———. N.d.*a* (1919?). "Annual Report for the Legal Aid Society" (by Maud Parcells Boyes, Superintendent).

———. N.d.*b* (1920s?). Memoranda on the Organization and Operation of the Legal Aid Bureau of the United Charities of Chicago (Civil Branch).

———. N.d.*c* (1923?). "The Legal Aid Bureau" (by Joel D. Hunter).

Chicago Legal Aid Society. 1908. *Annual Report*, 3.

———. 1910. *Annual Report*, 5.

———. 1914. *Annual Report*, 9.

———. 1917. *Annual Report*, 31.

Cicourel, Aaron V. 1964. *Method and Measurement in Sociology*. New York: Free Press of Glencoe.

Clark, Burton R. 1970. *The Distinctive College: Antioch, Reed and Swarthmore*. Chicago: Aldine.

Cloward, Richard A., and Piven, Frances Fox. 1966. "A Strategy To End Poverty." *Nation*, 2 May 1967, pp. 510–517.

"Community Counsel To Be Initiated." 1967. *Legal Aid Brief Case* (NLADA) 25:146–147.

Conover, D. S. B. 1898. "Chicago Protective Agency for Women and Children." *Charities Review* 8:287–288.

Coser, Lewis A. 1974. *Greedy Institutions: Patterns of Undivided Commitment*. New York: Free Press.

"Counsel to the Poor." 1980. *Newsweek,* 14 January, p. 89.

Cover, Robert M. 1975. *Justice Accused: Antislavery and the Judicial Process*. New Haven, Conn.: Yale University Press.

Cressey, Donald R. 1953. *Other People's Money: A Study in the Social Psychology of Embezzlement*. Glencoe, Ill.: Free Press.

Curran, Barbara A. 1977. *The Legal Needs of the Public: The Final Report of a National Survey*. Chicago: American Bar Foundation.

"Cut Off Vista Aid in Chicago, Pucinski Asks." 1968. *Chicago Tribune,* 18 April, sec. 1, p. 11.

Davies, William. 1971. "Getting Ghetto Justice." *Chicago Tribune Magazine,* 31 October, p. 24.

"Debate Transcript: Rivals for Presidency Discuss Views about Social Security." 1980. *New York Times*, 29 October, sec. A, p. 28.

Diesing, Paul. 1971. *Patterns of Discovery in the Social Sciences*. Chicago: Aldine-Atherton.

Donovan, John C. 1967. *The Politics of Poverty*. Indianapolis: Pegasus.

Drager, Kerry. 1979. "Foe of the Short-handed Hoe: CRLA Pioneers, Now Members of the Establishment." *California Journal* 10:146–147.

Ellis, William W. 1969. *White Ethics and Black Power: The Emergence of the West Side Organization*. Chicago: Aldine.

Epstein, Cynthia Fuchs. 1970. *Women's Place: Options and Limits in Professional Careers*. Berkeley and Los Angeles: University of California Press.

Erikson, Kai T. 1957. "Patient Role and Social Uncertainty: A Dilemma of the Mentally Ill." *Psychiatry* 20:263–274.

Erlanger, Howard S. 1978. "Lawyers and Neighborhood Legal Services: Social Background and the Impetus for Reform." *Law and Society Review* 12:253–274.

Ethical Culture Society. 1926. *The Fiftieth Anniversary of the Ethical Movement: 1876–1926*. New York: D. Appleton.

Etzioni, Amitai, ed. 1969. *Readings on Modern Organizations*. Englewood Cliffs, N.J.: Prentice-Hall.

Feeley, Malcolm M. 1979. *The Process Is the Punishment: Handling Cases in a Lower Criminal Court*. New York: Russell Sage.

Feyerabend, Paul K. 1975. *Against Method: Outline of an Anarchistic Theory of Knowledge*. Atlantic Highlands, N.J.: Humanities.

Fish, John H. 1973. *Black Power/White Control: The Struggle of the Woodlawn Organization in Chicago*. Princeton, N.J.: Princeton University Press.

Fisher, Kenneth P., and Ivie, Charles C. 1971. *Franchising Justice: The Office of Economic Opportunity Legal Services Program and Traditional Legal Aid*. Chicago: American Bar Foundation.

Fiss, Owen M. 1979. "Foreward: The Forms of Justice." *Harvard Law Review* 93:1–58.

Fitzgerald, Jeffrey M. 1975. "The Contract Buyers League and the Courts: A Case Study of Poverty Litigation." *Law and Society Review* 9:165–195.

Foote, Caleb. 1956. "Vagrancy-type Law and Its Administration." *University of Pennsylvania Law Review* 404:603–650.

Foucault, Michel. 1978. *Discipline and Punish: The Birth of the Prison*. New York: Pantheon.

Frankel, Marvin. 1965. "The War on Poverty: A Challenge to Legal Aid." *Legal Aid Review* 63:12–19.

Friedman, Lawrence M. 1968. *Government and Slum Housing: A Century of Frustration*. Chicago: Rand McNally.

Fuller, Lon L. 1969*a*. "The Morality That Makes Law Possible." In his *The Morality of Law*, rev. ed., pp. 33–94. New Haven, Conn.: Yale University Press.

———. 1969*b*. "Two Principles of Human Association." *Nomos* 11:3–23.

Garbus, Martin. 1971. "Mrs. Sylvester Smith against Ruben King and George Wallace." In his *Ready for the Defense*, pp. 143–208. New York: Farrar, Straus & Giroux.

Garfinkel, Harold. 1960. "The Rational Properties of Scientific and Common Sense Activities." *Behavioral Science* 5:72–83.

———. 1967. *Studies in Ethnomethodology*. Englewood Cliffs, N.J.: Prentice-Hall.

Gariepy, Marguerite Raeder. 1926. "The Legal Aid Bureau of the United Charities of Chicago." *Annals* 124:33–41.

Garson, Barbara. 1975. *All the Livelong Day: The Meaning and Demeaning of Routine Work*. New York: Doubleday.

Getzels, Mortimer. 1969. "Legal Aid Cases Should not Be Limited." *Legal Aid Brief Case* (NLADA) 27:203–206.

Gitlin, Todd, and Hollander, Nanci. 1970. *Uptown: Poor Whites in Chicago*. New York: Harper & Row.

Glaser, Barney G., ed. 1968. *Organizational Careers: A Sourcebook for Theory*. Chicago: Aldine.

Glaser, Barney G., and Strauss, Anselm L. 1967. *The Discovery of Grounded Theory: Strategies for Qualitative Research*. Chicago: Aldine.

Goffman, Erving. 1961. *Asylums: Essays on the Social Situation of Mental Patients and Other Inmates*. Garden City, N.Y.: Doubleday/Anchor.

———. 1971. *Relations in Public: Microstudies of the Public Order*. New York: Basic Books.

Gold, Raymond L. 1958. "Roles in Sociological Field Observations." *Social Forces* 36:217–223.

Goldman, Marion S. 1972. *A Portrait of the Black Attorney in Chicago*. Chicago: American Bar Foundation.

Gouldner, Alvin. 1955. "Metaphysical Pathos and the Theory of Bureaucracy ." *American Political Science Review* 49:496–507.

———. 1957. "Cosmopolitans and Locals: Toward an Analysis of Latent Social Roles." *Administrative Science Quarterly* 2:281–306.

Grant, Sally Deane. 1967. "Resort to the Legal Process in Collecting Debts from High Risk Credit Buyers in Los Angeles." *UCLA Law Review* 14:879–910.

Greenstone, J. David, and Peterson, Paul E. 1973. *Race and Authority in Urban Politics: Community Participation and the War on Poverty*. New York: Russell Sage.

Grønbjerg, Kirsten; Street, David; and Suttles, Gerald D. 1978. *Poverty and Social Change*. Chicago: University of Chicago Press.

Grusky, Oscar. 1960. "Administrative Succession in Formal Organizations." *Social Forces* 39:105–115.

Gusfield, Joseph R. 1955. "Field Work Reciprocities in Studying a Social Movement." *Human Organization* 14 (Fall):29–33.

Gussow, Zachary. 1964. "The Observer–Observed Relationship as Information about Structure in Small-group Research: A Comparative Study of Urban Elementary School Classrooms." *Psychiatry* 27:230–247.

Hale, William Henri. 1949. "The Career Development of the Negro Lawyer in Chicago." Ph.D. dissertation, University of Chicago.

Handler, Joel F. 1972. *Reforming the Poor: Welfare Policy, Federalism and Morality*. New York: Basic Books.

———. 1978. *Social Movements and the Legal System: A Theory of Law Reform and Social Change*. New York: Academic.

Handler, Joel F.; Hollingsworth, Ellen Jane; and Erlanger, Howard S. 1978. *Lawyers and the Pursuit of Legal Rights*. New York: Academic.

Hannon, Philip J. 1969. "The Leadership Problem in the Legal Services Program." *Law and Society Review* 4:235–253.

Hanson, Norwood Russell. 1958. *Patterns of Discovery: An Inquiry into the Conceptual Foundations of Science*. Cambridge: Cambridge University Press.

Harring, Sidney L. 1977. "Class Conflict and the Suppression of Tramps in Buffalo, 1892–1894." *Law and Society Review* 12:873–911.

Hazard, Geoffrey C., Jr. 1965. "Rationing Justice." *Journal of Law and Economics* 8:1–10.

———. 1969. "Social Justice through Civil Justice." *University of Chicago Law Review* 36:699–712.

Hearnshaw, Leslie S. 1979. *Cyril Burt, Psychologist*. Ithaca, N.Y.: Cornell University Press.

Helfgot, Joseph. 1974. "Professional Reform Organizations and the Symbolic Representation of the Poor." *American Sociological Review* 39: 475–491.

Hirschman, Albert O. 1970. *Exit, Voice and Loyalty: Responses to Decline in Firms, Organizations and States*. Cambridge, Mass.: Harvard University Press.

Hoffman, Paul. 1973. *Lions in the Street: The Inside of the Great Wall Street Law Firms*. New York: Saturday Review.

Hollingshead, August B., and Redlich, Frederick C. 1958. *Social Class and Mental Illness: A Community Study*. New York: Wiley.

Horsky, Charles A. 1952. *The Washington Lawyer*. Boston: Little, Brown.

Hunter, Albert. 1974. *Symbolic Communities: The Persistence and Change of Chicago's Local Communities*. Chicago: University of Chicago Press.

James, Marlise. 1973. *The People's Lawyers*. New York: Holt, Rinehart & Winston.

James, William. 1970. *The Meaning of Truth: A Sequel to Pragmatism*. Ann Arbor: University of Michigan Press.

Johnson, Earl, Jr. 1974. *Justice and Reform: The Formative Years of the OEO Legal Services Program*. New York: Russell Sage.

Johnston, Clement D., and Dudley, Henry A. 1964. "Conflicts of Interest in Business and Industry." *Federal Bar Journal* 24:344–350.

Johnstone, Quintin, and Hopson, Dan, Jr. 1967. *Lawyers and Their Work: An Analysis of the Legal Profession in the United States and England*. Indianapolis: Bobbs-Merrill.

Katz, Jack. 1975. "Essence as Moral Identities: Verifiability and Responsibility in Imputations of Deviance and Charisma." *American Journal of Sociology* 80:1369–1390.

———. 1978. "Lawyers for the Poor in Transition: Involvement, Reform, and the Turnover Problem in the Legal Services Program." *Law and Society Review* 12:275–300.

———. 1980. "The Social Movement against White-collar Crime." In *Criminology Review Yearbook*, vol. 2, ed. Egon Bittner and Sheldon L. Messinger, pp. 161–184. Beverly Hills, Calif.: Sage.

Kitsuse, John I. 1970. Editor's preface to "People-Processing Institutions." *American Behavioral Scientist* 14:163–165.

Kotre, John N. 1971. *The View from the Border: A Social-Psychological Study of Current Catholicism*. Chicago: Aldine.

Kuh, Richard H. 1961. "Careers in Prosecution Offices." *Journal of Legal Education* 14:175–190.

Ladinsky, Jack. 1963. "Careers of Lawyers, Law Practice, and Legal Institutions." *American Sociological Review* 28:47–54.

Langbein, John H. 1973. "The Origins of Public Prosecution at Common Law." *American Journal of Legal History* 17:313–335.

———. 1978. "The Criminal Trial before the Lawyers." *University of Chicago Law Review* 45:263–316.

"Law Technicality Snags Ruling on Cut on Medicaid." 1971. *Chicago Tribune*, 3 November, sec. 1, p. 2.

Leacock, Eleanor Burke, ed. 1971. *The Culture of Poverty: A Critique*. New York: Simon & Schuster.

Leff, Arthur Allen. 1970. "Injury, Ignorance and Spite: The Dynamics of Coercive Collection." *Yale Law Journal* 80:1–46.

"Legal Adviser for Charity Agency Dies." 1962. *Chicago Tribune*, 2 May, sec. 7, p. 10.

Legal Assistance Foundation. 1975–1980. Legal Assistance Foundation personnel files. Data supplied by Elnor Greenfield. Chicago.

———. 1979. "1978–1979 Docket of Federal Litigation, Appeals, and State Court Class Actions." Chicago.

———. 1979/80. "Federal Litigation, Appeals and State Court Class Actions." Annual Report. Chicago.

———. 1980. "Recent Decisions; New Cases Filed—No. 12—2/29/80 to 8/20/80."

Legal Services Corporation. 1977. Memorandum to "All Interested Persons," 2 March. "Analysis of Turnover Problem and Initial Proposals for Action" (by Clinton E. Bamberger, Jr. and Barbara Sard). Washington, D.C.

———. 1979. *Annual Report of the Legal Services Corporation, Fiscal Year 1979*. Washington, D.C.

———. 1980. *Legal Services Corporation News*, July-August, 1980.

Levine, Donald N.; Carter, Ellwood B.; and Gorman, Eleanor Miller. 1976

"Simmel's Influence on American Sociology." *American Journal of Sociology* 81:813–845; 1112–1132.

Levitan, Sar A.; Rein, Martin; and Marwick, David. 1972. *Work and Welfare Go Together*. Baltimore: Johns Hopkins University Press.

Levy, Nancy Duff. 1969. "The Aftermath of Victory: The Availability of Retroactive Welfare Benefits Illegally Denied." *Clearinghouse Review* 3:254; 285; 330.

Lindesmith, Alfred R. 1947. *Opiate Addiction*. Bloomington, Ind.: Principia.

———. 1968. *Addiction and Opiates*. Chicago: Aldine.

Lipsky, Michael. 1980. *Street-level Bureaucracy: Dilemmas of the Individual in Public Services*. New York: Russell Sage.

Lofland, John. 1976. *Doing Social Life: The Qualitative Study of Human Interaction in Natural Settings*. New York: Wiley.

Lortie, Dan C. 1959. "Laymen to Lawmen: Law School, Careers, and Professional Socialization." *Harvard Educational Review*, 29:352–369.

Lowenstein, Daniel H., and Waggoner, Michael J. 1967. "Neighborhood Law Offices: New Wave in Legal Services for the Poor." *Harvard Law Review* 80:805–850.

Lubove, Roy. 1965. *The Professional Altruist: The Emergence of Social Work as a Career, 1880–1930*. Cambridge, Mass.: Harvard University Press.

Lyons, Clinton. 1979. "Managing in the 1980's." *Legal Services Corporation News*, December, p. 2.

Mann, Jim. 1979. "High Court Backs Foster Care Aid to Children's Kin." *Los Angeles Times*, 22 February, sec. 1, p. 3.

Manning, Peter. 1978. "Analytic Induction." Unpublished paper. Michigan: Michigan State University, Department of Sociology.

Martin, George T., Jr. 1972. "The Emergence and Development of a Social Movement Organization among the Underclass." Ph.D. dissertation, University of Chicago.

Mathewson, Joe. 1974. *Up against Daley*. La Salle, Ill.: Open Court.

McCall, George J. 1969. "Data Quality Control in Participant Observation." In *Issues in Participant Observation*, ed. George J. McCall and J. L. Simmons, pp. 128–141. Reading, Mass.: Addison-Wesley.

McKelvey, Bill, and Sekaran, Uma. 1977. "Toward a Career-based Theory of Job Involvement: A Study of Scientists and Engineers." *Administrative Science Quarterly* 22:281–305.

McNeil, Kenneth, and Thompson, James D. 1971. "The Regeneration of Organization." *American Sociological Review* 36:624–637.

"Medicaid Benefits Restored." 1972. *Chicago Tribune*, 6 July, sec. 4A, p. 11.

Merton, Robert K. 1968. "Patterns of Influence: Local and Cosmopolitan Influentials." In his *Social Theory and Social Structure*, pp. 441–474. New York: Free Press.

Messinger, Sheldon L. 1955. "Organizational Transformation: A Case Study of a Declining Social Movement." *American Sociological Review* 20:3–10.

Michels, Robert. 1949. *Political Parties: A Sociological Study of the Oligarchical Tendencies of Modern Democracy*. Trans. Eden Paul and Cedar Paul. Glencoe, Ill.: Free Press.

Miller, Stephen J. 1970. *Prescription for Leadership: Training for the Medical Elite*. Chicago: Aldine.

Moskos, Charles C. 1967. *The Sociology of Political Independence: A Study of Nationalist Attitudes among the West Indian Leaders*. Cambridge, Mass.: Schenkman.

Moynihan, Daniel P. 1969. *Maximum Feasible Misunderstanding: Community Action in the War on Poverty*. New York: Free Press.

Myers, Vincent. 1977. "Toward a Synthesis of Ethnographic and Survey Methods." *Human Organization* 36:244–251.

Niebuhr, H. Richard. 1957. *The Social Sources of Denominationalism*. New York: World Publishing/Meridian.

Oberschall, Anthony. 1977. "The Decline of the 1960's Social Movements." In *Research in Social Movements, Conflict and Change*, vol. 1, ed. Louis Kriesberg, pp. 257–289. Greenwich, Conn.: JAI.

O'Gorman, Hubert J. 1963. *Lawyers and Matrimonial Cases: A Study of Informal Pressures in Private Professional Practice*. New York: Free Press of Glencoe.

Patner, Marshall. 1967. "Chicago Appellate Division: An Early View." *Legal Aid Brief Case* (NLADA) 25:141–145.

Perrow, Charles. 1972. *Complex Organizations: A Critical Essay*. Glenview, Ill.: Scott, Foresman.

Phillips, Derek L. 1973. *Abandoning Method*. San Francisco: Jossey-Bass.

Piven, Frances Fox, and Cloward, Richard A. 1971. *Regulating the Poor: The Functions of Public Welfare*. New York: Random House.

———. 1978. "Social Movements and Societal Conditions: A Response to Roach and Roach." *Social Problems* 26:172–178.

———. 1979. *Poor People's Movements: Why They Succeed, How They Fail*. New York: Random House.

Platt, Anthony, and Pollock, Randi. 1974. "Channeling Lawyers: The Careers of Public Defenders." *Issues in Criminology* 9:1–31.

Plomer, William. 1956. Introduction to *White Jacket*, by Herman Melville. New York: Grove.

Price, James L. 1977. *The Study of Turnover*. Ames: Iowa State University Press.

Project Advisory Group. 1979. *Project Advisory Group Report*, vol. 5, no. 4.

Pye, A. Kenneth, and Garraty, Raymond F., Jr. 1966. "The Involvement of the Bar in the War against Poverty." *Notre Dame Lawyer* 41:860–886.

Rabin, Robert. 1976. "Lawyers for Social Change." *Stanford Law Review* 28:207–261.

Radest, Howard B. 1969. *Toward Common Ground: The Study of the Ethical Societies in the United States*. New York: Frederick Ungar.

Reich, Charles A. 1964. "The New Property." *Yale Law Journal* 73:733–787.

Reiss, Albert J., Jr. 1968. "Stuff and Nonsense about Social Surveys and Observation." In *Institutions and the Person*, ed. Howard S. Becker, Blanche Geer, David Riesman, and Robert Weiss, pp. 351–367. Chicago: Aldine.

Riesman, David. 1976. "Some Questions about Discontinuities in American Society." In *The Uses of Controversy in Sociology*, ed. Lewis A. Coser, pp. 3–29. New York: Free Press.

Roach, Jack L., and Roach, Janet K. 1978. "Mobilizing the Poor: Road to a Dead End." *Social Problems* 26:160–171.

Roberg, Elena (de Laurentiis). 1957. *La Difesa del povero in America: Experienze di un avvocato Italiano a Chicago*. Milano: Giuffre.

Robinson, W. S. 1951. "The Logical Structure of Analytic Induction." *American Sociological Review* 16:812–818.

Rosett, Arthur I., and Cressey, Donald R. 1976. *Justice by Consent: Plea Bargains in the American Courthouse*. Philadelphia: Lippincott.

Roth, Julius A. 1966. "Hired Hand Research." *American Sociologist* 1:190–196.

Rothwax, Harold J. 1969. "The Law as an Instrument of Social Change." In *Justice and the Law in the Mobilization for Youth Experience*, ed. Harold H. Weissman, pp. 137–144. New York: Associated Press.

Roy, Donald F. 1959/60. "'Banana Time': Job Satisfaction and Informal Interaction." *Human Organization* 18:158–168.

Schaffer, S. Andrew. 1970. *Bail and Parole Jumping in Manhattan in 1967*. New York: Vera Institute of Justice.

Scheingold, Stuart A. 1974. *The Politics of Rights: Lawyers, Public Policy, and Political Change*. New Haven, Conn.: Yale University Press.

Schnaiberg, Allan, and Armer, Michael. 1972. "Measurement Evaluation Obstacles in Sociological Surveys: A Grounded Reassessment." Paper presented at the American Sociological Association meetings, August 1972, New Orleans.

Scott, W. Richard, 1965. "Field Methods in the Study of Organizations." In *Handbook of Organizations*, ed. James G. March, pp. 261–304. Chicago: Rand McNally.

Seid, Richard A. 1969. "A Reply to 'Choosing the Test Case in Welfare Litigation.'" *Clearinghouse Review* 1:3–4.

Selvin, Hanan C. 1957. "A Critique of Tests of Significance in Survey Research." *American Sociological Review* 22:519–527.

Selznick, Philip. 1949. *TVA and the Grass Roots: A Study in the Sociology of Formal Organization*. Berkeley and Los Angeles: University of California Press.

———. 1952. *The Organizational Weapon: A Study of Bolshevik Strategy and Tactics*. New York: McGraw-Hill.

———. 1957. *Leadership in Administration: A Sociological Interpretation*. New York: Harper & Row.

Shibutani, Tamotsu, and Kwan, Kian M. 1971. *Ethnic Stratification: A Comparative Approach*. New York: Macmillan.

Shils, Edward A. 1958. "The Concentration and Dispersion of Charisma: Their Bearing on Economic Policy in Underdeveloped Countries." *World Politics* 2:1–19.

———. 1975. *Center and Periphery: Essays in Macrosociology*. Vol. 1. Chicago: University of Chicago Press.

Sieber, Sam D. 1973. "The Integration of Fieldwork and Survey Methods." *American Journal of Sociology* 78:1335–1359.

Silberman, Charles E. 1964. *Crisis in Black and White*. New York: Random House.

Sills, David L. 1957. *The Volunteers: Means and Ends in a National Organization, a Report*. Glencoe, Ill.: Free Press.

Simmel, Georg. 1898. "The Persistence of Social Groups." *American Journal of Sociology* 3:662–698; 829–836; 4:35–50.

———. 1971. "Group Expansion and the Development of Individuality." In *Georg Simmel on Individuality and Social Forms*, ed. Donald N. Levine and trans. Richard B. Albares, pp. 251–293. Chicago: University of Chicago Press.

Smigel, Erwin O. 1964. *The Wall Street Lawyer: Professional Organization Man?* New York: Free Press of Glencoe.

Smith, Reginald Heber. 1919. *Justice and the Poor: A Study of the Present Denial of Justice to the Poor and of the Agencies Making More Equal Their Position before the Law with Particular Reference to Legal Aid Work in the United States*. New York: Carnegie Foundation for the Advancement of Teaching.

Smith, Reginald Heber, and Bradway, John S. 1936. *Growth of Legal Aid Work in the United States*. U.S. Department of Labor, Bureau of Labor Statistics Bulletin No. 607, rev. ed. Washington, D.C.: Government Printing Office.

Spector, Malcolm. 1972. "The Rise and Fall of a Mobility Route." *Social Problems* 20:173–185.

Starr, Paul. 1974. "Rebels after the Cause: Living with Contradictions." *New York Times Magazine*, 13 October, p. 31.

Steiner, Gilbert. 1966. *Social Insecurity: The Politics of Welfare*. Chicago: Rand McNally.

Sterling, Theodore D. 1959. "Publication Decisions and Their Possible Effects on Inferences Drawn from Tests of Significance—or Vice Versa." *Journal of the American Statistical Association* 54:30–34.

Strachan, Don. 1979. "In Search of Don Juan." *New West*, 29 January, pp. 90–91.

Stumpf, Harry P. 1975. *Community Politics and Legal Services: The Other Side of the Law*. Beverly Hills, Calif: Sage.

Stumpf, Harry P., and Janowitz, Robert J. 1969. "Judges and the Poor: Bench Responses to Federally Financed Legal Services." *Stanford Law Review* 21:1058–1076.

Stumpf, Harry P.; Schroerluke, Henry P.; and Dill, Forrest D. 1971. "The Legal Profession and Legal Services: Explorations in Local Bar Politics." *Law and Society Review* 6:47–67.

Suttles, Gerald D. 1978. "Street Gangs: The Perception of Political Power by the Politically Powerful." *Reports of the Division of the Social Sciences* (University of Chicago) 2:1–3.

Sykes, Gresham M. 1969. "Legal Needs of the Poor in the City of Denver." *Law and Society Review* 4:255–277.

Taylor, Graham. 1916. "Legal Aid: A Link between Social Justice and the Law." In *Proceedings of the National Alliance of Legal Aid Societies, 3rd Biennial Convention*, pp. 128–129. Boston: G. H. Dean.

Tullock, Gordon. 1959. "Publication Decisions and Tests of Significance: A Comment." *Journal of the American Statistical Association* 54:593.

Turner, Ralph H. 1953. "The Quest for Universals in Sociological Research." *American Sociological Review* 18:604–611.

Twining, William L. 1973. *Karl Llewellyn and the Realist Movement*. London: Weidenfeld and Nicolson.

Unger, Roberto Mangabeira. 1975. *Knowledge and Politics*. New York: Free Press.

United Charities of Chicago. 1922. *66 Years of Service*. Chicago.

———. 1957. *Yesterday-Today-Tomorrow: A Friend of the Family: 1857–1957*. Chicago.

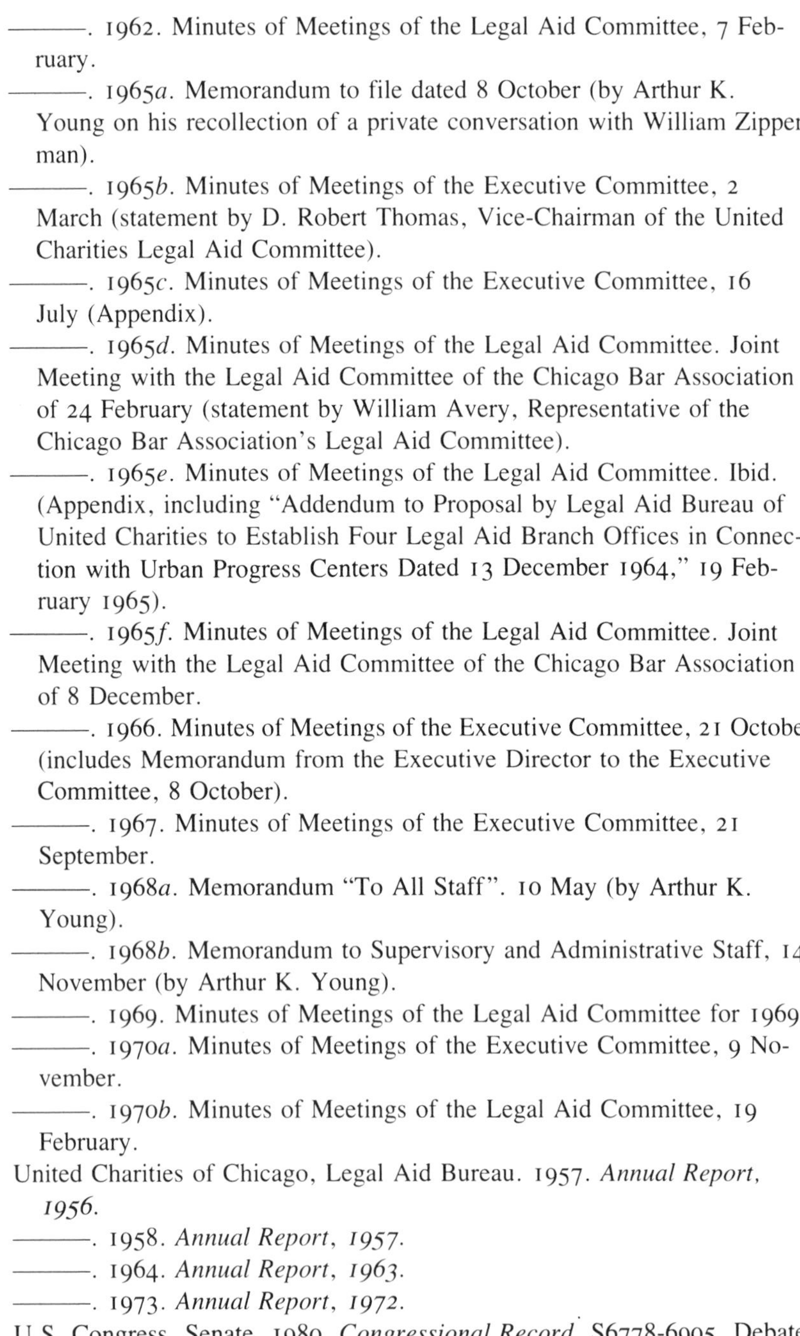

———. 1962. Minutes of Meetings of the Legal Aid Committee, 7 February.

———. 1965*a*. Memorandum to file dated 8 October (by Arthur K. Young on his recollection of a private conversation with William Zipperman).

———. 1965*b*. Minutes of Meetings of the Executive Committee, 2 March (statement by D. Robert Thomas, Vice-Chairman of the United Charities Legal Aid Committee).

———. 1965*c*. Minutes of Meetings of the Executive Committee, 16 July (Appendix).

———. 1965*d*. Minutes of Meetings of the Legal Aid Committee. Joint Meeting with the Legal Aid Committee of the Chicago Bar Association of 24 February (statement by William Avery, Representative of the Chicago Bar Association's Legal Aid Committee).

———. 1965*e*. Minutes of Meetings of the Legal Aid Committee. Ibid. (Appendix, including "Addendum to Proposal by Legal Aid Bureau of United Charities to Establish Four Legal Aid Branch Offices in Connection with Urban Progress Centers Dated 13 December 1964," 19 February 1965).

———. 1965*f*. Minutes of Meetings of the Legal Aid Committee. Joint Meeting with the Legal Aid Committee of the Chicago Bar Association of 8 December.

———. 1966. Minutes of Meetings of the Executive Committee, 21 October (includes Memorandum from the Executive Director to the Executive Committee, 8 October).

———. 1967. Minutes of Meetings of the Executive Committee, 21 September.

———. 1968*a*. Memorandum "To All Staff". 10 May (by Arthur K. Young).

———. 1968*b*. Memorandum to Supervisory and Administrative Staff, 14 November (by Arthur K. Young).

———. 1969. Minutes of Meetings of the Legal Aid Committee for 1969.

———. 1970*a*. Minutes of Meetings of the Executive Committee, 9 November.

———. 1970*b*. Minutes of Meetings of the Legal Aid Committee, 19 February.

United Charities of Chicago, Legal Aid Bureau. 1957. *Annual Report, 1956*.

———. 1958. *Annual Report, 1957*.

———. 1964. *Annual Report, 1963*.

———. 1973. *Annual Report, 1972*.

U.S. Congress, Senate. 1980. *Congressional Record*, S6778-6905. Debate

on the 1980 authorization act for the Legal Services Corporation, 12 June.
U.S. Department of Commerce, Bureau of the Census. 1950. *United States Census of Population,* vol. 2, *Characteristics of the Population*. Pt. 13. "Illinois."
———. 1960. *United States Census of Population,* vol. 1, *Characteristics of the Population*. Pt. 15, "Illinois."
Van Alystyne, W. Scott, Jr. 1952. "The District Attorney: A Historical Puzzle." *Wisconsin Law Review*, January, pp. 125–138.
Wallace, Anthony F. C. 1962. "Culture and Cognition." *Science* 135:351–357.
Weaver, Suzanne. 1977. *Decision to Prosecute: Organization and Public Policy in the Antitrust Division*. Cambridge, Mass.: M.I.T. Press.
Weisbrod, Burton, 1978. "What Might Public Interest Law Accomplish: Distributional Effects." In *Public Interest Law*, ed. Burton Weisbrod, pp. 102–147. Berkeley and Los Angeles: University of California Press.
Weissman, Harold H., ed. 1969. *Justice and the Law in the Mobilization for Youth Experience*. New York: Associated Press.
Wexler, Stephen. 1970. "Practicing Law for Poor People." *Yale Law Journal* 79:1049–1067.
Wheeler, Stanton. 1966. "The Structure of Formally Organized Socialization Settings." In *Socialization after Childhood*, by Orville G. Brim, Jr. and Stanton Wheeler, pp. 51–116. New York: Wiley.
"Why the SEC's Enforcer Is in over His Head." 1976. *Business Week*, 11 October, p. 70.
Wiebe, Robert H. 1962. *Businessmen and Reform: A Study of the Progressive Movement*. Cambridge, Mass.: Harvard University Press.
Wieder, D. Lawrence. 1974. *Language and Social Reality: The Case of Telling the Convict Code*. The Hague: Mouton.
Wills, Garry. 1972. *Bare Ruined Choirs: Doubt, Prophecy, and Radical Religion*. New York: Doubleday.
Wilson, James Q., ed. 1966. *Urban Renewal: The Record and Controversy*. Cambridge, Mass.: M.I.T. Press.
Wright, Eric. 1967. "Competition in Legal Services under the War on Poverty." *Stanford Law Review* 19:579–592.
Zald, Mayer N., and Ash, Roberta. 1966. "Social Movement Organizations: Growth, Decay and Change." *Social Forces* 44:327–341.
Zelditch, Morris, Jr. 1962. "Some Methodological Problems of Field Studies." *American Journal of Sociology* 67:566–576.
Znaniecki, Florian. 1968. *The Method of Sociology*. New York: Octagon.

Index

Aaronson, Mark, 180, 187–190
Abel, Richard L., 220n8
Agnew, Spiro T. (Vice President), 77, 194
Aid to Families With Dependent Children (AFDC), 184–185, 191, 231n35
Albert, Lee, 130
Alinsky, Saul, 100
Allen, Michael Patrick (and Panian and Lotz), 236n3
Alschuler, Albert W., 127
American Bar Association (ABA), 45, 77, 93, 104, 187, 223n9, 240n4
American Civil Liberties Union (ACLU), 156, 228n11
Armer, Michael (and Schnaiberg), 246n18
Ash, Roberta (and Zald), 227n5
Auchincloss, Louis, 225n18
Auerbach, Jerold S., 240n2
  (and Bardach), 43, 238n8

Balbus, Isaac D., 88, 232n3
Bamberger, Clinton, 139, 170
Bardach, Eugene (and Auerbach), 43, 238n8
Bass, Stan, 81
Beardsley, Charles A., 46
Becker, Howard S., 233n4, 244n4, 245n8
  (and Geer), 114, 231n36
  (and Geer, Hughes, and Strauss), 244n1
Bellow, Gary, 17, 161, 240n5, 240n10
Bennett, Michael (and Reynoso), 76
Bennett, Robert, 80
Berger, Bennett M., 235n10
Berkeley Center on Law and Society (University of California), 70
Bittner, Egon, 225n15
Black Panthers, 85, 94
Blackstone Rangers, 231n39
Blumenthal, Richard (and Soler), 98, 230n20, 232n3, 240n3
Blumer, Herbert, 229n14, 244n4
Bolton, John R. (and Holzer), 182
Boyes, Maud Purcells, 39, 47, 223n6
Bradley, Dan, 171
Bradway, John S., 223n7
  (and Smith), 41, 223n5, 223n10
Braverman, Harry, 236n5
Brennan, William J., Jr. (Justice), 79
Brill, Harry, 238n10
Brooks, Deton, 93–94
Brown, George (Senator), 195
Brownell, Emery A., 4, 46, 65, 134, 223n10
Bruyn, Severyn T., 244n4
Bureau of Justice, 15, 35–37, 82, 150
Burt, Cyril, 246n14
Burt, Moses C., Jr., 80
Businessmen for the Public Interest, 81

Cahn, Edgar S. (and Cahn), 70, 228n10
Cahn, Jean C. (and Cahn), 70, 228n10
California Rural Legal Assistance (CRLA), 76, 87, 161, 193, 195, 238n10, 240n3
Camus, Albert, 219n4
Caplan, Gerald M., 127
Careers
  balance between personal and collective interests in lawyers', 125–126, 133–134
  of blacks in legal assistance, 48, 52–53
  of cases, 111–113
  conflict between lawyer's, and

Careers, *continued*
needs of client organization, 102–103
contrast of Legal Aid and Legal Services lawyers', 52–56, 71, 105, 110–111
contrast of legal assistance lawyers' and board members', 46–48
of lawyers after leaving legal assistance, 17, 133, 172–173
lawyers' personal experience of, 13
legal assistance lawyers' expectations of, 18, 56, 105
legal assistance lawyers' motivations related to, 52–56, 71–76, 88, 105, 127–128
stepping-stone advancement in lawyers', 62, 105, 127, 173, 225n15
typical patterns in legal assistance, 46–49, 52–56, 62, 131
of women in legal assistance, 48, 52–53, 71, 224n14, 225n16
see also Involvement; Reform of poverty
Carlin, Jerome E., 69, 70, 180, 221n9, 224n13, 232n5
(and Howard), 70
Carter, Ellwood B. (and Levine and Gorman), 237n7
Carter, Jimmy (President) administration, 192
Castaneda, Carlos, 246n14
Catholicism, 73–74
Chavez, Cesar, 98
Chicago Bar Association (CBA), 41, 46, 86, 87, 142, 143, 159, 223n10, 225n17
Chicago Committee for Urban Opportunity (CCUO), 93–94, 137–138, 141–143, 145
Chicago Council of Lawyers, 86, 155
Chicago Historical Society, 39, 40, 41, 223n6, 223n9, 226n19
Chicago Housing Authority (CHA), 177, 187
Chicago Housing Tenants Organization, 87
Chicago Transit Authority, 175
Chicago Welfare Rights Organizations (CWRO), 170
Chicago Women's Club, *see* Protective Agency for Women and Children
Citizen Action Program, *see* Chicago Committee for Urban Opportunity
Citizen participation in anti-poverty organizations, 69, 84, 91, 92, 240n1
see also Clients
Clark, Burton R., 236n2
Clearinghouse Review, 174, 181, 183, 185, 242n16
Clients
demographics of, 49, 95
organizations as, 94, 95, 97–103, 143, 179
organized as National Clients' Council, 241n10
participation in directing legal assistance programs, 69, 78, 93, 95, 139, 150, 154–155, 158, 170, 240n1
perceived capabilities, 22, 25, 29, 221n10, 221n11, 222n13
racial and ethnic allocation to lawyers, 48, 49, 225n17, 226n19
typical legal problems, 21
see also Work problems
Cloward, Richard A. (and Piven), 85, 191, 192, 231n35, 232n7, 232n9, 233n10
Collective character
balance between members' and collective interests, 125–126
comparison between Legal Services' and Legal Aid's, 11, 52–56, 103, 133–135, 136, 151–159
contemporaneous distinctiveness, 66
dialectic between historical and contemporaneous distinctiveness, 66, 226n1, 227n4
extension to external constituencies, 124–125, 132–135, 172–178
external and internal differentiation, 226n1
historical distinctiveness, 66
influence on personal careers, 10, 59, 125
persistence of, 124–125, 126–132
reflected in collective philosophy, 11, 123–126, 129

shaped by individual careers of staff, 52, 82, 123–126
Collegial relations, 107, 113–122, 133–134, 165
Collins, James (Representative), 76
Columbia University, 70
Center on Social Welfare Policy and Law, 80
Community Chest, 45, 223n10
Community Fund, 45, 159
Community Legal Counsel (CLC)
creation of, 7, 15
merger with Legal Aid Bureau, 12, 135, 137, 148–159
reform goals and strategies of, 67–89, 91
staff characteristics, 108
work with organizations, 7, 67, 68, 84–85, 91, 97–104, 179
see also Legal Services
Community organizations
as clients, 94, 95, 97–103, 143, 179
leadership struggles within, 99
needs of, in conflict with lawyers' careers, 102–103
trend to federated format, 100–101
Connecticut Legal Services, 167
Conover, D.S.B., 35
Contract Buyers League, 81
Cook County Democratic Organization, 84, 86, 87, 93, 99, 136, 137, 143, 231n39
Cornfield, Gilbert, 80
Coser, Lewis A., 125
Cover, Robert M., 235n11
Cressey, Donald R., 245n7, 245n8
Curran, Barbara A., 219n5
Cushman, Robert S., 231n31

Daley, Richard J. (Mayor), *see* Cook County Democratic Organization
Dallas Legal Services, 76
Davies, William, *see* Donald Kerwin
Davis, Fred, 246n16
DePres, Leon (Alderman), 86
Diesing, Paul, 246n13
Dill, Forrest D. (and Schroerluke and Stumpf), 230n22
Donovan, John C., 94
Douglass, Frederick, 235n11
Drager, Kerry, 243n5
Dudley, Henry A. (and Johnston), 236n6

Economic impact of legal assistance litigation, 176–177, 180
Ehrlich, Thomas, 170
Ellis, William W., 100
Epstein, Cynthia Fuchs, 225n16
Equal Employment Opportunity Commission, 177
Equal justice
aggressive interpretation, 7, 9–10, 34, 36–37, 66, 68, 76–89, 165, 174, 181
passive interpretation, 5–6, 7, 9, 10, 37, 42–43, 50, 51
social construction of, 1–6
see also Reform of poverty
Erickson, A. Gerald, 158
Erikson, Kai T., 235n9
Erlanger, Howard S., 71, 72, 230n18
(and Handler and Hollingsworth), *see* The Wisconsin Study
Ethical Cultural Society of Chicago, 15, 35–36, 150
see also Bureau of Justice

Fair Employment Practices Commission, 177
Feeley, Malcolm M., 220n2
Feyerabend, Paul K., 244n2
Fish, John H., 84, 94, 100
Fisher, Kenneth P. (and Ivie), 95
Fitzgerald, Jeffrey M., 231n31
Foote, Caleb, 243n6
Ford, Gerald R. (President) administration, 7
Ford Motor Credit, 175
Foucault, Michel, 193, 220n9
Frankel, Marvin, 239n16
Friedman, Lawrence M., 191, 243n7
Fritzsche, Sybille, 80
Fuller, Lon L., 219n1, 227n4
Funding of legal assistance programs
government, 7, 15–16, 70, 162, 163–164, 170, 181, 194–196
as means to political control of program, 137, 138, 143, 146–148, 158–159

Funding of legal assistance programs, *continued*
 private, 4, 7, 15–16, 35–36, 45, 70, 146–148, 159, 163, 181

Garbus, Martin, 79–80, 230n25
Garfinkel, Harold, 226n4
Gariepy, Marguerite Raeder, 46, 223n10
Garraty, Raymond F. (and Pye), 230n22
Garson, Barbara, 17
Geary, Charles, 84, 228n8
Geer, Blanche (and Becker), 114, 231n36
 (and Becker, Hughes, and Strauss), 244n1
General Motors Acceptance Corporation, 175
Georgetown University, 70
Getzels, Mortimer, 240n5
Gitlin, Todd (and Hollander), 85, 94, 232n8
Glaser, Barney G., 236n2
 (and Strauss), 246n16
Goffman, Erving, 235n9
Goldman, Marion S., 225n17
Goldstein, Joseph, 70
Gorman, Eleanor Miller (and Carter and Levine), 237n7
Gouldner, Alvin, 227n5, 231n36, 237n7
Government support for legal assistance organizations
 and the conservative movement of the eighties, 5, 6, 16, 162, 194–196, 240n4
 in the sixties, 4, 7, 15
 in the seventies, 7, 16, 161, 170, 181
Grant, Sally Deane, 221n9
Great Society program, 172
Greenberg, Jack, 80
Greenstone, J. David (and Peterson), 84, 94
Grønbjerg, Kirsten (and Street and Suttles), 232n1
Grossman, Susan, 80
Grusky, Oscar, 236n3
Gurney, Edward (Senator), 76
Gussow, Zachary, 246n12

Hale, William Henri, 224n13, 225n17
Handler, Joel F., 85, 102
 (and Hollingsworth and Erlanger), *see* The Wisconsin Study
Hannon, Philip J., 98
Harring, Sidney L., 243n6
Harris, Patricia, 70
Harvard University, 37
Hazard, Geoffrey C., Jr., 182, 219n6
Hearnshaw, Leslie F., 246n14
Helfgot, Joseph, 227n5
Hirschman, Albert O., 236n4
History of Chicago legal assistance organizations
 chronology, 15–16
 expansion in the seventies, 7–8, 12, 89, 145–159, 160–178, 179–196
 fate in the conservative eighties, 6, 162, 194–196, 240n4
 isolation during the thirties, 50
 roots in the Progressive Era, 5, 7, 34–38, 49–50, 160
 transition to quiescence in the twenties, 5, 7, 10, 37–45, 50, 160
 within social movements of the sixties, 5, 7, 65–89, 90–104, 123, 136–144
 see also Social movements
Hoffman, Paul, 226n18
Hollander, Nanci (and Gitlin), 85, 94, 232n8
Hollingsworth, Ellen Jane (and Erlanger and Handler), *see* The Wisconsin Study
Holzer, Stephen T. (and Bolton), 182
Homans, George, 238n13
Hopson, Dan, Jr. (and Johnstone), 21
Horsky, Charles A., 28, 221n7
Howard, Jan (and Carlin), 70
Howard University, 70
Howell, Kenneth, 75, 82–83, 148, 151, 155–158
Hughes, Everett C. (and Becker, Geer, and Strauss), 244n1
Hunter, Albert, 100
Hunter, Joel D., 41, 45, 100, 223n9

Illinois Department of Corrections, 175
Illinois Department of Insurance, 177

Illinois Department of Public Aid (IDPA), 82–83, 175, 176
Independent Precinct Organization (IPO), 86
Independent Voters of Illinois (IVI), 86
Institutional analysis
of collective identity, 11, 124–125, 132–135, 163, 172–178
of Legal Aid/Legal Services struggle for dominance, 136–159
of organizational continuity, 11–12, 124–125, 126–132, 166
of organizational development, 166–171
of staff dissension, 168
vs. analysis of effects of social movements, 5–6, 104
see also Collective character; Organizational structure; Social movements; Staffs of legal assistance organizations
Involvement
as an active process, 106, 233n2
benefits to organization, 127–128
conditions necessary for, 11, 106–107, 108–109
defined, 13, 106
ending to, 115, 116–117, 234n7
personal experience of, 10, 105–122, 233n3, 233n4
self-discovery as a basis for, 18, 106, 127–128, 221n5, 233n4
see also Significance
Ivie, Charles C. (and Fisher), 95

James, Marlise, 232n4
James, William, 246n17
Janowitz, Robert J. (and Stumpf), 22
Jellinek, Donald, 79
Jenner, Albert, 81
Johnson, Earl, Jr., 70, 77, 92, 170, 180, 223n8, 227n3, 228n12, 239n15, 240n1, 240n3
Johnson, Lyndon B. (President), 77, 92
see also War on Poverty
Johnston, Clement D. (and Dudley), 236n6
Johnstone, Quintin (and Hopson), 21
JOIN, 85

Katz, Jack, 6, 168, 221n5, 221n6, 238n8, 242n11
Kennedy, John F. (President)
administration, 85
Kenwood-Oakwood Community Organization (KOCO), 84, 100, 228n8
Kerwin, Donald, 221n8
King, Ruben, 79
Kitsuse, John I., 220n4
Kotre, John N., 230n19
Kuh, Richard H., 127
Kwan, Kian M. (and Shibutani), 46

Ladinsky, Jack, 224n13
Landrieu, Moon (Secretary HUD), 176
Langbein, John H., 219n7
Lawndale People's Political Action Coalition, 84
Lawyers Committee for Civil Rights, 80, 156
Lawyer's Constitutional Defense Committee, 79
Lawyers in private practice
contrast of legal assistance lawyers to, 19–21, 26, 43, 47–48, 59, 70–71, 110–111, 122
relations of legal assistance lawyers with, 40–41, 155
relations with legal assistance organizations, 45–46, 47, 92–93, 138, 143–144, 159, 170, 178
ways of developing significance in work, 20
Leacock, Eleanor Burke, 222n13
Leff, Arthur Allen, 221n9
Legal Aid
advocacy styles compared to Legal Services, 68–69, 78, 86
balance of members' and collective interests compared to Legal Services, 125–126, 133–134
collective character compared to Legal Services, 52–56, 133–135
defined, 10, 13, 14
funding compared to Legal Services, 14, 45, 134–135
goals compared to Legal Services, 14, 65–66, 138–139, 140, 142–143
growth of, 65
location compared to Legal Services, 14, 67, 68, 95

Legal Aid, *continued*
organizational structure compared to Legal Services, 65, 67–70, 90, 136, 144, 162–165
philosophy compared to Legal Services, 123–126
staff compared to Legal Services, 52–56, 70–76, 90, 131, 134–135, 140–141
see also Equal justice; Legal Aid Bureau of United Charities of Chicago; Legal Services; Reform of poverty
Legal Aid Brief Case, 224n12
Legal Aid Bureau of United Charities of Chicago (LAB)
funding of, 13, 15, 45, 93, 163
in the seventies, 162–165
merger with Community Legal Counsel, 12, 135, 137, 148–159
movement toward Legal Services control, 137–143
Neighborhood Legal Services Program of, 15, 93, 97, 137–138
non-aggressive role toward reform, 10, 38–45, 46, 93
as oriented to "family service," 7, 38–39, 162
origins of, 15, 38
staffing patterns in, 46–48
see also United Charities of Chicago
Legal Aid Society of Chicago
becomes Legal Aid Bureau of United Charities, 38
during transition to quiescence in the twenties, 37–38, 160
origins of, 15, 36, 160
resurrection as vehicle for CLC and LAB merger, 15, 150–159, 160
"Legal assistance," defined, 14
Legal Assistance Association (New Haven), 70, 167
Legal Assistance Foundation of Chicago (LAF)
funding by Legal Services Corporation, 16, 163–164
in the seventies, 162–178, 179–196
origins of, 8, 14, 16, 135, 159
staff of, 108, 164
see also Legal Services Corporation
Legal realism, 43
Legal rights movement, 69–70, 78, 80, 81, 87, 88
Legal Services
advocacy style compared to Legal Aid, 68–69, 78, 86
balance of members' and collective interests, compared with Legal Aid, 125–126, 133–134
collective character compared to Legal Aid, 52–56, 103, 133–135, 136
criticisms of Legal Aid, 67–69
defined, 13–14
expansion in the seventies, 164
funding compared to Legal Aid, 14, 134–135
goals compared to Legal Aid, 14, 65–66, 90, 142–143
location compared to Legal Aid, 14, 67, 68, 69, 95
organizational structure compared to Legal Aid, 65, 67–70, 90, 136, 144, 162–165
staff compared to Legal Aid, 52–56, 65, 70–76, 90, 131, 134–135, 140–141
see also Community Legal Counsel; Equal justice; Legal Aid; Legal Assistance Foundation of Chicago; Legal Services Corporation; Reform of poverty
Legal Services Corporation
and balance of Legal Aid/Legal Service philosophies, 123, 170, 179
funding of Legal Assistance Foundation, 16, 163–164
national scope of, 181
origins of, 6, 7, 16, 161, 169
and the Reagan administration, 6, 16, 195–196
see also Legal Services; Office of Economic Opportunity
Levine, Donald N. (and Carter and Gorman), 237n7
Levitan, Sar A. (and Rein and Marwick), 243n2
Levy, Nancy Duff, 180
Lindesmith, Alfred R., 244n4, 245n7, 246n13
Lindsay, John (Mayor), 188

Lipsky, Michael, 188–189
Lloyd, Henry Demarest, 36
Lofland, John, 244n4
Lortie, Dan C., 224n13
Lotz, Roy E. (and Allen and Panian), 236n3
Lowenstein, Daniel H. (and Waggoner), 240n3
Lubove, Roy, 223n4

Mann, Jim, 176
Manning, Peter, 244n4
Martin, George T., Jr., 232n9
Martindale-Hubbell comparisons between ratings of lawyers and board members, 48, 223n3
Marwick, David (and Levitan and Rein), 243n2
Mathewson, Joe, 231n37
Matz, Rudolph, 35, 36, 37, 223n2
McCall, George J., 244n1
McKelvey, Bill (and Sekaran), 233n2
McNeil, E. Duke, 81
McNeil, Kenneth (and Thompson), 238n11
Merger of United Charities Legal Aid/Legal Services with Community Legal Counsel, 12, 13, 135, 137, 148–159
Merton, Robert K., 237n7
Messinger, Sheldon L., 236n4
Methodology, 13, 52, 71, 107, 162, 183, 197–217, 229n13, 242n12
Michels, Robert, 241n5
Miller, Stephen J., 220n3, 233n1
Mobilization for Youth (MFY), 70, 87, 227n5, 228n9, 239n16
Model Cities Plan, 81, 84, 89, 99
Mondale, Walter (Vice President), 7
Montrose Urban Progress Center, 94
Moskos, Charles C., 244n4
Moynihan, Daniel P. (Senator), 69, 94
Murphy, George (Senator), 76
Myers, Vincent, 244n3

NAACP Legal Defense Fund, 80, 228n11
Nader, Ralph, 78, 88
National Health Law Center, 167
National Labor Relations Board, 182
National Legal Aid and Defender Association, 15, 134, 137
Neighborhood Legal Services Program, *see* Legal Aid Bureau of United Charities of Chicago
Neighborhood Legal Services Project (Washington, D.C.), 70
Nelson, Robert F., 138, 139, 140
New York Legal Aid Society, 59, 167, 223n10, 239n16
Niebuhr, H. Richard, 227n4
Nixon, Richard M. (President)
- administration and legal assistance, 7, 89, 150, 161, 169
- and Family Assistance Plan, 192

Northwest Community Organization, 100
Northwestern University
- Center for Urban Affairs, 80
- School of Law, 41, 52, 71, 228n6

Oberschall, Anthony, 233n11
Office of Economic Opportunity
- Community Action Program, 78, 92, 94
- criticisms of Chicago legal assistance programs, 139, 143, 145, 150, 157
- dismantling of, 89, 158–159, 170
- requirements of Legal Services programs, 93–94, 138–139, 150, 179, 228n10
- resistance of Legal Services lawyers to control by, 92
- separation of Legal Services program from, 16
- *see also* Funding of legal assistance programs; Government support for legal assistance organizations; War on Poverty

Ogilvie, Richard (Governor), 82
O'Gorman, Hubert J., 222n13
Organization for a Better Austin (OBA), 100
Organizational structure
- changes in, resulting from Legal Aid/Legal Services struggle for dominance, 137–142, 144–145, 149–159, 163
- distance between legal assistance staffs and boards, 8, 35, 36, 45–49, 136, 149, 154–157, 160
- effects on individual careers, 61–62, 110–111, 236n5

Organizational structure, *continued*
as a homogenizing influence, 48–49, 52, 54–55, 71
and organizational continuity, 11, 128–132, 166–171, 172–173
as shaped by social influences, 67–70, 90, 104, 161, 166, 169
specialization, 62, 100–103, 163–165
and staff turmoil, 166–171
and staff turnover, 62, 130–132, 166–171, 172–174, 236n3
staffing patterns, 46–48, 70–71, 164–165, 166, 172, 241n6, 241n7, 242n12
see also Collective character; Institutional analysis; Legal Aid; Legal Services

Palm, Gary, 158
Panian, Sharon K. (and Allen and Lotz), 236n3
Parks, Jeanus, 70
Patner, Marshall, 67, 70, 80, 140
Paulson, Monrad, 70
People's Law Office, 94
Percy, Charles (Senator), 83
Perrow, Charles, 227n4
Peterson, Paul E. (and Greenstone), 84, 94
Phillips, Howard, 158
Piven, Frances Fox (and Cloward), 85, 191, 192, 231n35, 232n7, 232n9, 233n10
Platt, Anthony (and Pollock), 126
Plomer, William, 246n15
Polikoff, Alexander, 81
Political opposition to legal assistance programs, 5, 7, 76–77, 78, 161, 188, 194–196
Pollner, Mel, 246n14
Pollock, Randi (and Platt), 126
Poverty, legal institutionalization of, 8, 12–13, 50, 91–92, 180–181, 182–196
"Poverty lawyers"
defined, 13, 14
see also Legal Services
Powell, Lewis (Justice), 93
Price, James L., 236n3
Professionalism
appearance of, 42–43, 45, 49, 69, 146, 225n18
as a motivation, 17–18, 109–110, 178
and reform activities, 155, 193
see also Lawyers in private practice; Work problems
Professionalization of reform, *see* Reform of poverty
Project Advisory Group, 241n10
Protective Agency for Women and Children, 15, 34–36, 150
Pucinski, Roman (Representative), 86
Pye, A. Kenneth, 70
(and Garraty), 230n22

Quie, Albert (Representative), 94

Rabin, Robert, 224n11, 228n11
Racial and ethnic integration
of legal assistance clients, 225n17
of legal assistance staff, 48–49, 70–71
Radest, Howard B., 36
Radicalization, *see* Reform of poverty; Social movements
Reagan, Ronald (President), 6, 16, 195
as governor of California, 188
Reasonableness
as a career resource, 63
clients', 56–57, 58, 59
ethic of, 8, 10, 11, 56–59
and identification with local professional environment, 60–63, 148
Reform of poverty
as career motivation, 53–54, 71–76, 88, 105, 114, 122, 178
effects of social movements on personal commitment to, 72–76, 88
impediments in Legal Services programs for mobilizing, 90, 93–101
legislative, as an objective of legal assistance, 34, 36–37, 76–83
militance in achieving, 84–88, 89

objectives served by remedial laws and agencies, 39, 50, 77–78, 181, 191
opposition to, 76–77, 78, 87, 146
professionalization of, 8, 69–70, 178, 179–180, 186–190, 223n4
structural, as an objective of legal assistance, 7, 9–10, 34, 35, 76, 91, 179–186
sustaining individual commitment to, 5, 91, 105–106, 114–120, 132, 161
see also Economic impact of legal assistance litigation; Equal justice; Strategies to achieve reform
Reich, Charles A., 70
Rein, Martin (and Levitan and Marwick), 243n2
Reiss, Albert J., Jr., 244n3
Reynoso, Cruz (and Bennett), 76
Riesman, David, 245n9
Roach, Jack L. (and Roach), 232n6, 232n7
Roach, Janet K. (and Roach), 232n6, 232n7
Roberg, Elena (de Laurentiis), 226n2
Robinson, W.S., 245n10
Role
commitment and validation, 115, 235n9
distance, 118, 235n10
Roodman, Sheldon, 82, 171
Roosevelt, Theodore (President), 224n12
Rothwax, Harold J., 228n9
Roy, Donald F., 125

San Francisco Neighborhood Legal Assistance Foundation, 70
Schaffer, S. Andrew, 238n13
Scheingold, Stuart A., 232n41, 240n2
Schnaiberg, Allan (and Armer), 246n18
Schroerluke, Henry P. (and Dill and Stumpf), 230n22
Scott, Gordon H.S., 144, 145, 148, 156
Seid, Richard A., 130
Sekaran, Uma (and McKelvey), 233n2
Self
discovery of, as a basis for involvement, 18, 106, 127–128, 221n5, 233n4
social creation of, 110, 115, 234n6, 235n8, 235n9
Selznick, Philip, 125, 227n4, 236n2, 241n5
Shibutani, Tamotsu (and Kwan), 46
Shils, Edward A., 221n5, 227n4
Sieber, Sam D., 244n3
Significance
culture of, 8, 11, 107, 113–122, 133–134, 165
difficulties in sustaining, *see* Work problems
as experienced in sympathy for client problems, 120–122
lawyers' efforts to develop, 87–88, 103, 105–106, 108–109, 107–122
sustained through incredulity, 118
sustained through irony, 119–120
sustained through ridicule, 118–119
of work, for lawyers in private practice, 20
see also Involvement
Silberman, Charles E., 81
Sills, David L., 236n2
Simmel, Georg, 226n1, 227n4, 236n1, 237n7
Simpson, Dick (Alderman), 86
Singer, Bill (Alderman), 86
Smigel, Erwin O., 224n13, 235n10
Smith, Reginald Heber, 34, 37, 41–43, 46, 57, 58, 60, 64, 68, 219n2, 223n8, 223n10
(and Bradway), 41, 223n5, 223n10
Social class
legal assistance lawyers as intermediaries between upper and lower, 13, 38, 46
see also Racial and ethnic integration; Reform of poverty
Social movements
affecting personal commitment to reform, 72–76, 88, 96–97, 103–104, 161–162, 193
definition of, 72, 229n14
dependence of legal assistance movement on, 5, 6, 10, 13, 34, 50, 66–89, 90, 161, 171
growth of legal assistance as, 65

Social movements, *continued*
independence of legal assistance movement from, 5–6, 8, 10, 11, 13, 66, 89, 90–104, 122, 161–162, 171, 178, 193
shaping organizational structure, 67–70, 90
see also History of Chicago legal assistance organizations; Institutional analysis
Social work within legal assistance organizations, 39, 44, 223n7, 225n16
Soler, Mark I. (and Blumenthal), 98, 230n20, 232n3, 240n3
Sparer, Edward, 80, 233n10
Spector, Malcolm, 126
Sporkin, Stanley, 169
Staffs of legal assistance organizations
characteristics, 46–48, 52–56, 71–72, 73, 108, 164–166, 171, 172–173, 230n18
dissension within, 141–142, 166–171
recruitment, 68, 171, 173
size, 8, 11, 65, 163, 164, 181, 200
turnover, 47, 62, 108, 130–132, 133, 172–173, 239n14
see also Legal Aid; Legal Services; Organizational structure
Starr, Paul, 161
Steiner, Gilbert, 191
Strachan, Don, 246n14
Strategies to achieve reform, 36–37, 39, 78–88, 102–103, 174–177, 179–196
see also Reform of poverty; Work problems
Stratification
between legal assistance staff and boards, 45–49, 149, 154–157, 160
within legal profession, 47–48, 51, 52–56, 70
Strauss, Anselm L. (and Becker, Hughes and Geer), 244n1
(and Glaser), 246n16
Street, David (and Grønbjerg and Suttles), 232n1
Students for a Democratic Society (SDS), 85, 94
Stumpf, Harry P., 180
(and Janowitz), 22
(and Schroerluke and Dill), 230n22
Sullivan, Thomas, 81
Suttles, Gerald D., 231n39
(and Grønbjerg and Street), 232n1
Sykes, Gresham M., 219n5

Taft, William Howard (President), 224n12
Taylor, Graham, 37
Terry, Burton, 140
Thompson, James D. (and McNeil), 238n11
Thorpe, Joyce, 80, 230n23
Tobey, Frank, 36
Tower, John (Senator), 76
Turner, Ralph H., 244n4, 245n7
Twining, William L., 43

Unger, Roberto Mangabeira, 219n3
United Charities of Chicago, 7, 15–16, 38–39, 41, 45, 137–143, 157, 163
see also Legal Aid Bureau of United Charities of Chicago
United Farm Workers, 76, 98, 193
University of Chicago, 101
Law School, 67, 70, 140, 158, 173, 228n6
Uptown Coalition, 84–85
Urban Progress Center, 138, 141, 143

Van Alystyne, W. Scott, Jr., 219n7

Waggoner, Michael J. (and Lowenstein), 240n3
Wallace, Anthony F.C., 246n11
Wallace, George (Governor), 79
War on Poverty, 5, 7, 65, 69, 74, 77, 84, 88, 89, 91, 137, 178
Warren, Earl (Chief Justice), 230n25
Watergate scandals, 6, 172
Weaver, Suzanne, 168
Weisbrod, Burton, 180
Weissman, Harold H., 239n16
Welfare rights movement, 79, 80, 82, 100, 102, 170, 179, 191–192, 232n6
Western Center on Law and Poverty, 167

West Side Organization, 100
Wexler, Stephen, 102
Wheeler, Stanton, 236n2
White collar crime
  and equal justice, 3, 172
  in the seventies, 6, 172
  in the eighties, 6, 238n8, 242n11
Wiebe, Robert H., 37
Wigmore, John, 41
Wills, Garry, 230n19
Wilson, James Q., 84
Wilson, Woodrow (President), 224n12
Wisconsin Study, The, 71–72, 226n20, 226n1, 230n21
Woodlawn Organization, The (Two), 81, 84, 94, 100–101, 228n8
Work problems
  client lies, 31–32, 59–61
  demoralization, 95–96, 113–114
  discontinuities between cases, 9, 18, 26–29, 103
  discontinuities within cases, 9, 18, 29–32
  free service and client motivation, 32, 221n11
  heavy caseloads, 17, 21, 165, 220n2, 221n9
  lawyers' struggles for case control, 110–113, 161
  limited significance, 8, 9, 17, 18, 19–29, 33, 51, 59, 87, 103, 107–108
  negotiating client demands, 23–29
  organizational discontinuities, 129–131, 166
  routine, 9, 17–33, 96, 107, 125, 220n1, 220n2, 236n5
  short-term client relations, 28–29
  see also Reasonableness; Reform of poverty; Significance; Strategies to achieve reform
Wright, Eric, 227n3, 239n16

Yale University, 70
Young, Arthur, 52, 62, 138, 141, 142, 144, 146, 157
Young Lords, 231n39
Young Patriots, 85, 231n39

Zald, Mayer N. (and Ash), 227n5
Zelditch, Morris, Jr., 244n3
Zipperman, William, 138
Znaniecki, Florian, 245n5